GEORGE BUSH
VS.
SADDAM HUSSEIN

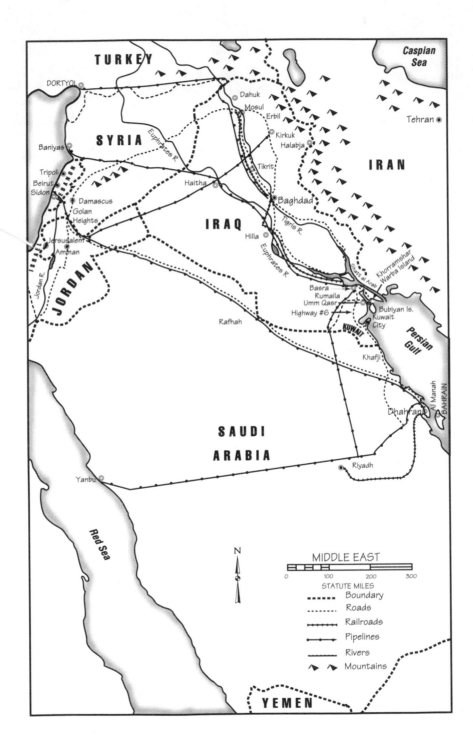

TURKEY

Caspian
Sea

DORTYOL

Dahuk
Mosul
Erbil

SYRIA

Kirkuk
Halabja

IRAN

Baniyas

Euphrates R.

Tehran

Tripoli
Beirut
Sidon

Tikrit

Haitha

Baghdad

Damascus
Golan
Heights

IRAQ

Tigris R.

Jerusalem
Amman

Hilla

Euphrates R.

Khorramshar
Warba Island

JORDAN

Basra
Rumaila
Umm Qasr
Highway #6

Bubiyan Is.
Kuwait
City

Rafhah

KUWAIT

Persian
Gulf

Khafji

Jordan R.

SAUDI

Al Manah
Dhahran
BAHRAIN

ARABIA

Riyadh

Yanbu

Red Sea

N

MIDDLE EAST

0   100   200   300
STATUTE MILES

········ Boundary
-------- Roads
+++++++ Railroads
———— Pipelines
~~~~~ Rivers
ʌ ʌ Mountains

YEMEN

GEORGE BUSH
VS.
SADDAM HUSSEIN

Military Success! Political Failure?

ROGER HILSMAN

LYFORD
Books

LYFORD Books
Published by Presidio Press
505 B San Marin Drive, Suite 300
Novato, CA 94945

Library of Congress Cataloging-in-Publication Data

Hilsman, Roger.
    George Bush vs. Saddam Hussein : military success! political failure? / by Roger Hilsman.
        p.   cm.
    Includes bibliographical references and index.
    ISBN 0-89141-470-3
    1. Persian Gulf War, 1991. 2. Middle East—Politics and government—1979-   3. Iraq—Politics and government. 4. Middle East—Foreign relations—United States. 5. United States—Foreign relations—Middle East. I. Title. II. Title: George Bush versus Saddam Hussein.
DS79.72.H56   1992
956. 704'3 —dc20   92-11929
                                                                        CIP

Typography & maps by ProImage

Printed in the United States of America

To the memory of the fallen
—on both sides—
—military and civilian—
men, women, and children

The Institute of War and Peace Studies
School of International Affairs
Columbia University

This book was prepared under the sponsorship of
The Institute of War and Peace Studies
of Columbia University's School of International Affairs

In addition to *George Bush vs. Saddam Hussein,* the Institute of War
and Peace Studies has sponsored five other books by Roger Hilsman:
*To Move a Nation: The Politics of Foreign Policy in the Administra-
tion of John F. Kennedy* (1967); *The Politics of Policy Making in Defense
and Foreign Affairs* (1971); *The Crouching Future: International Politics
and U.S. Foreign Policy, a Forecast* (1975); *The Politics of Governing America* (1985); and *The Politics of Policy Making in Defense and
Foreign Affairs: Conceptual Models and Bureaucratic Politics* (1st ed.,
1987; 2d ed., 1990).

The Institute of War and Peace Studies sponsors the publication of
works in international relations, international institutions, and American
foreign and military policy. Among its studies of policy and the policy
process by other authors are: *The Common Defense* by Samuel P.
Huntington; *Strategy, Politics, and Defense Budgets* by Warner P.
Schilling, Paul Y. Hammond, and Glenn H. Snyder; *Planning, Prediction, and Policy Making in Foreign Affairs* by Robert Jervis; *How
Nations Behave* by Louis Henkin; and *Economic Statecraft* by David
Baldwin.

CONTENTS

ACKNOWLEDGMENTS

For help in research, editing, and advice, the person to whom I owe the most is Eleanor H. Hilsman. She also did the index. My gratitude is deep.

Alan Platt read an early draft and gave some very useful advice.

Leavenworth Holden sketched out the maps, digging out the locations of some of the more obscure towns and villages and sorted out the variety of spellings that anyone writing about the Middle East invariably encounters.

Dale Wilson gave invaluable advice at every step of the editing process—including a heroic job of reducing one chapter from an unmanageable 11,000 words to a more appropriate 6,000. I am very grateful.

Finally, special thanks to Barbara Feller-Roth for her careful eye during the copyediting of the manuscript.

PREFACE

This book originated from a series of articles and talks analyzing events in the Middle East beginning shortly after Iraq invaded Kuwait in August 1990. In the aftermath of the war, it seemed important to try to understand why all the many attempts to bring about a negotiated settlement failed and the invasion led to war—a war that resulted in a great number of Iraqi casualties, mind-boggling devastation of the Iraqi economy, and long-range political consequences for the Middle East, for Israel, and for the United States' position in the Middle East—a war whose fateful results are just beginning to be recognized.

The method of analyzing how decisions on both sides were reached is one that looks at the making of national decisions as the result of a political process—what has been called "the politics of policy making"—developed by a number of analysts in the period since World War II.*

This book applies these methods to the Gulf War by:

(1) Tracing briefly the historical origins of the war.
(2) Examining the attempts that both the contenders and neutrals made to avoid war in order to try to understand why these

---

*Robert J. Art, in an article entitled "Bureaucratic Politics and American Foreign Policy: A Critique," (*Policy Sciences*, December 1974), credits the development of this method of analysis to two "waves" of theorists. The first wave was Richard E. Neustadt, Gabriel A. Almond, Charles E. Lindblom, Warner R. Schilling, Samuel P. Huntington, and Roger Hilsman, the present author. The second wave was Graham T. Allison, Morton H. Halperin, I. M. Destler, and Alexander L. George. The authors in both the first and second waves have written a number of books and articles that either elaborated and sharpened the general analytical method or used it to analyze a particular series of events, such as the Vietnam War or the Cuban missile crisis.

efforts failed and, in particular, why two very promising plans for a negotiated settlement were not pursued.

(3) Determining why, after the Iraqi invasion of Kuwait, such short shrift was given to two alternatives that would have avoided using predominantly American forces to fight the war and thus escaped the long-range political consequences of having Americans kill Arabs—the first alternative being to give responsibility to a United Nations (U.N.) force and the second being to give responsibility to a combined Arab and Third World force commanded by an Arab general.

(4) Tracing the political and military decisions made by both sides as the struggle progressed.

(5) Examining the negotiations to end the war itself and trying to understand why the settlement ended up the way it did—that is, with Saddam Hussein still in power and with Iraq still in control of substantial military forces.

(6) Reviewing the negotiations aimed at establishing peace for the whole of the Middle East, including settlement of the Arab-Israeli dispute.

(7) Examining what the long-run political and economic consequences of the war might be.

The first four chapters trace the historical origins of the war.

Chapter 1 sketches the period from ancient times: the successive conquests by Persians, Arabs, and Turks; how Britain and France carved the present-day Middle East out of the old Ottoman empire after World War I; and how in doing so they planted the seeds of today's rivalries and war.

Chapter 2 looks at the crisis during the Carter administration that followed the seizure of the American embassy in Iran by militants who made hostages of its staff—events that not only ensnared the United States in the rivalries of the Middle East, but deeply influenced where it would stand in the later struggles.

Chapter 3 briefly reviews the Iran-Iraq war and analyzes how it set the stage for the events that followed.

Chapter 4 recounts the events immediately preceding the Iraqi attack on Kuwait—what the American ambassador, April Glaspie, under instructions from Washington, told Hussein; how Hussein interpreted what the ambassador said; the Iraqi invasion; and the United States' decision to send troops to Saudi Arabia.

Chapter 5 discusses alternatives debated in Washington and elsewhere that the United States did *not* take:

(1) To head off an invasion by negotiating a settlement of Iraq's grievances.
(2) After the invasion, to defend Saudi Arabia with Arab and Third World troops rather than American (thereby avoiding the political consequences of Westerners once more killing Arabs, which Arabs feel has happened all too often in modern times) and to emphasize sanctions rather than a military offensive.
(3) After the original dispatch of U.S. troops had headed off an Iraqi attack on Saudi Arabia, gradually to withdraw the Americans and turn responsibility over to a U.N. force—and again to emphasize sanctions rather than a military offensive.
(4) If the U.N. would not accept responsibility, to employ an Arab–Third World force, again emphasizing sanctions rather than a military offensive.

Chapter 6 offers a brief history of the diplomacy of building the Allied coalition—how the decisions were made in Washington, and the diplomacy of dealing with the Arab Allies, with the U.N., and, most importantly, with the Soviet Union.

Chapter 7 traces the road to war. First, it examines how the goals were changed—from defending Saudi Arabia and the emirates to evicting Iraq from Kuwait; destroying Iraq's military potential, including its budding nuclear potential; and removing Saddam Hussein from power. It describes the decision to double the U.S. forces to give them an offensive capability, the diplomatic moves designed to obtain U.N. approval for an Allied invasion, and the political maneuvering on the U.S. domestic scene that culminated in Congress' narrow vote authorizing the use of force.

Chapter 8 describes the strategy, tactics, and consequences of the air war against Iraq; Chapter 9 does the same for the ground invasion.

Chapter 10 tells the story of the Shiite and Kurdish rebellions against Baghdad and Saddam Hussein—how they came about and how they ended.

Chapter 11 describes the tension between the military and the press resulting from the very strict rules that the military imposed on the press—rules that the military felt were essential as a result of what they regarded as their bad experience with the press in the Vietnam War.

Chapter 12 is a postmortem on the war. It reviews, first, the military operations—and finds them superbly planned and executed. It also discusses three negatives: the Patriot missile, the decision to stop the war at a moment that left Iraq with its elite forces still largely intact (forces that Hussein used to put down the rebellions), and postwar events in Kuwait—and the political liabilities that they created for the United States.

Chapter 13 examines the fifth point listed above, that is, how the peace negotiations with Iraq ended up the way they did, leaving Saddam Hussein still in power and Iraq with substantial military forces intact.

Chapter 14 looks in detail at the thorny question of Iraq's nuclear potential—what its intentions were, what kind of help it had gotten from other countries, who those countries were, how far Iraq had gotten toward realizing its intentions, and what kind of nuclear threat it would have posed if the war had not intervened.

Chapter 15 examines the diplomatic effort to build a lasting peace for the whole of the Middle East, including settlement of the Arab-Israeli dispute.

Chapter 16 discusses the political aftermath of the war, which it does not find as satisfactory as the military conduct of the war. Hussein remained in power. Only a handful of Americans and Allied soldiers were casualties, but something like two hundred thousand Iraqi soldiers and civilians were either killed in the war or died as a direct result of the war—because of the bombing of water purification plants, sewage systems, electrical generating plants (which meant that the hospitals could not refrigerate medicines), and so on. The chapter also discusses the consequences of the destruction of Iraq's entire industrial infrastructure—which, as the U.N. inspection team said, reduced Iraq to an underdeveloped country.

Epilogue I argues that the observer of the Gulf War is left with three unanswered questions: Why did the war go so well for Bush, the United States, and its Allies and so badly for Hussein and Iraq? Why did Saddam Hussein take the course he did? Why did George Bush turn his back on at least four alternatives to making the Persian Gulf conflict an American war (as described in Chapter 5)? The chapter concludes that the Gulf War was, more than any other war in modern history, a personal struggle between two men, Saddam Hussein and George Bush.

Epilogue II analyzes Saddam Hussein, the alternatives he had before him, and why he chose the course he did.

Epilogue III does the same for George Bush.

Roger Hilsman

INTRODUCTION

At 2:00 A.M. on August 2, 1990, Iraqi forces crossed the Kuwaiti border in force. Within six hours they had occupied the entire country.

Saddam Hussein, the president of Iraq, announced that Kuwait had been annexed to Iraq and that it was an "eternal merger." A small part of Kuwait was being incorporated into an existing province, and the rest was being formed into a new one.

The following weekend, on August 4, U.S. President George Bush convened a small circle of advisers at Camp David, the presidential retreat in Maryland, and decided to move a massive U.S. military force to the Middle East—the largest American deployment since the Vietnam War. In keeping with the president's preference for making important decisions in secret, only one congressional leader, Sen. Sam Nunn of Georgia, chairman of the Senate Armed Services Committee, was consulted in advance.

Over the next few days, the president spent hours on the telephone with various heads of state, seeking allies and support. In particular, it was vital that King Fahd of Saudi Arabia grant permission to station U.S. troops in his country. Once the king gave his permission, Bush ordered ground and air troops to Saudi Arabia, as well as additional naval forces to the Gulf.

As part of the flurry of diplomatic activity in those few hectic days, the United States persuaded the members of the U.N. Security Council to vote to condemn the invasion of Kuwait and to call for worldwide economic sanctions against Iraq, to pressure it to withdraw to its own borders.

Most members of Congress, a majority of the American people, and almost all of the leaders of the anti-Iraqi coalition favored giving economic sanctions time to work, even though most of them conceded that it might take a year or more. Yet, within a few weeks Bush and his closest advisers came to the conclusion that sanctions alone would not be sufficient to force Saddam Hussein to withdraw. Accordingly, the United States successfully pressed for a U.N. resolution setting a deadline of January 15, 1991, for Iraq to withdraw and, if it did not comply, authorizing U.N. members to use military force to make it do so.

Saddam Hussein and Iraq remained unmoved. The deadline passed, and on January 16, 1991, Bush ordered an all-out air assault on Iraq and the Iraqi troops in Kuwait. The war had begun.

At the outbreak of World War I, the outgoing chancellor of Germany, Prince von Bülow, said in puzzlement to his successor, "How did it all happen?" "Ah," was the reply, "if we only knew!" Many Americans feel the same way about the war with Iraq. Understanding why things happened as they did requires a brief look at the historical background.

The Historical Background[1]

Today's Iraq was the heart of the ancient "fertile crescent"—the place where civilization based on agriculture first arose. It lies between two mighty rivers, the Tigris and the Euphrates, and the Greeks accordingly called it Mesopotamia, "the land between the rivers."

Three thousand years before Christ, the Sumerians, who lived in the area just south of what is now Baghdad, developed the first known system of writing. The Babylonians, who lived farther south in the second millennium B.C., developed the beginnings of astronomy and, under Hammurabi, produced the world's first systematic set of laws. Assyria rose as Babylon's rival near the present-day city of Mosul, developing a standing army and a full-time bureaucracy.

The Persians, led by Cyrus the Great, conquered Babylon and Assyria about 500 B.C., and for more than a thousand years the land was ruled alternately by Persians or the heirs of Alexander the Great's Greek generals.

The Coming of the Arabs

In A.D. 637 the Arabs, spreading Islam by the sword, drove out the Persians and gave Iraq the name it bears today. But they split over the succession to the prophet Muhammad. One faction, the Shiites, favored Muhammad's son-in-law, Ali. The other faction, the Sunnis, sought the support of the old aristocracy of Mecca.

Almost a century of civil war followed. Finally the governor of Syria, Muwayah, won out over the Shiites. Utterly ruthless, he brought peace by annihilating the opposition.

Muwayah founded the Umayyad dynasty, and his successors built Baghdad as their capital. From 750 until 1258, Iraq was ruled by the Abbasid Caliphate, and the country flourished. It was prosperous and enjoyed a flowering of creativity in astronomy, mathematics, medicine, and other sciences.

But a series of weak caliphs brought in Turkish soldiers to keep themselves in power and, by the end of the ninth century, the Turks became the real rulers of the country.

Still the prosperity and creativity continued until the thirteenth century, when Iraq was sacked by the Mongols. The next few hundred years were a dark age. The Ottoman Turks invaded in 1534, and Iraq became a battleground between the Ottomans and the Persians. It was not until 1638 that the Ottomans finally won.

The Creation of Modern Iraq

The British and the French created modern-day Iraq in the Sykes-Picot agreement of 1916, when they decided how to divide the Ottoman empire following their anticipated victory in World War I. Britain formed Iraq out of three former Ottoman provinces. One of Iraq's borders, that with Iran, is ancient. It marked the boundary between the Ottoman empire and Persia. The border between Iraq and Turkey was a provincial boundary of the Ottoman empire, and it split the Kurds, leaving some in Turkey and some in Iraq (some Kurds also live in both Syria and Iran). The borders with Syria and Jordan in the west are lines that the British drew in the sand, as is the southern border between Iraq and Saudi Arabia.

Then, in 1923, Britain deliberately drew the border between Iraq and Kuwait so as to deny Iraq a port and safe access to the Persian Gulf. Britain gave Kuwait two uninhabited islands in the Shatt-al-Arab, Warba and Bubiyan, which blocked Iraq's route to the open sea. As it happened, the border also put the tip of the Rumaila oil field, which had not yet been discovered, inside Kuwait, and this became a cause of future trouble between Kuwait and Iraq.

Geography and Peoples

Iraq is slightly larger than the state of California, centered, as already mentioned, between the Tigris and the Euphrates. The Tigris flows south from Turkey. Baghdad lies on its banks. The Euphrates rises in Syria and meets the Tigris just above Iraq's second largest city, Basra. The combined waters from their juncture to the sea are called the Shatt-al-Arab, the "river of the Arabs." From just south of Basra to the sea the river forms the border between Iraq and Iran.

Northern Iraq is mountainous. It is inhabited mainly by Kurds, who are Sunni Muslim in religion but not ethnically Arab. They constitute about 20 percent of the Iraqi population of eighteen million. The area north of Baghdad between the rivers is inhabited by Sunni Arabs, who make up another 20 percent of the population. Saddam Hussein was born a Sunni Arab. Shiite Arabs, who make up 55 percent of the population, live in the extremely fertile area between the rivers south of Baghdad. The western portion of Iraq is part of the Great Syrian Desert. It is lightly populated by Bedouin Arab tribes, who make up the remaining 5 percent of the total population.

The British Install a King

After World War I the British installed Faisal, a prince of the Hashemite family, as king of Iraq. Faisal surrounded himself with Sunni Arabs, in both the government and the army, and Sunni Arabs have maintained their dominance ever since. Iraq became independent in 1932, although the British maintained military bases and great political influence. With independence came the dream of pan-Arabism, at least for the Sunni officers of the Iraqi army—the dream that Iraq could become the instrument for creating a single Arab state. After World War II and the departure of the British from the bases they had maintained between the wars, the dream grew.

During the 1948 Arab-Israeli war, Iraq sent a contingent of troops, and Israel's victory was the source of much bitterness in Iraq, as it was throughout the Arab world.

The Monarchy Overthrown

When Egyptian President Gamal Abdel Nasser turned back the British and French invasion in 1956 (with a huge political assist from President Eisenhower), he became a hero to the Arab masses throughout the Middle East. Two years later a group of nationalist Iraqi army officers, led by Gen. Abdul Karim Qassim and his close collaborator, Col. Abdul Salam Arif, seized the opportunity to overthrow the Iraqi monarchy, brutally gunning down the entire royal family in the palace courtyard.

Qassim, the son of a Sunni Arab father and a Kurdish mother, did not share the pan-Arabist dreams and pro-Nasser attitude of most of the Iraqi military. The military, including Arif, wanted to follow Nasser's vision and merge with Egypt, as did Syria for a time. Qassim's ambitions were for Iraq itself.

Shortly after Qassim and Arif took power, they quarreled violently in Qassim's office over the issue of merging with Egypt. Arif reached for his pistol, but Qassim and another officer wrestled him to the floor. Contrary to the usual custom in Iraq, Qassim did not have Arif executed, but merely jailed.

Qassim then turned on the other pan-Arabist advocates of a merger with Egypt, relying on the Communists for help. In March 1959, pan-Arabist, nationalist officers rose up in the city of Mosul, in the north. Qassim put down the rebellion in one of the bloodiest repressions in modern Iraqi history.

A relatively obscure but ruthless political party, the Baathists, then ambushed Qassim's car on October 7, 1959, wounding him badly. Qassim's retaliation against the Baathists was vicious, and for the next four years the opposition to his rule went underground and seemed no longer to pose much of a threat.

CHAPTER 1

The Rise of Saddam Hussein

Saddam Hussein rose to power by climbing through the ranks of the Baathist party. The party was founded in Syria in the 1930s as a pan-Arab nationalist movement—*baath* means rebirth in Arabic. Their slogan was "One Arab nation with an eternal mission."

All over the world nationalism has historically found some of its strongest supporters among secondary school teachers, the keepers of the language and literature of the mass of the people and of the traditions of the lower middle class. True to this tradition, the principal leaders of the infant Baathist movement were two Damascus high school teachers, Michel Aflaq and Salah Bitar.

Initially these two were attracted by the marriage of nationalism and socialism espoused by the German Nazi party; like the Nazis, they were violently anti-Communist. Their ideas spread in the Arab world, and in the period following World War II a Baathist party was formed in Iraq. It remained small, however, and probably had fewer than a thousand members when Saddam Hussein joined its ranks.

Saddam Hussein's Background

Saddam Hussein was born on April 28, 1937, in the small town of Tikrit on the banks of the Tigris River. Tikrit is located in the heart of central Iraq, the homeland of Sunni Muslims, who constitute, as mentioned earlier, about 20 percent of the Iraqi population and who have long been dominant in both the military and the government. In the Middle East, one's first loyalty is to the clan and to the place of birth, and Tikrit came to play an important role in both Hussein's rise to power and his ability to stay in power.

Hussein's father died before Saddam's birth, and his mother sought shelter with her brother, Khairallah Talfah. In a twist that turned out to be peculiarly appropriate, the child was given the name Saddam: "one who confronts."

Saddam Hussein spent the first few years of his life with his uncle; it was long enough for the boy to come to look upon him as a father. Khairallah was an army officer and a nationalist. In 1941, the Iraqi officer corps looked to Hitler and Nazi Germany to free Iraq from British domination; when the British sought to transfer troops through Iraqi territory, the army rebelled. The British soundly beat them and restored the king to the throne. Many nationalist officers who had participated in the rebellion were executed. Others, of whom Hussein's uncle was one, were cashiered and jailed—in Khairallah's case for five years. The effect on young Saddam Hussein was to ignite a lifelong hatred of both the monarchy and the Western countries that had put it back in power.

For the next few years Saddam Hussein lived in a small village near Tikrit with his mother and her new husband. His stepfather was cruel, and the children of the village treated young Saddam as an outsider. Some of Saddam Hussein's biographers believe that it was this experience that lies behind his suspicious nature and his ultimate reliance on his own inner counsel.

When his uncle was released from prison in 1947, Saddam Hussein returned to Tikrit to go to school. His uncle was fond of him, and his best friend was his uncle's son, Adnan, whom Saddam Hussein was one day to make minister of defense. Shortly after young Saddam graduated from primary school, the family moved to Baghdad, where Saddam Hussein entered high school. Wanting to follow in his uncle's footsteps, Saddam applied to the Baghdad Military Academy, Iraq's West Point, but failed the entrance examinations.

Already active politically, Saddam Hussein joined the infant Baathist party. It is not known just why he chose this particular party, whose nationalism and pan-Arabism were shared by other better-known, larger, and more powerful parties. But the clue may well lie in the fact that his uncle's cousin, Ahmad Hassan al-Bakr, also from Tikrit, was a high-ranking Baathist.

Saddam Hussein's contribution to the Baathist cause at this early stage was to organize his high school classmates into a gang that the party occasionally used to beat up its political opponents. Hussein was, in fact, implicated in the murder of a government official in Tikrit and spent six months in jail before he was released for lack of evidence.

When Qassim and his fellow army officers overthrew the monarchy in 1958, the Baathist party applauded the coup and actually participated in Qassim's government. But the Baathists were sympathetic to Arif and his pan-Arab, pro-Nasser views, so when Qassim and Arif quarreled and Arif was jailed, many Baathists were also jailed. The rest of the party went underground and reorganized for a coup attempt.

The Baathists decided that their best course of action was to assassinate Qassim. On October 7, 1959, a group of young Baathist party members, including Saddam Hussein, ambushed Qassim's car, badly wounding him.

A large number of Baathists were arrested and put on trial. In an ironic twist, however, the party itself benefited. During the trial, the Baathists were defiant. Their courage attracted attention, and they went from a small, virtually unknown fringe group to a party that commanded widespread public respect.

Saddam Hussein escaped. In later years, stories of his courage and heroism circulated widely, although how true they are is open to question. In any case, Hussein made his way to Syria, whose leaders at the time were also Baathist. There he met and apparently became something of a protégé of Michel Aflaq, who was, as described earlier, one of the founders of the Baathist party. Aflaq's influence apparently helped Hussein get elected to the Regional Command of the Iraqi party, the highest of its decision-making bodies, in 1964.

After three months in Syria, Hussein went to Cairo—at that time a city seething with pan-Arab political activists in exile from all over the Middle East. He stayed there from February 1960 to February 1963. He joined Egypt's Baathist party but spent most of his time going to school. Hussein completed his high school education in 1961, and in 1962 enrolled in the University of Cairo to study law. However, the university experience seems to have had little effect on Hussein's politics or outlook. Under Nasser, the university was not a hotbed of radicalism but a fearful community of "stifling uniformity."

On his return to Iraq in 1963, Saddam Hussein married his cousin, Sajidah Talfah. Sajidah, like Hussein, had also grown up in their uncle Khairallah's house, where they had been like brother and sister. However, their grandfather had betrothed Sajidah to Saddam Hussein when they were still children.

Several of Hussein's biographers have concluded that he studied Nasser's methods and political tactics during his years in Egypt and later copied them, especially Nasser's establishment of a one-party state and a puppet parliament and his pragmatism in international affairs. But whereas Nasser was an emotional speaker, a rabble-rouser similar to Adolf Hitler, Hussein was a dull speaker and a behind-the-scenes manipulator more like Josef Stalin.

The First Army-Baathist Coup

What made Hussein's return to Iraq possible was the bloody 1963 coup against Qassim. The coup was staged by nationalist army officers led by Arif in alliance with the Baathists, led by Col. Ahmad Hassan al-Bakr, the cousin of Hussein's uncle.

Qassim was captured and taken to the television station in Baghdad. He begged for a chance to talk to Arif, his former comrade whose life he had spared. But Arif refused to meet with him, and Qassim was executed on the spot. Qassim's supporters would not believe he was dead, so the Baathists propped his body in a chair, focused a TV camera on it, and a soldier repeatedly pulled his limp head up by the hair and let it drop—proving to the TV audience that Qassim was indeed dead.

With Qassim out of the way, Arif became president and Bakr was given the considerably less important post of prime minister.

In spite of Hussein's participation in the earlier attempt against Qassim, he was able to land only a minor position in the new government. But he immediately established himself as a prominent member of Bakr's personal faction.

Although Arif was president, the Baathists were strong in the Revolutionary Council, which was nominally the ruling body, and succeeded in passing a number of resolutions of which Arif did not approve.

The Baathists also busied themselves with expanding their influence in the National Guard and recruiting new members for the Guard from Baathist ranks. It was not long before both Arif and the army saw the Baathists as a threat to their own power and position.

The success of the Iraqi coup encouraged the Baathists in Syria, and in March 1963 they succeeded in overthrowing the Syrian regime— also in alliance with pan-Arab, nationalist, army officers.

Being advocates of Arab unity, the new rulers in both Syria and Iraq sought Nasser's approval and persuaded him to call a conference in Cairo in April. Embittered by Syria's 1961 withdrawal from the United

Arab Republic, which he had formed, Nasser used the talks mainly to try to discredit the Baathists.

In the meantime, the Baathist-led Iraqi National Guard was arresting people without warrants and using torture during interrogations. One of the torturers was young Saddam Hussein.

Arif, increasingly alarmed by the growing Baathist strength, ordered the army to seize control of Baghdad and arrest the Baathist leaders in November 1963.

Hussein, however, was apparently considered too junior and unimportant to be arrested, and he used the period that followed to very good advantage, picking up responsibilities that would normally have belonged to his jailed superiors.

When Bakr was finally released from jail, his group was the dominant faction in the party, and as he rose in power, so did Saddam Hussein. In 1964, when a provisional Regional Command was established, Hussein was chosen to be a member. When it became a permanent body, he was again a member.

Later in 1964, Hussein was in a position to plot a coup against Arif. One plan was to infiltrate a group into the palace and assassinate the entire Arif leadership. But the officer of the Republican Guard who was to let them in was suddenly transferred to another post. The second plan was to have an escort fighter shoot down the president's plane. But one of the pilots recruited by the Baathists was actually a member of Arif's secret service. Arif again jailed the Baathist leaders, including Bakr.

Saddam Hussein once more escaped arrest. The Baathist National Command in Syria instructed him to flee to Damascus, but Hussein chose to remain in Iraq. He apparently sensed a great political opportunity. As one of the ranking Baathists not in jail, he could continue the effort to oust Arif. If successful, he would be at the top. If the attempt failed and he remained free, his reputation would grow. If it failed and he was arrested, the worst he expected was that he would join the other Baathist leaders in jail.

As it turned out, Arif's security forces found Hussein's hideout and, after a brief exchange of fire, Hussein ran out of ammunition and surrendered. He spent two years in jail.

According to the legend that Hussein himself has cultivated, he then devised an escape plan. When he and two other prisoners were driven to a court appearance they persuaded the guards to stop for lunch. Then, while one of the prisoners tried to encourage the guards to defect, Hussein and the other prisoner went to the lavatory and from there to the back alley, where Hussein's cousin was waiting with a car.

Following his escape, Hussein played a key leadership role in the Baathist underground. Almost immediately, a coup in Syria brought an ardently pro-Marxist faction of the military into control, and Michel Aflaq and others among Hussein's allies were jailed. Hussein called an Extraordinary Regional Congress to decide what should be done; the result was a permanent schism between the Syrian and Iraqi Baathists. The hatred and conflict between Syria and Iraq that began at that time continues today.

In the period that followed, Hussein concentrated on party security. The job gave him the opportunity to get rid of opponents on both the left and the right and to put his own loyalists, many from Tikrit, into key positions. When Bakr was released from jail, Hussein continued his activities but as a dutiful subordinate.

Arif kept the Baathists in prison for a time but then released them, although he took care to keep them powerless. The Nasserites in the army, however, remained relatively strong. They attempted a coup against Arif in 1965, but failed.

In April 1966, Abdul Salam Arif died in a helicopter crash, and his brother, Abdul Rahman Arif, took over as president. The army Nasserites attempted another coup in June 1966, and it too failed. This time the Baathists actively supported the new President Arif, and gained even more freedom as their reward.

The new President Arif was not the strongman his brother had been, but weak and vacillating. Not only was he lax in heading off the Baathist reach for power, but he even attempted at one point to buy their co-operation with positions in his government.

The Second Army-Baathist Coup

Two years later, in 1968, an ambitious Republican Guard officer, Col. Abd al-Razzaq al-Nayif, deputy director of military intelligence, began to plan a coup. The Guard was responsible for the security of the president and of the city of Baghdad. Ironically, Guard officers were personally picked by Arif himself. Nayif promised high positions to the Guard's top officers in exchange for their help. But he needed allies outside the Guard as well and finally decided upon the Baathists.

The coup was successful. Nayif rewarded the Baathists by giving their secretary-general—Hussein's sponsor, Ahmad Hassan al-Bakr—the post of president, since Nayif intended that the president would be little more than a figurehead anyway. Nayif took the post of prime minister, and the commander of the Republican Guard, Col. Ibrahim al-Daud, became minister of defense.

But the Baathists had learned much from their defeat at Arif's hands following the earlier coup. Less than two weeks after this new coup, while Daud was out of the country, Bakr invited Nayif to the palace. At one point, Bakr left the room and shortly afterward Saddam Hussein and another officer entered. Hussein drew his pistol and used it to whip Nayif repeatedly across the face while cursing him as the "son of a whore." Nayif broke down and begged for his life. Within hours he was flown into exile in Morocco, and the Baathists proceeded to eliminate all of his allies. Daud never returned to Iraq, and ten years later Nayif was assassinated by Hussein's agents while he was in exile in London.

The Baathists in Power

The new Baathist government was headed by Bakr as president and a Revolutionary Command Council consisting of Bakr and four Baathist generals. Saddam Hussein was deputy secretary-general of the party, but he remained behind the scenes. In fact, what he did over the next few years was to concentrate on building a personal base among the intelligence arm and eliminating other political parties.

In 1973, Gen. Nahim Kzar, who had been a Baathist from early on, attempted a coup against Bakr. It was to have begun with Bakr's assassination at the airport, but Bakr's plane was late and the coup failed. Saddam Hussein was one of those who helped put the coup down. In so doing, he was able to eliminate a number of personal rivals within the Baathist party itself. By 1973, Bakr was the only military officer left in high office, and Hussein was the most powerful of the remaining officials. He did not turn on Bakr personally, but he succeeded in moving Bakr's personal supporters to less influential positions. By 1974, Bakr was isolated; he was little more, in fact, than a figurehead. But until 1979, this suited Hussein's purposes more than becoming president himself. From 1974 on, it was Hussein who held the power and made the decisions.

The Kurdish War

In the meantime, beginning in 1969, an internal war against the Kurds had begun in earnest. With the help of the Soviet Union, Iraq reached a negotiated settlement with the Kurdish leader, Mustafa Barzani. The arrangements were supervised by Saddam Hussein, who met personally with Barzani in Kurdistan.

Iraq, however, apparently had no intention of abiding by the agreement. Some of Hussein's henchmen tried to assassinate Barzani's son a short time later. The following year some religious sheiks were scheduled to meet with Barzani, and Hussein duped them into taking a bomb disguised as a recording device with them to the meeting. When they turned it on, one of the sheiks and a servant were killed, but Barzani was unharmed.

In 1972, Iraq signed a "Friendship Treaty" with the Soviet Union, and again it was Saddam Hussein who conducted the negotiations. In the months that followed, the Soviets pressed both Hussein and the Iraqi Communists to form a united front. In 1974, the Iraqi Communists reluctantly agreed.

Because of the "Friendship Treaty," the United States and the shah of Iran launched a covert campaign to help the Kurdish rebellion and "destabilize" Iraq. Fighting in Kurdistan escalated.

However, in 1975, Saddam Hussein, ever the pragmatist, with the help of Egypt and Algeria, reached an agreement with the shah in which Iran would withdraw its support from the Kurds and Iraq would recognize Iran's claim to half the Shatt-al-Arab. Iraq immediately launched a massive attack on the Kurds, and Barzani fled the country.

Relations With Other Middle Eastern Countries

Virulently anti-Israel, the Baathist regime from 1968 on supported the most radical Palestinians, including the notorious Abu Nidal, who had mounted more than a dozen terrorist attacks in Europe and whose organization the U.S. State Department described as "the most dangerous terrorist organization in existence."

In 1973, although Bakr was reluctant, Hussein insisted on sending a substantial Iraqi army force to fight against Israel on the Golan Heights.

By that time, Hussein and Syrian President Hafiz al-Assad were bitter rivals. When Syria and Egypt negotiated a cease-fire, Hussein withdrew the Iraqi troops and denounced the agreements.

Following the 1973 Arab-Israeli war, oil prices soared and Iraq prospered enormously. It became increasingly independent of the Soviet Union, even going so far as to condemn the Soviet invasion of Afghanistan. At the same time, it increased trade with the United States, although rebuffing the Carter administration's overtures to renew diplomatic relations.

Saddam Hussein's Maneuverings

Saddam Hussein could undoubtedly have removed Bakr and become president as early as 1974. Publicly, Hussein was deferential to Bakr, but in the words of Efraim Karsh and Inari Rautsi in their authoritative biography of Saddam Hussein, "Lurking behind his seemingly deferential reticence were the practical and patient considerations of a fundamentally cautious man who would only risk supplanting the President when he felt confident of success."[1] Karsh and Rautsi speculate that Hussein viewed Bakr as neither devious nor powerful enough to stop Hussein, but at the same time Bakr had an "impeccable revolutionary record" that provided a formidable shield for Hussein to consolidate his power until he was totally certain that a move to replace Bakr as president would succeed.

Hussein's greatest weakness was the fact that he had never served in the military and had few allies in its ranks. So he had Bakr appoint him to the rank of lieutenant general in 1976 and fill key military positions with a number of Hussein's relatives and cohorts from Tikrit. Systematically, Hussein maneuvered to have Bakr's closest supporters transferred, ostensibly promoted, or removed. Bakr himself was minister of defense, but in October 1977 Hussein persuaded him to give up the post and appoint Col. Adnan Khairallah Talfah instead. As mentioned earlier, Talfah was Hussein's boyhood friend and favorite cousin. He was also Bakr's son-in-law.

The move was a vital one on Hussein's road to the presidency, for Talfah apparently saw his own future with Hussein and not Bakr. In the summer of 1978, Talfah, at Hussein's direction, purged a number of high-ranking officers, including the air force commander and a number of division commanders. Sixty of the officers removed were executed.

Until that time, Hussein had not been willing to accept the offers that the Soviet Union and other countries had made to sell Iraq arms. But, confident of his control over the military, and to soften the blow of the purges, Hussein embarked on a program to obtain tanks, self-propelled guns, bombers, helicopters, and transport aircraft from the Soviet Union and Mirage fighters and Gazelle antitank helicopters from France.

Hussein also moved to strengthen his following among the mass of the people as well. Iraq's oil revenues were $476 million in 1968; by 1980 they were $26 billion. Hussein launched a huge economic development program. He cut taxes, raised wages, and subsidized basic foods. He took land from the wealthy and gave it to peasants. He launched impressive housing, health, and education programs. Free education was established from kindergarten to the university. Eliminating illiteracy became the target of a large-scale effort. He also launched an ambitious program to emancipate women—a remarkable move in an Arab country—including equal pay and outlawing job discrimination on the basis of sex.

Development, however, was uneven, and the gap between rural and urban populations widened. To try to deal with this problem, Hussein decided to revise the Baathist commitment to a centrally controlled socialist economy to permit and even encourage private enterprise, both domestic and foreign.

Saddam Hussein Becomes President

By the early summer of 1979, Hussein apparently believed that he had done everything necessary to ensure that a bid for the presidency had the support of both the Iraqi military and the people. But what apparently triggered his decision to replace Bakr as president was the situation in Iran.

Following Hussein's deal with the shah of Iran in 1975 to call off Iran's support of the Kurds in exchange for Iraqi recognition of Iran's right to half of the Shatt-al-Arab, Hussein had cultivated the shah's friendship. Ayatollah Ruholla Khomeini had been living in Iraq in exile, but in October 1978, at the shah's request, Hussein expelled him, and the Ayatollah went to live in Paris. By 1979, Khomeini was back in Iran and in power, the head of a fundamentalist Shiite regime that promised trouble for its neighbors. It was apparently this threat from Iran that made Hussein decide that he could no longer delay taking over the presidency.

In the spring of 1979, Hussein embarked on a hectic tour of towns, the countryside, military posts, and even the Shiite and Kurdish areas; his trip resembled nothing less than an old-fashioned American whistle-stop presidential campaign. As he traveled, the government propaganda mills ground out his praises.

Then, on July 16, 1979, President Bakr dutifully appeared on television and announced that, because of his continued poor health, he was resigning as president. Within minutes Saddam Hussein was sworn in as his successor.

CHAPTER 2

Iran and the Hostage Crisis

Saddam Hussein became president of Iraq in the summer of 1979. But it was events in neighboring Iran that dictated his agenda.[1]

The Fall of the Shah

Shah Mohammad Reza Pahlavi had taken dictatorial power in Iran in August 1953 as a result of a coup that was assisted by the U.S. Central Intelligence Agency (CIA). For the next twenty years, Iran was allied with the United States, which supplied it with large amounts of military aid and equipment.

But the shah was tyrannical and arbitrary, alienating many segments of Iranian society, and by 1978 the shah's position had deteriorated badly. The great majority of Iranians are Shiite Muslims, and the shah's chief opponent was the top Shiite religious leader, Ayatollah Ruholla Khomeini (ayatollah is a priestly title). As already mentioned, Khomeini had been expelled from Iraq and was living in exile in Paris. Many U.S. diplomats, including the ambassador to Iran, William H. Sullivan, advised the Carter administration that the shah was doomed and urged the United States to establish relations with the ayatollah. But the Carter administration continued to support the shah.

The shah continued to lose domestic support, and when it became clear in January 1979 that even the army was no longer loyal, he went into exile. Ayatollah Khomeini arrived in Iran on February 1. Khomeini's choice for prime minister, Mehdi Bazargan, took office on February 11. The next few months saw a bitter struggle for power between the Shiite priests—the mullahs—and the politicians who had been their allies in overthrowing the shah. During the struggle a variety of

19

different factions attempted to manipulate the attitudes of the Iranian people toward the United States and toward the Sunni Muslims who controlled Iraq and its large population of Shiites.

In the days following the arrival of Khomeini and Bazargan, bands of armed revolutionaries roamed the capital city, Teheran. One band launched an assault on the American embassy. However, the deputy prime minister, Ibrahim Yazdi, and other officials of the new regime, including an ayatollah, came immediately to the embassy with a rescue force. The American personnel actually surrendered to a group containing both attackers and rescuers. Within hours, order was restored.

The shah, who was in Mexico, had become increasingly ill with cancer and asked for permission to come to the United States for medical treatment. The American embassy personnel in Teheran opposed admitting the shah to the United States, arguing that the wiser course would be to send a team of American doctors to Mexico. Even if the shah was admitted to the United States, they argued, his trip should be delayed until steps could be taken to protect the embassy from terrorists. The embassy personnel also warned that if the shah were granted entrance, the Iranians might take Americans hostage. Nevertheless, the Carter administration allowed the shah to come to the United States for treatment on October 22, 1979.

The Seizure of the American Hostages

On November 4, 1979, during a march in Teheran demonstrating against the United States, a small group of militants broke away from the march, took control of the American embassy, and seized about a hundred embassy personnel as hostages. The militants demanded that the shah be returned to Iran to stand trial. The next day Khomeini condoned both the takeover and the militants' demand. A few days later, he directed the release of all black and female hostages, reducing the number to fifty-three. Those fifty-three hostages were held for 444 days.

What made these events unique in modern history was the fact that the Iranian government sanctioned holding the hostages in violation of both international law and almost five hundred years of diplomatic tradition and custom. Terrorists have taken American embassy personnel hostage a number of times in history, and most frequently in the decades since World War II. But in every other case the government of the country, even when it was extremely anti-American and sympathetic to the seizure, either negotiated the hostages' release or rescued them by military force—although on some occasions, the rescue resulted in some of the American hostages being killed.*

The Carter Administration's Explanation

The Carter administration, the press, and the American public could not help but wonder: Why was Iran behaving so differently?

The administration developed a threefold answer. First, the argument went, the Soviet military buildup over the preceding fifteen years had made many Iranians wonder whether their alliance with the United States offered as much security as it once had. Iran, after all, was particularly exposed, situated as it was on the Soviet border and on the path to the Middle East's oil. Showing direct hostility toward the United States by taking hostages would signal a concrete step toward a policy of independence.

Second, the Carter administration's argument continued, the new Iran was ambitious. It aspired to leadership in the Muslim world, and a display of hostility toward the United States helped to establish that leadership. Taking the hostages not only demonstrated independence but also suggested that the United States was, in former President Richard M. Nixon's phrase, a "pitiful, helpless giant" in the face of Ayatollah Khomeini.

Third, the Carter administration's argument concluded, seizing the hostages carried an ideological appeal. By confronting and defying a superpower and getting away with it, the leaders of the Iranian revolution were trying to show that they stood on the side of the downtrodden peoples of the Third World.

In its public announcements and in its policies, the Carter administration added one more point. In addition to these essentially strategic and geopolitical motives, another motive attributed to Iran was revenge for U.S. support of the shah over the years and for the more recent decision to let him come to the United States for medical treatment.

---

*A notorious example was when the American ambassador to Afghanistan, Adolph Dubs, was abducted by Muslim terrorists in January 1979. American officials pleaded with the Afghan authorities to negotiate. The authorities ignored the pleas and stormed the hotel, killing Ambassador Dubs in the course of the attack. It was alleged that the attacking forces were accompanied by their Soviet advisers, but the Soviet Union vehemently denied the charges.

In hindsight, the Carter administration seemed to feel that the argument that revenge was a motive was less persuasive than it had been at the beginning of the crisis, principally because the shah's subsequent death seemed to make no difference in the negotiations. To the Carter people, however, the strategic and political motives seemed even more persuasive, since it was the various pressures, especially economic, that seemed to bring Iran to an agreement.[2]

A Rival View

Such were the conclusions of the Carter White House about the Iranians' motives for taking the hostages. But another group of analysts saw it differently.[3] They argued, first, that the principal threat to the new Iranian government was not really a direct attack from the Soviet Union, which the shah had feared, but instead was from the Iranian Communists, the Tudeh party, who might attempt a coup or, with Soviet help, start a guerrilla insurgency along the lines of that in Vietnam. A friendly United States could give massive aid to the government. This aid, combined with the ayatollah's religious and patriotic appeal to the Iranian people, could ensure a different outcome from that in Vietnam, where the leaders in the South lacked any such fundamental popular support. But by expressing hostility to the United States in permitting the militants to continue to hold the hostages, Iran would make it difficult for the United States to give its support if the Tudeh party decided to move.

Second, they pointed out that the ayatollah's regime was also in a precarious economic position. The Soviets might be pleased that Iran was establishing its neutrality, but this alone would probably not be enough to convince the Soviets that they should solve Iran's economic problems—which the Soviet Union probably did not have the economic capability of doing in any case. The United States and the West, on the other hand, did have the resources to provide a solution, but if Iran continued to hold the hostages, the Americans and their allies would find it politically impossible to offer such help.

Finally, they concluded, defying a superpower might earn cheers from the Third World, but those cheers would provide neither the butter to solve Iran's economic problems nor the guns to solve its security problems.

While proponents of this argument admitted that the Iranians might not see it just this way—perhaps because revenge for the Americans' past support of the shah might be a more important motive than some

Americans thought—they argued that the implications of this analysis for U.S. policy were that even if the Iranians persisted in holding the hostages, the United States should not have adopted the punitive measures followed by the Carter administration, such as freezing Iranian assets. Such moves only angered Iran and at the same time put it in a position in which agreeing to free the hostages would mean a loss of prestige. On the contrary, they concluded, the United States should work behind the scenes to offer such carrots as help with Iranian economic problems, while quietly trying to persuade other Muslim countries to convince Iran that holding the hostages discredited all Muslims throughout the world.

A Third Explanation

Still others analyzed quite differently the Iranian motives for seizing and holding the hostages—although none of the proponents of this particular analysis were inside the Carter administration, but in the Congress, among the press, and in academia. The proponents of the arguments described above saw the Iranians' motives as strategic and geopolitical. The proponents of this third view saw them as the product of a power struggle inside Iran itself.

The groups contending for power inside Iran, according to this argument, were quite obvious. Ayatollah Khomeini and his immediate supporters were the most prominent. The old business, commercial, industrial, military, and governmental elites also continued to exercise some power, even though they had been weakened by the purges of both the shah and the new revolutionary government.

In addition, it was clear that a power struggle was going on inside the new revolutionary government itself. The shah's overthrow had been accomplished by a coalition of militant mullahs, of whom Ayatollah Khomeini was the most prestigious and the acknowledged leader. Other contending power centers inside the Iranian government included more moderate mullahs, mostly in outlying districts; a group of mullahs who were fanatically Muslim but at the same time extremely left wing, almost Marxist; and moderate laymen of the national front. Prime Minister Mehdi Bazargan was the leader of one of the latter groups. A rival group was headed by a man who had been a close lay adviser to Khomeini during his exile, Abol-Hassan Bani-Sadr, who was elected president of Iran under the new constitution in January 1980.

The Carter administration, however, saw Iran as a state like all other states. The administration viewed Iran as a country with a working government and political system. It would negotiate with what it assumed was the government of Iran, reach an agreement with it, and then be infuriated when the government did not live up to its side of the agreement and produce the promised results. The fact is, however, that Iran did not have a working government and political system in which the policies were bargained out among the power centers, agreement reached, and the policies then implemented more or less as they were decided upon. Thus when the United States reached an agreement with what was ostensibly the government of Iran, the other contending groups proceeded to do something that would in fact sabotage or nullify the agreement. The militants, for example, refused to obey orders from President Bani-Sadr on several occasions and at least once from the Revolutionary Council, the highest government body. The militants may well have been able to ignore a direct order to free the hostages from Ayatollah Khomeini himself, their professed leader.

The truth, in sum, is that while the hostages were being held, Iran was in anarchy. Rival power centers struggled against each other, with none of them certain of their power or authority. As Gertrude Stein said of her birthplace, Oakland, California, "There was no there there."

The story of the struggle for power inside Iran seemed to reveal that the hostages were taken and held not for strategic, geopolitical reasons but for use as a weapon in this internal struggle.[4]

The Course of Events

The policies adopted by the Carter administration flowing from its analysis of the situation in Iran combined both carrots and sticks. On the one hand, the administration tried to negotiate with Iran through the United Nations, the Iranian ambassador to Washington, special emissaries to Iran, the Swiss and Algerian governments, and the Vatican. On the other hand, the Carter administration froze several billion dollars in Iranian assets held in American banks, boycotted Iranian oil, dispatched naval units to the Arabian Sea, ordered a reduction in the number of Iranian diplomats in the United States, ran an immigration check on the tens of thousands of Iranian students in America, and put pressure on its allies to join in economic sanctions.

At several stages the administration believed it had reached an agreement for the release of the hostages, but each time, Iran failed to carry out its side of the bargain. On April 7, 1980, the United States broke off diplomatic relations.

The Attempt to Rescue the Hostages

On April 25, the Carter administration mounted a military operation with helicopters and transport aircraft in an attempt to rescue the hostages by force—an attempt at a coup de main. The rescue force rendezvoused at an isolated spot in the desert some distance from Teheran to refuel the helicopters for its dash to the embassy, but an equipment failure led to the collision of two rescue aircraft, causing the mission to be canceled. Eight American servicemen were killed in the accident.

The shah died in July. Many observers, especially those who thought that revenge was one of the Iranian motives, believed that with the shah dead, negotiations would be successful. The Carter administration renewed its attempts to negotiate the release of the hostages with the help of Algeria, but there was still no progress. It was not until after the American election in November that the Algerian effort began to show results. An agreement was reached just forty-eight hours before the inauguration of the new president, Ronald Reagan, and the hostages were released immediately afterward.

In the months following his appointment as prime minister, Bazargan attempted to pursue a moderate course. He called for calm, emphasized reconstruction, and opposed extreme antagonism toward the United States. He said that the benefits of the revolution could come only when the economy was back on its feet, and he deplored the preoccupation with American "conspiracies." Khomeini, however, continued to preach violent anti-Americanism.

The exact occasion that triggered the seizure of the hostages illustrates its link with the internal power struggle. Bazargan traveled to Algeria for its independence day celebrations and, while he was there, met with Zbigniew Brzezinski, Carter's national security adviser. Bazargan's rivals in Iran arranged for pictures of the meeting to appear on Iranian TV. There was a mass demonstration protesting Bazargan's meeting with a representative of the "Great Satan," as Khomeini called the United States, and a group of militants broke off from the march, occupied the American embassy, and took the hostages.

The evidence is that their action had not been directed by either the government or Khomeini. The militants made a public appeal for Khomeini's approval, which he gave the next day, saying that the embassy was a "lair for spies" and that the Americans had expected to bring the shah to the embassy and "engage in plots." Apparently the militants' only intention at the time was to take advantage of the pictures of the Bazargan and Brzezinski meeting to stage a sit-in to embarrass

Bazargan and his supporters. They seem to have had no plan to actually occupy the embassy and hold the hostages for any length of time.

What changed the militants' mind and led them to hold the hostages for 444 days was the worldwide publicity, especially on TV. This publicity made holding the hostages a useful tactic in the power struggle inside Iran by giving the militants who were backing the Khomeini group a prominence of which they never dreamed.

In time, the American press itself realized that it had been a primary cause for the hostages being held so long. During the entire fourteen months that the Americans were held captive, Walter Cronkite, anchor of the CBS evening news, ended each broadcast with a solemn and sonorous intonation: "This is the [umpteenth] day of the captivity of the American hostages in Iran." Following the aborted rescue attempt, James Reston of the *New York Times* criticized President Carter for giving in to the pressure to "do something" rather than being patient and letting the inevitable factionalism within Iran bring about the captives' release. But Reston quickly added that the pressure on Carter had been enormous, with not the least of the pressure coming from "my old buddy, the Ayatollah Walter Cronkite."[5]

The most biting criticism of the role of the press during the hostage crisis was made by still another news reporter, Digby Whitman:

> The hostages fully deserve our sympathy and respect. . . . They have been callously exploited by the Iranian [government] . . . for political, mercenary, and venal purposes. But it seems to me that they have also and equally cynically been exploited for the same purposes in their homeland.
>
> During the fourteen months of their internship [sic], the plain fact is that there have been exactly three pieces of hard news. The first was the news of their seizure. The second was the news of the imbecilicly bungled attempt by our military to bring them away by force. The third was the news of their release.
>
> These three islands of actual, factual news have been almost submerged in a 400-day sea of wildly speculative, usually inaccurate, and often flatly wrong newspaper blather and noisy network commentary: it has been authoritatively reported, it has been learned from reliable sources, an unidentified official at the State Department (or the White House) has said, it is believed in the Pentagon that—with every week's reportage contradicted or reversed next week, and in its totality nothing being reported at all.

The whole fourteen-month "crisis" has been ruthlessly utilized to attract and hold readers and viewers and listeners.

Even today, in the happy hour of the hostages' homecoming it is worth noting that while they pushed the regular programs off the channels, they didn't displace any commercials. They are simply perceived and used as a vehicle superior to "Ironsides" or "Captain Kangaroo" for the movement of beer and toilet tissue, toothpaste and pantyhose.[6]

The Triumph of the Mullahs

In any event, as part of a power struggle the militants' move was successful. The Bazargan government had promised to protect the American embassy and criticized its occupation. Thus when Khomeini gave public approval to the action, the government resigned.

In January 1980, Bani-Sadr was elected president. In February he began to try to assert his authority over the militants by saying that the "government within a government" that they were attempting to create was "intolerable." As a result of negotiations, a U.N. commission was appointed to investigate the shah's regime as part of an agreement to bring about the release of the hostages. Bani-Sadr then told an interviewer that the hostages would be freed as soon as the commission issued its report.

Ayatollah Khomeini immediately announced that the decision on the fate of the hostages would be made by the Islamic Assembly, which was not scheduled to meet until May. The U.N. commission arrived in Teheran shortly after Bani-Sadr's announcement, and on March 6 it was announced that the hostages would be placed in the custody of the government of Iran. The militants refused. Khomeini then seemed to uphold their decision by announcing that the U.N. commission would not even be allowed to see the hostages until their report was submitted to and approved by Iran.

At this point the Carter administration decided to break diplomatic relations and launch its aborted rescue attempt. Immediately afterward, Secretary of State Cyrus Vance resigned because he had opposed the raid.

Bani-Sadr had been elected president in January with 75 to 80 percent of the vote. But in May, when the results of the election of the Islamic Assembly were announced, the Islamic Republican party, the party of the militant leaders of Iran's eighty thousand mullahs, took a clear majority of the seats.

Although Bani-Sadr was still nominally in charge, Khomeini's group had won the power struggle. They launched a purge of all but the most devout fundamentalists in the bureaucracies, the universities, the army, and elsewhere. There were many executions, public stonings of sinners, and so many arrests that the jails were as full as they had been under the shah at the worst of times.

By the end of the summer, the power struggle was over. Although some extremists talked of putting the hostages on trial as spies to humiliate the United States even more, now that the power struggle had been won the hostages were no longer useful. All that was needed was a graceful way out. This was provided by President Carter's defeat in the 1980 election. The negotiations began to make headway immediately after Carter's loss, although they were probably deliberately slowed down so that the actual release did not occur until after he had left office.*

---

*William Casey, Reagan's campaign manager and later director of the CIA in his administration, allegedly held several meetings with Ayatollah Khomeini's representatives in which Casey promised to give Iran arms if it would delay the release of the hostages until after the election. See Gary Sick, "The Election Story of the Decade," the *New York Times* (April 15, 1991): 17; and Leslie H. Gelb, "A New Iran Hostage Scandal?" the *New York Times* (April 17, 1991): 23. Bani-Sadr, in an interview in Washington on May 6, 1991, said that he did not have firsthand knowledge of contacts between the Reagan campaign team and Iranian religious leaders to delay the release of the hostages, but that in the month before the 1980 election many people in Iran's ruling circles were openly discussing the fact that a deal had been made between the Reagan campaign team and Iranian religious leaders to delay the hostages' release in order to help bring about Jimmy Carter's defeat [the *New York Times* (May 7, 1991): A 11]. In August 1991 Congress began an investigation into the question of whether or not such a deal had been made.

CHAPTER 3

The Iran-Iraq War

Saddam Hussein's problems with Iran began at about the same time that President Carter's did. Immediately after Ayatollah Khomeini returned to Iran on February 1, 1979, he launched a series of fiery speeches calling for the export of Iran's Islamic revolution to other Muslim countries and made a special effort to appeal to Shiite Arabs in those countries. Hussein responded in two ways. First, he began stirring rebellion in the Iranian province of Khuzestan, whose inhabitants were mainly Arab rather than Persian. Second, he sent military and financial aid to Kurds living in Iran, which was ironic, since he had been warring against his own Kurdish minority for years.

The Carter and Hussein "Doctrines"

When the Soviet Union invaded Afghanistan, President Carter announced what was quickly dubbed the "Carter doctrine"; that the United States would come to the aid of Saudi Arabia and the emirates against foreign (that is, Soviet) aggression. Not to be outdone, Hussein announced a "Pan-Arab Charter," dubbed just as quickly the "Hussein doctrine." It was an appeal for collective Arab defense against any aggression and for Arab states to refrain from using armed force against any other Arab state.

The Shiite Daawa Rebellion

In April 1980 a revolutionary Shiite party, al-Daawa, attempted to assassinate Iraq's deputy prime minister, Tariq Aziz. Aziz survived, but his companions were killed. At the funeral for the victims, the Daawa party attacked a second time.

Saddam Hussein responded by making membership in the Daawa party a crime punishable by death. About twenty thousand urban, middle-class Shiites were arrested and deported, as were some fifteen thousand Shiite Kurds. The leading Shiite cleric, Ayatollah Sadr, and his sister were arrested and tortured. Sadr died in the process.

The Iran-Iraq War[1]

Iraq by this time was full of refugees from Iran, many of them former high-level officials from the shah's regime. They convinced Saddam Hussein that the Iranian army would not fight for Khomeini's regime, and Hussein decided on war. In front of the television cameras, he tore up the agreement by which he had given Iran half the Shatt-al-Arab and ordered an invasion.

However, the Iranian air force and most of the ground forces remained loyal. An Iraqi ground attack across the Shatt-al-Arab captured the city of Khorramshahr, but then bogged down. The war settled down to a stalemate similar to the World War I western front.

At this stage Iraq felt the full impact of Britain's 1923 decision to draw the Kuwaiti borders so as to deny Iraq a port. Kuwait, cowed by Iran, refused to give Iraq permission to use the channel, cutting off Iraq's access to the sea. Iraq had to export its oil via two pipelines, one that went to Syria and a second to Turkey. As the war went on, Iraq built two more pipelines for export, while depending on truck convoys from Jordan, Kuwait, and Turkey for incoming supplies.

In spite of the war effort, Iraq was able to build some new war industries. One of these was a nuclear reactor that Hussein hoped to use to produce nuclear weapons. But Israel destroyed the plant in a bold air attack on June 7, 1981.

Iran Strikes Back

By this time, the clerics had won the internal struggle for power in Iran. Hundreds of thousands of teenagers were recruited for the army. They were armed, given a minimum of military training, and indoctrinated with the Shiite religious belief that death in a holy war was a passport to paradise. Then, led by fanatic mullahs, they went into battle in human waves. The loss of life was appalling, but the Iraqi forces were pushed back to the border.

In December the Iranians took a key road junction, and a month-long Iraqi assault failed to take it back. In March 1982 Iranian forces pushed the Iraqis thirty miles farther back, capturing fifteen thousand Iraqi soldiers in the process. Three months later Iran recaptured the city of Khorramshahr, taking twenty-two thousand Iraqi soldiers prisoner.

Saddam Hussein's Countermoves

Saddam Hussein, as usual, was both flexible and clever. On June 6, Israel invaded Lebanon to destroy the Palestine Liberation Organization (PLO) bases there. Less than a week later Hussein ordered a unilateral cease-fire in the war with Iran and pulled back all the Iraqi troops still in Iranian territory. He then proposed that Iran and Iraq join in helping Lebanon resist the attack by Israel.

These public moves were clever enough, but there is reason to believe that Hussein had also engineered the Israeli attack. Yassir Arafat, the PLO leader, knew that the Israeli government was looking for an excuse to move against the PLO bases in Lebanon, and he had done everything possible to avoid giving them a pretext. Hussein seems to have provided it.

On June 3, an attempt had been made in London to assassinate the Israeli ambassador to the Court of St. James. This gave the Israelis the excuse they were looking for to attack the PLO bases in Lebanon, but the man the British arrested and tried for organizing the assassination attempt turned out to be an Iraqi intelligence colonel.

Ayatollah Khomeini rejected Saddam Hussein's overture, and Iran launched another offensive on July 14, this time into the Iraqi homeland. Fighting on their home ground made the Iraqi troops more determined, and the attack failed. What probably disappointed Khomeini even more was that the Iraqi Shiites showed no sign of rebellion.

During the years since 1979, Hussein had expelled more than three hundred thousand Iraqi Shiites, mainly middle class and mainly to Iran. This left the Shiite peasants leaderless. They lived in fear of Hussein and his repression, but at the same time they had no stomach for living under a fundamentalist priestly rule like that in Iran, even if it was Shiite.

Saddam Hussein Launches a New Party Line

In June 1982, coincident with the withdrawal of troops from Iranian territory, Saddam Hussein shifted the party line. He downplayed pan-Arabism in favor of Iraqi nationalism. He developed closer ties to both Egypt and Jordan. He made overtures to Morocco, Saudi Arabia, and the other Arab monarchies that he had previously condemned as feudal and reactionary. The United States also began to "tilt" toward Iraq, benefiting Hussein greatly, although he did not agree to normalize relations.

Iran's Yearly Offensives

For the rest of the war, Iraq stayed on the defensive. Iran, on the other hand, launched at least one offensive each year.

In February 1984 Iran attacked across the marshes in southern Iraq, which had previously been considered impassable. Although Iranian casualties were high, the offensive did well. For the first time, Saddam Hussein ordered the use of chemical weapons against Iran.

Another Iranian offensive across the marshes in 1985 also made significant progress, and again Hussein ordered the employment of chemical weapons.

Iran launched still another offensive in February 1986, and this time its forces took the whole of the Fao peninsula, near the Iraqi military port of Umm Qasr. Iraqi counterattacks failed to retake the peninsula, and the Iraqis suffered perhaps as many as fifteen thousand casualties.

Iraq retaliated by attacking Iranian shipping in the Gulf. Iraq had no shipping in the Gulf, so Iran attacked the shipping of Iraq's supporters, principally Kuwait.

The Iran-Contra Affair[2]

In early November 1986, the so-called Iran-Contra affair became public. The Reagan administration had been actively urging U.S. allies not to sell arms to Iran. Its own policy was to "tilt" toward Iraq. Behind the scenes, however, the Reagan administration, with the help of Israel, had secretly been selling arms to Iran and, using roundabout channels, sending the profits to support the Contras rebelling against the pro-Communist government of Nicaragua.

The Reagan White House saw the Middle East as an area of prime strategic importance. First, it had oil, the most strategic of all commodities in today's world. Second, the Middle East is a vital crossroads of world communications routes. Finally, just as the north German plain was seen as an avenue for the Soviets into Western Europe, so was Iran seen as an avenue for the Soviets into the Middle East and Africa.

The Iran-Iraq war was at its height at the time, threatening the stability of the entire Middle East. The Reagan administration's analysis recognized that the cause of the war was mainly religious, rooted in the ancient rivalry between the Sunni and Shiite Muslims and Iran's encouragement of the Iraqi Shiites to rebel against the Sunni-dominated Iraqi government.

Nevertheless, in spite of its fears about the instability that the war was creating, the Reagan administration followed a policy of neutrality. Iran under Ayatollah Khomeini had been actively hostile to the United States. After the fifty-three American hostages were released, Iran sponsored terrorist attacks on individual American citizens and on U.S. installations. Iraq, for its part, had not been quite so hostile as Iran, but it had certainly not been friendly. The Reagan administration "tilted" toward Iraq because it judged Iran the greater threat. But it still maintained a basic neutrality and actively lobbied its allies and others not to sell arms to either side, especially Iran. In addition, the Reagan administration sought to isolate Iran both economically and politically.

Secretly, however, early in 1982 the Reagan administration began giving military aid to Iraq and intelligence information garnered from satellite photography and other sources.[3] Although the avowed U.S. policy was to be neutral in the Iran-Iraq war, its real policy was to try to make sure that neither side won a clear victory by secretly arming both. After the Gulf War, officials who served in the Reagan administration conceded that while the purpose that they intended to accomplish with U.S. aid, that of preventing Iran from defeating Iraq, had been achieved, U.S. aid—along with aid from the Soviet Union—had helped Iraq grow powerful enough to invade Kuwait in 1990.

At the time of the Iran-Contra affair, three or four Americans were being held hostage in Middle Eastern countries by groups under the influence of Iran, if not under its actual control. In dealing with the problem, the Reagan administration had followed the policy set by Israel: "Never negotiate with terrorists under any circumstances. If you make a deal with terrorists to release one hostage, they will only be encouraged to take more."

What seemed to worry the Reagan administration most about the continuing Iran-Iraq war was the instability it created for the whole of the Middle East. The administration's greatest fear was that this instability would provide an opportunity for the Soviets to increase their political influence in the region, or even provide an excuse for military intervention.

At this point an opportunity arose to negotiate with "moderate" elements in Iran by offering to trade arms for hostages. The Reagan administration, according to its own account, saw in this opportunity a chance to kill two birds with one stone: strengthening the Iranian moderates and obtaining the release of American hostages. The administration, in utmost secrecy, began to negotiate such a deal, in spite of its declared policy of pressing U.S. allies not to sell arms to Iran under any circumstances.

As for the Contra side of the Iran-Contra affair, the connection developed when the arms deal generated surplus funds. The Boland amendment passed by Congress had specifically forbidden military aid to the Contras, so additional appropriations were impossible. Admiral John Poindexter, Reagan's national security adviser, and Marine Corps Lt. Col. Oliver North, a member of the National Security Council (NSC) staff, thought it would be a "neat idea" to get around the Boland amendment by using the money to supply arms to the Contras.

When the story of the Iran-Contra affair was leaked, White House staff members tried to avoid embarrassing the president by telling the press that he had not been informed about these machinations. The historical parallel here is Henry II and the murder of Thomas à Becket, the archbishop of Canterbury. King Henry had not ordered the murder of Becket. Rather, annoyed to the point of exhaustion by the archbishop, the king had only said—rhetorically—"Is there not one who will rid me of this low-born priest?" Two Norman knights hastened to do just that and thus to please the king.

The Reagan Administration Reasoning

The Reagan administration offered three reasons for its actions in the Iran-Contra affair—two strategic or geopolitical and one humanitarian. The first strategic-geopolitical reason was that selling arms to Iran would encourage the moderates in the Iranian government and thereby help end the Iran-Iraq war. Ending the war would in turn bring stability to the Middle East and block an avenue for the Soviets to increase their political influence in the region, if not their actual military presence there.

The second strategic-geopolitical reason was that using the money generated by selling arms to Iran to aid the Contras would help them overthrow the pro-Communist Nicaraguan government. The Reagan administration was convinced that continued Communist control of Nicaragua would provide both the Soviet Union and Castro's Cuba vital

political opportunities in Central America, and eventually bring Soviet submarine and missile bases right to the United States' doorstep.
The humanitarian reason was the possibility of freeing the hostages.[4]

This, in sum, was the Reagan administration's reasoning behind its
decision to sell arms to Iran. But critics of the administration's action
came to quite opposite conclusions.

The Critics' Counterargument

First, the critics argued, there were no "moderates" in the Iranian
government. All of the moderates had long since been eliminated, and
the officials who remained were religious zealots. This was the one
country in the world, the counterargument continued, where the priests
truly ruled. Furthermore, even if there were moderates in Iran, selling arms to Iran when the government of the United States had been
pressuring its allies and everyone else not to do so would destroy the
world's confidence in the U.S. government, its statements, its policies,
and its integrity.

As for the humanitarian motive, the counterargument was that even
if the United States did free a few hostages by trading arms to Iran,
the Iranians would simply tell their minions to take a few more. Finally, according to this group of critics, any fool should have realized
that word that the United States was sending arms to Iran would leak
out, for the simple reason that the Iranians were in on the deal and
would broadcast the details whenever it suited their purpose, as it surely
would sooner or later.

For the Contra side of the affair, the argument was that the Sandinistas
who ruled Nicaragua were only superficially Communists. They were
nationalists first and Communists second. They were fighting against
the long exploitation of the peasants by the oligarchs and would seek
help wherever they could find it.

If all this was so, the counterargument continued, then the only hope
for a solution to the Nicaragua problem was negotiation, preferably
multilateral and spearheaded by the Central American and Latin American
countries themselves.

Finally, these critics concluded, even if no solution could be found,
the worst that could happen was that Nicaragua would be a minor
annoyance, as Castro's Cuba had been, and not a vital threat. The Soviets
already had a submarine base in Cuba. The Cuban missile crisis had
taught them not to put nuclear weapons near the United States;

furthermore, even if they forgot that lesson at some point in the future, missile technology had advanced to the point where missiles based in the Soviet Union or on submarines lurking under the arctic and antarctic ice packs were more effective than missile bases in the Americas.

A Third Explanation

As more and more evidence became available about the internal maneuvers in the White House that led to the Iran-Contra affair, a third explanation surfaced: an explanation centering more on struggles inside the Reagan administration than with strategic and geopolitical factors.

The Reagan administration's Iran-Contra decisions were made by a very small group of people who had successfully excluded those who had legitimate responsibilities and knowledge that might have shown the weaknesses of the operation. These few people were not actually members of the NSC itself, which is composed of the secretaries of the major departments, such as State, Defense, and Treasury. They were members of the NSC staff, principally Robert C. McFarlane, who held the post of national security adviser at the beginning of the affair; his successor, Admiral Poindexter; and Lieutenant Colonel North. McFarlane and Poindexter seem to have been motivated by both ideological convictions and personal ambitions to play as large a role in the NSC as their predecessors, Henry A. Kissinger and Zbigniew Brzezinski. North, on the other hand, apparently was not only highly ideological but was also like the two Norman knights referred to earlier—what the military call a "can-do" personality or a "loose cannon," that is, a highly energetic person, eager to please, who charges off in all directions to accomplish what he thinks his leaders want, but who exercises little judgment in doing so.

As for President Reagan's role, the Henry II analogy seems to have been only partly true. Reagan's critics suggested that the entire affair reminded Reagan of an old movie plot that had all the elements for a box-office success: anti-Communist fervor, intrigue, and, most importantly, the sentimental human element provided by the hostages. It was precisely the kind of operation, the argument ran, that would pique Reagan's interest.

But the limited evidence so far available is that all this is only part of the story. What is known hints that the person who was in control, who knew all the details and pulled all the strings, was CIA director

William Casey. During World War II Casey had served in a very active post in the Office of Strategic Services, the CIA's World War II predecessor. He was a hard-line anti-Communist and a firm believer in the covert actions and behind-the-scenes maneuvering of secret intelligence. Unfortunately, the extent of his role in the Iran-Contra affair may never be known: He died of cancer in the middle of the investigation.

In any case, as more than one observer has remarked, Saddam Hussein's charges that the American imperialists and the Israeli Zionists were constantly engaged in plots and conspiracies seem to have been borne out by the actual facts.

The Reflagging of Kuwaiti Tankers

While the convoluted story of the Iran-Contra affair was just beginning to unfold, Iran launched an offensive against the Iraqi city of Basra in January 1987 and got close enough to lob artillery shells into it. Iran had broken through four of the five Iraqi defense lines, and the Iraqis could not help but believe that the Iranian success was due in large part to the fact that they were equipped with American Hawk antiaircraft missiles and TOW (tube-launched, optically sighted, wire-guided) antitank missiles.

When Iran began attacking its shipping, Kuwait asked for American protection. The Reagan administration was in no hurry to provide it, so the Kuwaitis threatened to turn to the Soviets for the help they needed. The Reagan administration then promptly agreed to reflag Kuwaiti tankers as American merchant vessels and to provide naval escorts for them, beginning in July 1987.

Faced with American power in the Gulf, Iran shifted its attack to the north, working with the Iraqi Kurds. In March 1988 Iranian forces reached Halabja, and Hussein countered once more with chemical weapons.

Iraq Takes the Offensive

Then, in April 1988, it was Iraq's turn again. Iraqi forces launched an offensive and in less than two days took back the Fao peninsula. The next month, they attacked and forced back the Iranians facing Basra.

The Iranians completely lost heart. A U.N.-sponsored cease-fire was proposed, and on July 18, 1988, Ayatollah Khomeini felt that he had no choice but to accept, saying as he did so that accepting was "more lethal for me than poison."

The Iraqi people celebrated for more than two weeks; the Iranian people were glum. The Iraqi government claimed victory; the Iranian government remained silent.

Aftermath

Iraq, although it claimed victory and its people celebrated, had paid a very high price: The dead numbered 120,000 and the wounded 300,000— out of a population of 17,000,000. For a country with the population of the United States, the equivalent figures would have been 1,764,000 killed and 4,411,000 wounded. Iraq had a foreign debt of $35 billion to Arab countries and another $35 billion to others. Iran held 65,000 Iraqi POWs. Iraq had gained no territory, and although Iraq claimed the whole of the Shatt-al-Arab, it remained closed.

The negotiations with Iran bogged down. The exchange of POWs ceased. Prices in Iraq soared. One-third of Iraq's army of one million men were demobilized, but there were no jobs for them. Hussein tried to persuade Kuwait and other oil-rich Arab states to bail Iraq out of its difficulties, but without success.

CHAPTER 4

The Attack on Kuwait and the U.S. Response

In 1975, when Iraq sent troops against the Kurds, one of its own minority people, the Soviet Union stopped shipping arms to Iraq. As already mentioned, the Carter administration saw the cooling of Soviet-Iraqi relations as an opportunity and approached Iraq about renewing diplomatic relations. Iraq was not interested, but during the hostage crisis with Iran, informal diplomatic contacts between the United States and Iraq increased significantly.

Reagan Restores Diplomatic Relations With Iraq

After its war with Iran began to go badly, it was Iraq that sought to renew diplomatic ties. Dreading an Iranian victory, the Reagan administration was eager to help. The problem was that American law forbade normalizing relations while Iraq remained on the list of terrorist states, and the Reagan administration could hardly remove it from the list so long as Iraq was harboring the notorious Abu Nidal.

As already mentioned, the State Department considered Abu Nidal's terrorist organization the most dangerous of them all. Nidal had been a member of Arafat's PLO but broke with it after the October 1973 Arab-Israeli war. Arafat decided to focus terrorist attacks within Israel and the occupied territories; Nidal wanted to attack Jews everywhere in the world, as well as any government that was sympathetic to them. Nidal not only broke with Arafat, he threatened to kill him. When the Austrian and Italian governments showed sympathy for Arafat, Nidal's terrorists attacked airport lounges in Vienna and Rome with submachine guns and hand grenades. The Abu Nidal organization continued its terrorist attacks in the years that followed. One of the most brutal of these attacks was in 1986 on the El Al ticket counter in Rome, where terrorists killed twelve people and wounded sixty others. An eleven-year-old American schoolgirl was one of those killed.

Despite this, the Reagan administration struck some sort of deal with Hussein. Abu Nidal moved to Damascus, Syria, and in March 1982 the Reagan administration removed Iraq from the list of terrorist states.

In December 1982 the Reagan administration granted Iraq credits of $300 million for the purchase of rice and wheat, and in the following years Iraq bought more than $5.5 billion worth of American farm products. In November 1984, the administration restored diplomatic relations with Iraq and exchanged ambassadors.

Reagan Administration Aid to Iraq

To help Iraq further in its war with Iran, the CIA passed to Iraqi intelligence services information on Iran gathered by its spy satellites. The United States extended additional agricultural credits to Iraq, and American banks were encouraged to lend the Iraqis money.

The Reagan administration remained silent when Iraq used intermediate-range ballistic missiles against Iranian cities. The administration's protests about the use of poison gas against Iranian troops were mild. It also approved the shipment of $730 million worth of sensitive technological products to Iraq—some of which, U.S. officials now believe, were diverted to Iraq's nuclear, chemical, and missile programs.

After U.S. troops were sent to the Middle East a joke going around the Pentagon was that if an American soldier got shot, it would probably be with a Soviet bullet. But if he was wounded by a chemical or biological warhead, the missile would probably have been designed by an American computer.

When news of the Iran-Contra affair was leaked in November 1988, Saddam Hussein was outraged. The Reagan administration apologized profusely. Shortly after that the administration agreed to reflag the Kuwaiti oil tankers. The move, motivated mainly by fear Kuwait might otherwise turn to the Soviet Union, was done partly to placate Saddam Hussein.

In 1987, it was Saddam Hussein's turn to apologize. An Iraqi airplane hit the USS *Stark* with a French-made Exocet missile, killing thirty-seven crewmen. Hussein not only apologized, but paid $27 million to the victims' families.

Strains in U.S.-Iraq Relations

Immediately after the cease-fire between Iran and Iraq in August 1988, Saddam Hussein renewed his attack on Iraq's Kurdish minority—this time with poison gas. Secretary of State George Schultz lodged a strong protest and Hussein promised to refrain from such acts in the future.

Early in the Bush administration, in 1989 and early 1990, several other incidents strained Western relations with Iraq. A British journalist in Iraq looking into rumors of a renewed Iraqi effort to build nuclear weapons was arrested, tried, and executed for spying.

Another incident concerned Gerald V. Bull, the world's foremost designer of modern artillery. Iraq had in its arsenal a number of artillery pieces designed by Bull. One, for example, was the ERFB (extended-range full-bore) gun, which had a range six miles greater than that of the artillery in the American arsenal. Bull was engaged in building a 450-foot-long supercannon with a more than 1,000mm bore (more than three feet), which was capable of hurling a shell more than a thousand miles. Components for such a gun were intercepted on their way to Iraq and confiscated. Then, in March 1990, Bull was assassinated outside his apartment in Brussels, Belgium—presumably by Israeli agents.

Even more ominously, devices that serve as triggers for nuclear weapons were also intercepted on their way to Iraq.

Iraq also began stockpiling grain purchased through a $300 million line of credit from a bank in Bahrain.

Hussein renewed his efforts to make a formal peace agreement with Iran. He proposed a summit meeting with Iran's president, Rafsanjani, but the Iranians refused.

Although Iraq had claimed victory in its war with Iran, there had been no profit in it. Iraq was having a difficult time recovering from the war. As already mentioned, Hussein sought help from Kuwait, the emirates, and Saudi Arabia. Iraq's long and costly war with Iran, he argued, had not been Iraq's private business but the defense of the entire Arab world against Iran's Shiite fundamentalism. He had five demands.

First, Hussein wanted the three to forgive their loans to Iraq.

Second, he wanted them to grant Iraq new loans totaling $30 billion.

Third, he demanded that Kuwait pay Iraq $2.4 billion for the oil stolen from Iraq through the slant wells dug into the Rumaila oil field on Iraq's side of the border.

Fourth, he demanded that the Arab states that had been violating the Organization of Petroleum Exporting Countries (OPEC) quotas cease doing so. Although Hussein did not name Kuwait, in his mind it was undoubtedly the major offender. Kuwait's OPEC quota was 1.5 million barrels a day, but for some time Kuwait had actually produced 2.4 million barrels a day, which was considered a major factor in depressing the price of oil. The oil glut, Hussein argued, had depressed prices, and the low prices were making it impossible for Iraq to recover economically. War, he said, is fought by soldiers, but it is also waged by economic means. The violation of oil quotas, Hussein argued, "is in fact a kind of war against Iraq."

Finally, Hussein argued that the market technicians had set the price of oil too low. He urged that the price be raised immediately to $18 a barrel. Each one-dollar drop in the price, he said, cost Iraq $1 billion a year. Western experts, he went on, said that the client states were prepared to pay up to $25 a barrel.

All of Hussein's demands were rejected by his fellow Arab leaders, with the emir of Kuwait in the lead. Hussein denied that he was bent on war; after eight years of war with Iran, he said, Iraq knew what war meant. But he also said, ". . . we have reached a point where we can no longer withstand pressure."

Nevertheless, Hussein continued to assure both his fellow Arab leaders and the United States that he had no intention of invading Kuwait. He continued to make those assurances until July 25, 1990.

Did the United States Give Hussein a Green Light?

In spite of the strains in U.S.-Iraq relations, Hussein, ironically, seems to have had good reason to believe that the United States had given him a green light to invade Kuwait. A few days before the Iraqi attack on Kuwait, Hussein called in the American ambassador, April Glaspie. He repeated his complaints that Kuwait had violated the OPEC agreements on oil supplies and prices and that Kuwait had stolen Iraqi oil by digging slant wells under the border to tap the oil deposits on the Iraqi side of the Rumaila oil field. Also clearly on Hussein's mind was the fact, mentioned earlier, that in 1923 Great Britain fixed the borders of Iraq in such a way as to deny Iraq a port on the Gulf, that is, by giving Kuwait the two uninhabited islands that blocked the approach to the Iraqi port.

Hussein obviously thought he had a strong case for moving against Kuwait. Afterward, several third-party commentators observed wryly that it was probably better in both moral and international legal terms, for example, than the case the United States had for invading Panama—an attack that was condemned by the U.N. General Assembly by a vote of seventy-five to twenty, with thirty-nine abstentions, and unanimously condemned by the Organization of American States. Hussein also made the same point afterward, asking why the United States had not responded with equal vigor when Israel and Syria invaded and occupied neighboring territories.

In his meeting with Ambassador Glaspie, Hussein launched into a tirade, threatening to use force not only against Kuwait but also against the United States if it tried to stop him. Ambassador Glaspie, acting on instructions from President Bush and the State Department, replied that the United States had "no opinion" on Arab vs. Arab conflicts such as Iraq's dispute with Kuwait, although it opposed the use of force and continued to support its friends in the region.

On her return to the United States, Ambassador Glaspie told the American press that no one in the administration had anticipated that Iraq would take all of Kuwait. Her statement implied that the administration *did* expect Iraq to take a slice that would include the port that Iraq had been denied and probably the Kuwaiti territory encompassing the tip of the Rumaila oil field. She conceded that Hussein probably understood the policy statement she had delivered to him to be a green light to settle his differences with Kuwait by force.

Some seven months later, however, Glaspie claimed that the account released by Iraq had been toned down—that she had been tougher than the account suggested. On the other hand, a few days after Glaspie met with Hussein, John Kelly, the assistant secretary of state for the Middle East, said in testimony before Congress just about the same thing that Glaspie was supposed to have said to Hussein—that Iraq's quarrel with Kuwait was an affair for the Arabs themselves to settle. Similarly, the day before Glaspie's meeting with Hussein, Margaret Tutweiler, the State Department spokesperson, said that the United States was committed to supporting the individual and collective self-defense of American friends in the Gulf, but she added that "we do not have any defense treaties with Kuwait, and there are no special defense or security commitments to Kuwait." It is also significant that Secretary of State James Baker refused to declassify Glaspie's original report of her conversation with Hussein. Leaks from the State Department suggested that the reason for Baker's refusal was that Glaspie did what she was ordered to do and that what she was ordered to do was fairly accurately described in the Iraqi account.

In July 1991 the State Department gave the Senate Foreign Relations Committee copies of Glaspie's cables sent immediately after her session with Hussein. The chairman of the committee, Claiborne Pell (D., Rhode Island), wrote to Secretary of State Baker demanding an explanation of "inconsistencies" between what Glaspie's cables reported and what she had testified before the committee. In particular, Pell continued, Glaspie had said in her testimony that she had told Hussein that even though the United States took no position on his dispute with Kuwait, "we insist that you settle your disputes with Kuwait nonviolently" and that she had assured Sen. Joseph R. Biden, Jr. (D., Delaware), that her reporting cable included that phrase. However, Pell's letter continued, the cable had not included that phrase. Senator Alan Cranston (D., California) said, "April Glaspie deliberately misled the Congress about her role in the Persian Gulf tragedy." Other senators charged angrily that her testimony, in which she said that she had been tougher than the Iraqi version reported, was actually not true—that her cables and what was released by the Iraqi government were essentially the same.

At the same time, the committee was also given a copy of the cable that President Bush had sent to Hussein on July 28 to follow up on Glaspie's July 25 meeting. This cable said that any use of force by Iraq would be "unacceptable," but it emphasized that "My Administration continues to desire better relations with Iraq." The cable, in the words of newspaper columnist Leslie Gelb, was "an echo of the weak Glaspie line," lacking any "steel" and even failing to mention the one hundred thousand Iraqi troops massed on the Kuwaiti border.[1]

The Bush administration apparently expected Iraq to take the disputed islands that blocked its port and the part of the oil field that stuck into Kuwait, but was shocked when Iraq took all of Kuwait. Hussein, on the other hand, probably thought that taking the entire country was only prudent. Doing so would give him bargaining chips to keep the islands and the oil field, and he just might get lucky and end up with the whole of Kuwait as well.

The Invasion of Kuwait

As already described, Iraqi forces crossed the Kuwaiti border in force at 2:00 A.M. on August 2, 1990, and occupied the entire country within six hours, after which Hussein announced that Kuwait was being incorporated into Iraq in an "eternal merger."

The U.S. government was caught by surprise. Although the U.S. intelligence community had kept track of the Iraqi buildup and correctly predicted that Iraq would invade, the White House chose to ignore repeated warnings. On August 1, the CIA's Charles E. Allen, whose title was National Intelligence Officer for Warning, issued a "final warning" to the NSC staff responsible for Middle Eastern affairs that an invasion would come in twenty-four hours. It did, and the top White House and Pentagon officials were at home in bed.[2]

President Bush's first public statement after the Iraqi invasion proclaimed that the United States had no intention of intervening militarily.

That same afternoon Bush met with British prime minister Margaret Thatcher, who lectured him sternly. "Remember, George," she said, "this is no time to go wobbly."[3] Hussein, she said, must be stopped. Accordingly, Bush changed his mind and announced that military intervention was indeed being considered.

Shortly afterward, President Bush telephoned King Fahd. Since Fahd knew that the Iraqi troops had pulled back from the Iraq-Saudi border, he was greatly surprised when Bush argued that Saddam Hussein would not stop with Kuwait but would continue on to conquer Saudi Arabia. It was some days before Fahd could be convinced that he should permit American troops to enter his country.

While Saddam Hussein may have intended attacking Saudi Arabia at some future date, it is now clear that he had no plans to do so at that time. Months later, General Powell told the press that during the three weeks following President Bush's announcement that the Allies had decided to send troops, Saudi Arabia was virtually defenseless. "We were scared to death . . . ," General Powell said, "there was no way we could have stopped him."

However, President Bush's TV announcement of the planned deployment not only repeated the argument that Iraq was about to attack Saudi Arabia, but suggested that the idea of sending American troops had originated with King Fahd.

As already mentioned, on the weekend of August 4, President Bush convened a small circle of advisers at Camp David, the presidential retreat in Maryland, including Secretary of Defense Richard Cheney; the chairman of the Joint Chiefs, Gen. Colin Powell; the national security adviser, retired air force Lt. Gen. Brent Scowcroft; and Gen. H. Norman Schwarzkopf, commander of the U.S. Central Command.[4]

General Schwarzkopf briefed the group on Iraq's military capabilities and the plan for a deterrent force: 200,000 to 250,000 American army, navy, air force, and Marine troops—the largest deployment since the Vietnam War. Once permission was obtained from the king of Saudi Arabia, it would take approximately seventeen weeks to get the troops in place.

General Scowcroft noted that Kuwait was not popular among Arabs; Bush responded that that was why the focus had to be on the defense of Saudi Arabia. Bush was not only worried about the fate of Saudi Arabia, but also about the likelihood that the Saudis would accept Iraq's annexation of Kuwait and buy their way out of any perceived threat to themselves.

The decision was to pressure King Fahd into accepting U.S. troops stationed in Saudi Arabia. In keeping with the president's preference for making important decisions in secret, only one congressional leader, Sen. Sam Nunn (D., Georgia), chairman of the Senate Armed Services Committee, was consulted in advance.

On Sunday, August 5, General Powell was watching TV as the president stepped off the helicopter on the White House lawn. In answer to a question, Bush said that he was determined to reverse the Iraqi aggression. "This will not stand," he said. "This will not stand, this aggression against Kuwait." According to journalist Bob Woodward, Powell was stunned. There had been no staff study of the situation, no NSC meeting, no consultation with Powell and the other chiefs of staff. Bush had set a new, much larger goal: to oust Iraq from Kuwait, as well as to defend Saudi Arabia. And he had done so in a personal and emotional declaration. To reverse an invasion was one of the most difficult military tasks imaginable, yet the highest ranking U.S. military adviser had been given no opportunity to offer his assessment. "Powell marvelled at the distance Bush had traveled in three days," Woodward writes. "To Powell it was almost as if the president had six-shooters in both hands and was blazing away."[5]

Bush then dispatched Secretary of Defense Cheney and a team of advisers, including General Schwarzkopf, to brief the king and obtain his permission to send troops to Saudi Arabia. In his meeting with the king, Cheney outlined a two-part strategy. The first part was to station U.S. and other troops in Saudi Arabia to deter an Iraqi attack. The second was economic strangulation. The troops would be important to deter not only an immediate attack, but to prevent Hussein from lashing out when the economic sanctions began to pinch. The king finally granted his permission.

A spokesperson for the administration said that, like Reagan, Bush considered the War Powers Act unconstitutional, so he was sending Congress "a notification [of the dispatch of troops] consistent with the Act," rather than the formal document the act requires.

Bush then got on the telephone and, with unbounded energy and a dazzling display of personal diplomacy, orchestrated an impressive international political consensus condemning Iraq's aggression. A formidable force of naval, air, and ground forces was assembled to block an Iraqi attack on Saudi Arabia, and the U.N. was persuaded to condemn Iraq's aggression and call for a worldwide economic boycott to pressure it to withdraw to its own borders.

The United States' Goals

President Bush said that the mission of the American troops was defensive. "A line has been drawn in the sand," he said, against any invasion of Saudi Arabia. The American ambassador to the U.N., Thomas R. Pickering, hailed the decision to draw such a line as "an historic moment." One of his Arab colleagues at the U.N. agreed. "Now let us pray," he said, "that we can control the winds."

The theme of Bush's August 8 speech to the nation was the need to stop further aggression:

America does not seek conflict. Nor do we seek to chart the destiny of other nations. But America will stand by her friends. The mission of our troops is wholly defensive. Hopefully, they'll not be needed long. They will not initiate hostilities but they will defend themselves, the Kingdom of Saudi Arabia and other friends in the Persian Gulf.

Although his main theme was the need to oppose aggression, Bush did refer to the importance of oil. Iraq, Bush said, has the world's second largest oil reserves, and the United States imports nearly half of the oil it consumes.

In an August 15 speech to Pentagon employees, Bush discussed the ramifications of Hussein ever gaining control of Saudi Arabia: "Our jobs, our way of life, our own freedom and the freedom of friendly countries all around the world would suffer if control of the world's great oil reserves fell into the hands of Saddam Hussein."

Bush also compared Hussein to Hitler: "A half a century ago, our nation and the world paid dearly for appeasing an aggressor who should, and could, have been stopped. We are not going to make the same mistake again."

Arab Reaction to the Iraqi Invasion

The Arab reaction to Iraq's invasion showed little sympathy for Kuwait. Newspapers around the world carried pictures of demonstrations supporting Kuwait in London, Geneva, and the Riviera, but there were no demonstrations in Arab countries.

In the eyes of the Arab man in the street, Kuwait was the spoiled rich kid of the Middle East, enjoying the highest per capita income in the world while most of the Arab countries were mired in poverty.

Also, no Arab can forget that when Great Britain was carving up the Ottoman empire after World War I, it installed as the rulers of certain states, including Kuwait, people whom many Arabs viewed as feudal potentates, chosen because they would serve British neocolonialist interests. As one British authority on the Middle East said, not only did the Western powers pick the leaders of the Arab states, but around those leaders a class of people grew up with a vested interest that is different from the interest of the ordinary Arab. "There is a very deep schism," he added, "between what the man in the street feels and how the regimes function." As an Arab put the same point, "It is one thing to say that Saddam is wrong. But it is another to say that American intervention is good."[6]

Elaborating on this theme, Edward Said, a professor at Columbia University and an American of Palestinian descent, said that Saddam Hussein is "a tyrant and an aggressor, who seems nevertheless to speak to hidden emotions and frustrations in the collective Arab soul."[7]

The truth is that the Arab man in the street had considerable sympathy for the Iraqi position. An Arab professor, Kamel S. Abu Jaber, director of the Jordan Center for Middle Eastern Studies, explained the reaction in an op-ed piece in the *New York Times* on August 10, 1990. He complained of the somewhat selective reaction that the West seemed to have to aggression in the Middle East. Jordan, he pointed out, had been the most steadfastly pro-Western state in the region. Yet when Israel seized Jerusalem and the West Bank, the West offered no help. If Saddam Hussein had learned anything from the behavior of Israel toward the women and children of the Palestinian Intifada and the indifference of the West, Jaber argued, it was that might makes right. "A feeling has developed that Arabs' lives, resources and even their souls are free for the taking, and that whether the Arabs are moderate or radical, their treatment by the West is ultimately the same."

Jaber went on to say that most Arabs were grateful to Iraq for protecting them against the extremism of Iran. "Iraq protected the entire Arab world, even the West, in a bloody and costly battle with Iran. Where would the world be had Iran's revolution spilled beyond its borders?" The Gulf crisis, he concluded, should be understood not only as a dispute over borders and Arab interests, but as "the outcome of pan-Arab hostility toward industrial nations preoccupied with preserving the flow of cheap oil."

The view that oil was the motive behind Bush's decision to send troops to the Middle East was not confined to Arabs. In another *New York Times* op-ed piece, on August 12, Thomas L. Friedman argued that the United States did not send troops to the Middle East to defend democracy. Saudi Arabia, after all, is a feudal monarchy where women are not even allowed to drive cars. On the contrary, Friedman argued, the war was about money, about protecting governments loyal to the United States and punishing those who are not, and about who would set the price of oil. Iraq and Kuwait account for 20 percent of the world's known oil reserves. If Iraq were to dominate Saudi Arabia, it would then have price influence over 45 percent. "In other words, by the price argument, one reason that the Bush Administration is sending 100,000 soldiers to Saudi Arabia is for the sake of five cents a gallon. . . ."

But, Friedman argued, the administration's judgment was misguided. Saddam Hussein has a stake in selling oil, and if the price is too high the world will go elsewhere for its oil. Texas wells will reopen, and Canada and Venezuela will move as fast as they can to fill the gap.

Friedman also rejected the argument that even if the price of oil did not justify the U.S. response, the need to deter aggression did. Secretary Baker, for example, said: "If might is to make right, then the world will be plunged into a new dark age." Friedman's answer was that the United States was not consistent in this policy. In Cambodia, it approved of bringing back into the ruling coalition the murderous Khmer Rouge—the people who killed more than a million Cambodians.

"Laid bare," Friedman concluded, "American policy on the Gulf comes down to this: troops have been sent to retain control of oil in the hands of a pro-American Saudi Arabia, so prices will remain low." Friedman said that a cartoon in the Boston *Globe* had it right: The vital interest at stake may be to make the world safe for gas guzzlers; the principle the United States holds dear is eighteen miles per gallon.

An American international banker made the same point, saying that if Syria, which has no oil, had been the aggressor, the United States would not have intervened.

As reported by Harrison J. Goldin, an American businessman who visited Yemen, Syria, Egypt, Jordan, and Saudi Arabia in late August 1990, these attitudes were not confined to the Arab man in the street but were shared by many Arab journalists, academics, professionals, and other intellectuals.[8] Although these people did not deny the menace of Hussein, they rooted for him to succeed in Kuwait—first, because they resented the Kuwaitis' arrogant display of their wealth and, second, because of a desire to see the United States humbled. The basic reason behind this attitude was a "deep-seated sense of inferiority and persecution." Each day that Saddam Hussein held the mighty West at bay, "the Islamic world holds its head higher and walks just a bit more erect." That American military might would ultimately prevail was an accepted certainty to these people, but "equally sure is that the indignity of an American victory will intensify the Arabs' quest for some ultimate, undefined violent vindication."

Because of these attitudes among the Arab people, the leaders of the Arab states lined up against Iraq stressed that their goals were defensive—to protect Saudi Arabia and the emirates from an Iraqi invasion. Some Arab leaders hinted rather broadly that their forces would not participate in an invasion of Iraq, and some said so publicly and in so many words. "Egyptian forces in Saudi Arabia," their commanding general said flatly, "will not participate in any offensive." Some time later, Prince Sultan Ibn Abdul-Aziz, the Saudi defense minister, repeated the point. The United States, he said, would not be allowed to mount any offensive action from Saudi soil against a "brother Arab state."

Reaction in the United States

In the United States, opinion was clearly divided about Bush's policies.

In an address to Congress on September 11, 1990, Bush named as one of his goals in the Middle East the establishment of a "new world order . . . in which nations recognize the shared responsibility for freedom and justice." But, as his critics pointed out, neither at that time nor in the months that followed was Bush any more specific about just what he meant by a "new world order."

Bush's critics argued that a step toward such a goal would be to turn over responsibility for the Gulf crisis to a regional organization or to the United Nations. But Bush bluntly rejected U.N. command of the forces in the Middle East and said nothing about even the more modest step of having the Allied forces fight under the U.N. flag, as they did in the Korean War.

Bush's critics suggested that with the end of the cold war, the implication was that what Bush meant by a "new world order" was a unipolar world dominated by the United States.

Opinion Among the Allies

America's Western Allies were skeptical about Saddam Hussein's takeover of Kuwait qualifying as an international aggression. In France, for example, many people thought of Kuwait not as a country but as "a multinational company headquartered in London" whose stockholders were the United States and Great Britain. Other critics pointed out that the emir of Kuwait had forty-seven wives and seventy-six children; that there were five Pakistani, Filipino, Iraqi, or Egyptian servants in Kuwait for every Kuwaiti citizen; and that because of all this, restoring sovereignty to Kuwait could hardly be described as furthering the cause of democracy.

Bush vs. Hussein

For George Bush the struggle against Iraq seemed to become a personal one, focusing on Saddam Hussein himself. What is ironic is that for years, as mentioned earlier, both the Reagan and Bush administrations had supported Hussein, preferring him to Iran's Ayatollah Khomeini. It was only when Hussein attacked Kuwait that Bush began to liken him to Hitler and called upon the Iraqi people to overthrow him.

Hussein is indeed a villain in the mold of Hitler. But in the sense of being a threat to the United States and the world, the comparison is ridiculous. Hitler commanded a highly industrialized nation with a population larger than any other in Western Europe. Germany had a long history of military excellence in terms of both its generals and its soldiers. Germany under Hitler conquered Europe, and threatened both the Soviet Union and the United Kingdom. Iraq had little industry except for its chemical, biological, and budding nuclear capacity, and it had only eighteen million people. As the dictator of such a country, Hussein was a threat to his neighbors—and to reserves of cheap oil— but nothing more.

In a word, Bush's comparison of Saddam Hussein to Hitler trivialized Hitler and inflated Saddam Hussein. Most observers found that removing Hussein was an inappropriate goal.

Attitude of the Arab Man in the Street

The ordinary Arab fully understands that Saddam Hussein is a ruthless dictator, a butcher, and a tyrant. But such a leader is no stranger to the Middle East. To Arabs it seems cynical that President Bush should call Hussein a Hitler but welcome as an ally Hafiz al-Assad, Syria's dictator, who is no less a monster than either Hitler or Hussein. Assad's support made possible the terrorist bombing of Pan Am Flight 103, in which 189 Americans died, as well as many other terrorist attacks in which Americans were killed.

In Arab eyes, what tends to outweigh Hussein's crimes is the fact that he has been trying to break the neocolonialist shackles imposed on the Arab peoples. To the Arab man in the street, Hussein, for all his villainies, is the preeminent spokesman of Arab nationalism, ranking second in the pantheon of Arab heroes only to Gamal Abdel Nasser and Saladin, who crushed the crusaders in Palestine in the twelfth century.

CHAPTER 5

Alternatives Not Taken

As the Gulf crisis continued, the Bush administration's goals changed. When President Bush sent troops to Saudi Arabia and launched an economic boycott of Iraq, he said that the troops were to serve "purely defensive purposes" and that the goals were to forestall an Iraqi invasion of Saudi Arabia and the emirates and to put enough economic pressure on Saddam Hussein to make him agree to withdraw from Kuwait. At the same time, Bush denied any intention of invading either Kuwait or Iraq, saying that he was confident that the combination of economic pressure and world opinion would force Hussein to give in.

However, on three key points, uncertainty and some confusion reigned:

(1) Whether the goals as originally stated should not be expanded.
(2) If so, whether stationing troops and naval forces in the Middle East in a posture limited to defending Saudi Arabia could achieve the expanded goals.
(3) If not, what means would accomplish the expanded goals?

At first, everyone in the administration seemed confident that the dispatch of U.S. and Allied troops would deter Hussein from attacking Saudi Arabia and the emirates. Within a few days, however, some administration insiders began to think that economic sanctions might take so long to become effective that holding together the various members of the coalition might become difficult.

Remove Hussein?
As these doubts grew, leaks from inside the Bush administration made the point that even if Hussein did withdraw from Kuwait, he would

still control Iraq's battle-hardened army of a half million men, plus another half million reservists; its fifty-five hundred tanks; an air force of one hundred French Mirage jets, armed with the Exocet missile (the type of French missile that sank the USS *Stark* in the Gulf in 1987 with heavy loss of American lives, and a British cruiser in the Falklands War with even heavier loss of life); thirty British Hunter fighters; about four hundred Soviet MIGs, many of which were modern; its stockpile of chemical and biological weapons; and its potential for developing nuclear weapons.

The conclusion suggested by these leaks was that if Iraq merely withdrew from Kuwait, the threat that Hussein posed would remain and, because of Iraq's nuclear potential, would actually increase over time. If so, the only sensible way to accomplish the American purposes in the Middle East, the administration seemed to be suggesting, would be to remove Saddam Hussein from power, force a reduction in Iraq's armed forces, and destroy Iraq's chemical and biological facilities and weapons and its potential for building nuclear weapons.

The Strategy: Bomb Iraq

Administration thinking about how to accomplish the goals of removing Hussein and destroying Iraqi war potential was revealed in an interview with the press by the air force chief of staff, Gen. Michael J. Dugan. According to Dugan, the Joint Chiefs of Staff and the commander of the forces in the Middle East, Gen. H. Norman Schwarzkopf, were all agreed that the only way to avoid a bloody land war that would destroy Kuwait in the process was a massive bombing of "downtown Baghdad," with Saddam Hussein, his family, and his mistress the principal targets.

In addition, General Dugan said, all the usual military targets would be bombed at the same time: military bases, air defense systems, airfields, Iraqi armor concentrations, command and communications centers, industrial sites producing conventional, chemical, and biological weapons, and the facilities with a potential for producing nuclear weapons. Targets would also include power stations, communications systems, bridges, roads, and railroads.

It was obviously indiscreet of General Dugan to speak so frankly about U.S. war plans, and Defense Secretary Cheney fired him shortly afterward. But neither Cheney nor any other member of the Bush administration denied that Dugan's remarks were an accurate description of the administration's thinking about war plans.

Leaks from the White House suggested, in fact, that not only was Dugan's description of the strategy correct but that the timetable had been stepped up.

At about the same time, the White House began to worry about still another aspect of the boycott. A long, drawn-out boycott would most likely strain the coalition. It might not be possible to hold it together for the time it would take to make a boycott work. In addition, suppose having Iraq withdraw from Kuwait was not the only goal. Suppose that the U.S. and Allied goals were also to remove Saddam Hussein, to reduce his army and air force to a point that they would no longer threaten Iraq's neighbors, and to dismantle Iraq's chemical and biological capabilities and its potential nuclear capability. A boycott did not seem likely to accomplish these additional goals. It would, in fact, offer no real solution at all. If these additional goals were the true U.S. interest, what would be needed to accomplish them was a full-scale military offensive. If so, a long, drawn-out boycott would only give Iraq the opportunity to strengthen its defenses.

In the meantime, Iraqi troops were devastating Kuwait, and the White House decided it could wait no longer. On September 28, Brent Scowcroft, Bush's national security adviser, raised the possibility of another U.N. Security Council resolution that would include specific mention of the use of military force against Iraq. President Bush himself suggested that the present stalemate could be allowed to continue only so long before "additional steps" would have to be taken.

The implication of all these hints and innuendos was that the administration was planning for at least an air attack on both Kuwait and Iraq—and planning for it to be launched sooner rather than later.

Doubts About the Bush Policy

Pondering the implications of these events—General Dugan's remarks, Scowcroft's suggestion of a U.N. resolution authorizing force, and the White House leaks—some observers began to have qualms about the administration's plans. On October 1 the *New York Times*, which had enthusiastically supported sending troops to Saudi Arabia, voiced alarm at what both the "doves" and the "hawks" were saying—the doves calling for immediate negotiations and the hawks calling for a preemptive military attack. The *Times* thought that the United States should stick to what the U.N. had authorized; that is, continuing the strategy of "squeezing" Iraq by an economic boycott.

Leaks from the capitals of a number of states that had so far supported U.S. policy indicated that they shared the *Times'* fears. The chief of the Soviet General Staff, Gen. Mikhail A. Moiseyev, said in an interview that the Soviet Union could not agree with an attempt to resolve the crisis by military force. The boycott, he maintained, was beginning to hurt Iraq and to force Hussein to seek a diplomatic solution. In any case, General Moiseyev argued, if the United States and its Allies did resort to force, such action should first be approved by the U.N.

An Extended Stalemate

But the policy of relying on an economic boycott also had its critics—critics on the hawk side of the discussion. Their argument was that the most that could be gained from a boycott would be a prolonged stalemate, with both sides dug into the desert along the border. Such a stalemated confrontation could last for years. The cost would be $30 to $50 billion a year, which would more than eliminate the "peace dividend" that was supposed to come with the easing of tensions with the Soviet Union and the end of the cold war. It would add significantly to the pressures already pushing the United States and the world into an economic recession.

In addition, the hawkish critics argued, if the two sides were dug in facing each other for an extended period, the tension would be high, fraught with the danger that a single slip or misunderstanding would escalate into war. As time went on, support for the policy in the Arab world, among the other Western powers, and in the American public would steadily erode.

What was worse, the hawkish critics concluded, was that if the United States and its Allies did bow to the pressure to sit tight in order to "give the boycott time to work," the initiative would pass to Saddam Hussein.

Hussein's Options

One initiative open to Hussein was to carefully choose the time to announce that he had intelligence regarding secret Israeli plans to invade Jordan. Reminding the world that King Hussein of Jordan had been Iraq's good friend and supporter, Hussein could argue that he was duty bound to send Iraqi troops to Jordan to forestall the Israeli move.

Israel had remained in the background of the crisis. But if Hussein had sent troops to Jordan, the Israelis would have had no choice but to invade. The Arab world would then have been faced with what they feared more than anything else: a coalition of Israeli and American forces on the ground in the Middle East.

Some of the Arab states would most likely have responded by simply withdrawing their military contributions to the coalition force in Saudi Arabia. Those who did not could expect to be wracked with protest and riot. Any of those not withdrawing that were headed by feudal potentates would likely be threatened by coups or even open rebellion. Some of the Arab states that withdrew might well cross over to the other side and support Iraq. The result, in time, might well have been that Israel, the United States, and possibly the United Kingdom would find themselves pitifully alone—facing, perhaps, a coalition of Arab states lined up beside Iraq.

What should not be forgotten, the argument continued, is that one of the main factors that has enabled Israel to survive is the disunity in the Arab world. If the Arab world were ever united, the odds against Israel would be 180 million Arabs against 4.7 million Israelis, of which one million are actually Arabs. If the confrontation were to become Muslim against Jew, rather than Arab against Jew, the odds would increase by 55 million Iranians.

Another option available to Hussein, the argument went on, would be to attack the coalition forces in Saudi Arabia. Hussein commanded a formidable force made up of soldiers who had been hardened in eight years of war. The coalition forces might eventually be beefed up to comparable numbers, critics conceded, but they had no such battle experience.

The critics also pointed out that the strategy outlined by General Dugan suggested that the United States and its Allies did not intend to put enough ground forces in Saudi Arabia to hold along the border, but instead would rely on air power. If Hussein struck with a ground attack, U.S. air superiority would cause many Iraqi casualties, but the critics doubted that it could prevent Hussein's armies from occupying a considerable portion of Saudi Arabia.

The critics pointed out that Hussein could then use his huge stockpile of chemical weapons to lay down a miles-wide belt of nerve gas and other chemicals across Saudi Arabia that humans could enter only in full protective gear. Fighting in such gear in the desert is next to impossible, and the only troops in the world who have had any experience doing so are Iraqi.

A high-level Iraqi official, the critics reminded everyone, had threatened that if war came, the Americans would come home in large numbers—but in body bags. It might well be, the argument went, that Hussein thought that after their experience in Vietnam, the American people, faced with high casualties, would demand an end to the war. Since this war would be perceived not as a crusade to stop Communist aggression but as a crass and venal attempt to keep the price of oil low, the critics argued, Hussein might turn out to be right. But, in the short run at least, the critics argued, casualties would be more likely to anger the American people into supporting an air attack on the Iraqi homeland. If so, the United States would undoubtedly follow the strategy outlined earlier by General Dugan.

The critics argued that strategic bombing alone was not likely to succeed in forcing Iraq to surrender. Air power's historical record was not that promising. The Reagan administration's attack on Libya and its leader, Muammar Qaddafi, succeeded in killing Qaddafi's three-year-old daughter, knocking down a lot of buildings, and perhaps damaging some of Libya's war industry. These results may well have persuaded Qaddafi to curtail his support for various terrorist organizations, but that was far different, the critics argued, from forcing Iraq to withdraw from Kuwait, remove Hussein from power, and give up its chemical, biological, and nuclear capabilities.

To the critics, in other words, bombing Iraq did not seem to be any more likely to end the war on U.S. terms than had bombing North Vietnam.

The results of bombing Iraq, the critics continued, would not further U.S. long-term goals, but damage them. The air assault described by General Dugan would kill many of the five thousand American and Western hostages that Hussein had quartered on his military bases and around the targets described previously. Since Baghdad and other cities would be given a high priority, tens of thousands of civilians—men, women, and children—would also be killed and maimed.

The critics concluded that the results would be, first, to unite the mass of the Arab people against the United States and against the Arab rulers who had allied themselves with it. A second result would be to provoke a cry of horror and outrage from the Third World, muted but intense disapproval from the peoples of the developed countries, and, as the results became known, the stunned shock of the American people. This shock would be followed, if Hussein and Iraq did not quickly capitulate, by increasingly active domestic opposition to Bush and his administration and an America even more divided than it was in the latter stages of the Vietnam War. This time, the critics argued, opposition to the war would be easier because it would be perceived not as a crusade to stop Communist aggression but, as mentioned above, as a crass and venal war to keep the price of oil at its preinvasion level.

Given the worldwide outrage that bombing Iraq would create, the critics contended, Hussein might well choose not to retaliate. If, on the other hand, he did choose to retaliate, he could not do much harm to the U.S. seaborne forces, but his chemical and biological weapons could inflict horrendous casualties on U.S. ground forces stationed in Saudi Arabia. The Saudi Arabian oil fields that the American intervention was designed to protect might also be heavily damaged by conventional bombs. If so, oil would then cost something in the neighborhood of seventy dollars a barrel, compared to the preinvasion cost of less than twenty dollars a barrel.

Although it would undoubtedly turn the world against him as nothing else would, Hussein could also unleash his chemical and biological weapons on Israel.

However, the argument continued, the probability was that Hussein would not retaliate but would instead try to make the most of the world's disgust at the American bombing of Iraq. No matter how heavy the U.S. bombing, if the United States did not use nuclear weapons, it would probably fail to force Hussein to surrender. If the bombing did include nuclear weapons, it could, of course, destroy every living thing in the entire country. But the political consequences to the United States of that sort of attack are simply unimaginable. No sane president would order such an attack, and if an insane president did so, it is doubtful that the American military would carry it out.*

The critics conceded that it could be safely assumed that an American air attack on the Iraqi homeland would be with conventional

---

*There is an historical example that tends to confirm the point. In the period just before Richard M. Nixon resigned as president, when the House Judiciary Committee voted to recommend that Nixon be impeached, the secretary of defense and members of the Joint Chiefs of Staff were apparently worried about the possibility of an American version of the incident in which Hitler staged the Reichstag fire as an excuse to arrest opposition leaders.

An American equivalent of the Reichstag fire might be, for example, that either the president himself or one of his aides would telephone lower-ranking officers commanding battalions and regiments in and around Washington and order them, say, to occupy the Capitol and arrest the president's congressional opponents on the grounds that they were secret Communists. To guard against some such incident, the secretary of defense and the Joint Chiefs of Staff quietly issued instructions that no weapons. But what could be expected from such an attack? The world's experience with "strategic bombing"—that is, bombing cities, factories, bases, and lines of communication—is that such bombing is a valuable adjunct to land and sea warfare, but that it does not win wars by itself.

The German bombing of England in World War II stiffened British resistance more than it hurt their war effort. The United States Strategic Bombing Survey (USSBS), conducted shortly after World War II, concluded that German war production peaked in 1944 in spite of the sustained Allied bombing campaign. As for Japan, the USSBS concluded that it was not the bombing that brought Japan to its knees, but the combination of attrition on the battlefield and the mind-boggling toll that submarine warfare took on the ships that carried raw materials going to Japan and the war supplies going to their troops in the field.

In the Korean War, the critics continued, the United States had total air superiority from the Yalu River south. Its constant, unimpeded bombing and strafing slowed down the movement of men and supplies to the front, but it did not stop it. It took the Communist side longer than it would have without the bombing to build up the stockpiles for an offensive, but they were still able to do so.

In Vietnam, the United States dropped more bombs on the enemy than were dropped by both sides in the whole of World War II—but it was the Communists who won the war.

Bombing Iraqi cities, industries, and lines of communication, the critics concluded, did not seem likely to force Hussein to capitulate. To accomplish that goal, a ground offensive would be needed.

If the reaction in the Third World, the developed countries, and among the American people was anything like that described above, the critics argued, it would be extremely difficult for Bush to take that next step—an all-out ground invasion of Iraq. Furthermore, if he did order an invasion, the critics predicted, the casualties would probably

---

presidential order was to be obeyed unless it came through the proper channels. It seems probable that the American military would behave in much the same way if it received an order to launch a surprise nuclear attack against a country such as Iraq—and especially if they suspected that the president was not sane. [Sources: Theodore H. White, *Breach of Faith: The Fall of Richard Nixon* (New York: Atheneum, 1975), 22–23; and personal interviews.]

be horrendous. Attacking prepared defensive positions is difficult in any circumstances, but when the defender has chemical and biological weapons in his stockpile and is willing to use them, it can prove disastrous, or so they argued.

The critics found it difficult to imagine that President Bush would make such an obviously risky decision. In Vietnam, when bombing failed, neither Lyndon Johnson nor Richard Nixon believed they could survive the political backlash to an invasion of North Vietnam—and the North Vietnamese had neither chemical nor biological weapons.

What options would be open to Bush at that juncture, the critics asked? Presumably, he would call for negotiations. But with Iraqi forces in control of half of Saudi Arabia, Iraqi cities in ruins and casualties in the tens of thousands, world opinion outraged, and America itself divided, what would be the incentive for Hussein to agree? The obvious course for Hussein to follow would be to respond that no talks could take place until U.S. and other Western forces withdrew completely from the Middle East.

Alternative Policies Open to Bush

The critics pointed out that it was not as if Bush had not had alternatives before the crisis erupted that would have had a good chance of keeping Iraq from invading Kuwait in the first place.

One alternative suggested by antiwar critics was to get ahead of events. The four problems facing Hussein and Iraq, to repeat, were (1) the two uninhabited islands blocking Iraq's access to the sea that Britain had given to Kuwait for exactly that reason; (2) Kuwait's pirating oil from the Rumaila field; (3) Kuwait's violating the OPEC oil quotas and the resulting low price of oil, which hampered Iraq in paying off its debt; and (4) Iraq's need for a loan to tide it over the financial crisis resulting from the Iran-Iraq war.

The problem of the two uninhabited islands could be met by either transferring sovereignty to Iraq or simply by internationalizing them. The problem of Kuwait pirating oil was only slightly more complicated. Only a small tip of the Rumaila oil field extends into Kuwait, and with all Kuwait's other oil fields, giving up this tip would not be a great sacrifice. If Kuwait balked at this solution, the problem could be solved by the other Arab states supervising operations at that field on both sides of the border. The question of raising the price of oil and sticking to the new level would have required the Arab countries to develop a policing method, which would probably have required nothing more than the rest of the Arab countries agreeing to isolate Kuwait if it again stepped out of line. If more pressure was required, it could be supplied by oil-consuming states, such as Germany and Japan, agreeing to boycott Kuwaiti oil unless Kuwait adhered to the agreements. Finally, the Arab states alone could have managed a loan or restructuring of Iraq's debt to Kuwait and others to tide it over the financial crisis resulting from the Iran-Iraq war. If not, the oil-consuming states could have helped. And, if that was not enough, the United States and Great Britain certainly could have been persuaded that a loan would be preferable to—and cheaper than—war.

Such arrangements would have met Saddam Hussein's immediate needs. Once those needs were met, he would be unlikely to invade Kuwait and isolate himself from the other Arab states. His greatest ambition for a long time has been to be one of the principal leaders of the Arab world, and nothing would so quickly and effectively destroy that possibility as turning his back on a "brotherly" Arab solution. These critics argued that it seemed well within the realm of possibility that the United States and the Arab states could have probably made a settlement with Iraq that would have avoided the invasion of Kuwait, at least for several years to come.

As we have seen, however, instead of heading off Hussein by midwifing a settlement, the Bush administration indicated that the United States would not interfere if Iraq seized the two islands and the Rumaila oil field, and was outraged when Hussein understood the message to be that he had U.S. permission to take all of Kuwait.

Once Iraq invaded and annexed Kuwait, the critics conceded, the task of persuading Iraq to withdraw was much more difficult. But, they argued, there were alternatives better suited to today's realities than sending American troops to Saudi Arabia.

To most observers familiar with the Middle East, there was one absolutely fundamental criterion that any action attempting to deal with Iraq's conquest of Kuwait and threatened conquest of Saudi Arabia and the emirates had to meet: Given the long history of Western countries oppressing Arabs, if anyone had to kill Arabs it should not be Americans and Europeans but other Arabs.

Keeping this criterion central, the most promising policy open to Bush after Iraq invaded Kuwait, according to the critics, was three-fold.

First, Bush could have said that any great power intervention in the Middle East was just as unacceptable as Hussein's threat to Saudi Arabia. The problem was an Arab problem and should be dealt with by Arabs. The United States could give both military and economic aid to those Arab countries threatened by Iraq, but it would not send troops.

The rise of nationalism in the Third World, the argument continued, convinced most Western leaders that the days of military intervention in Asia, Africa, Latin America, and the Middle East were over. It took defeat at the hands of Vietnamese peasants "clad in black pajamas" to make Lyndon Johnson understand this elemental fact. One hopes, said the critics, that a similar disaster would not be needed to convince George Bush.

Second, Bush could have said that the United States should not be the architect of a boycott of Iraq, but that it could and would join such a boycott if the Arab states chose to organize one.

Third, and most important, the critics argued, Bush could have coupled these policy statements with a far-reaching program to make the United States not only less dependent on Middle Eastern oil, but totally independent of it.

The consequence of keeping the cost of oil at about twenty dollars a barrel is that although in 1976 the United States got about 26 percent of its oil from the Middle East, by 1990 the figure was about 46 percent. If the price were raised to twenty-five dollars a barrel, a substantial number of American wells could again become economically competitive, Venezuela and Canada would increase production, and imports of Middle Eastern oil could be discouraged by a substantial import tax.

A higher price for oil would also reduce consumption. Europeans pay three to four times as much for gasoline as Americans, which is partly the reason that they consume less than half as much oil per capita.

The critics pointed out that these measures would leave a shortfall of something between one million and two million barrels of oil a day for several years, which is how long it would take for longer-run measures to reduce U.S. dependence on Middle Eastern oil to take effect. This gap, the argument continued, could be filled by doling out the necessary oil from the one billion barrels of oil in the U.S. Strategic Reserve, supplemented by expanded oil production in Canada,

Venezuela, and Mexico—as soon as they learned how to cash in on their wonderful new opportunities.

The first of the longer-run measures the critics advocated that would free the United States from its dependence on Middle Eastern oil was energy conservation. One suggestion was to reinstitute the fifty-five-mile-per-hour speed limit—and enforce it. Another was to use tax incentives to cut down on the number of gas-guzzling cars and increase fuel efficiency. There is no technical reason why cars could not be built that get fifty miles to the gallon. Public transportation could be vastly increased, reducing U.S. dependence on private automobiles.

The world's oil consumption is about fifty-five million barrels a day. The Middle East contains an estimated 50 percent of the world's oil reserves, but its current production of oil is only about twelve million barrels a day.

So long as gasoline prices remain low, the incentive to look into the possibility of alternative fuels for automobiles is also low. Methanol and compressed natural gas would help a lot. So would synthetic fuel, which, with the present technology, can be produced for about forty dollars a barrel. Incentives could also be devised to encourage the use of battery-powered automobiles in large metropolitan areas, which would not only reduce U.S. dependence on oil but also reduce pollution.

Work has already gone far on an even more exotic fuel—hydrogen. The *Hindenburg* disaster—the explosion of the German dirigible that used hydrogen for lift—discouraged research into using hydrogen as a fuel. But hydrogen can now be stored in hydrides contained in a tank the size of one of today's automobile gasoline tanks. The hydrogen cannot be released without the application of heat, making it considerably safer than gasoline. Experts say that if the price of gasoline were four dollars a gallon, hydrogen would be competitive even with current technology. Further research promises to make hydrogen as a fuel for automobiles even cheaper and more practical. An enormous bonus is that hydrogen would be almost totally nonpolluting, since the product would be simply water.

The second long-run conservation measure cited was converting oil-using electrical generating plants to coal, with only a modest increase in the price of electricity and, with modern technology, an actual decrease in pollution. Much could also be done to increase the production of electricity by water power, tidal power, geothermal power, wind power, and solar radiation. Solar energy is particularly promising. Giant machines to convert sunlight to heat could be sited in the American deserts and the electricity they generate could be transmitted all over the United States. Although the initial expense would be large, it would probably still be smaller than the long-term cost of American intervention in the Middle East.

Third, switching from oil to other energy sources for home heating would bring an enormous reduction in the use of oil. The solar energy program abandoned in the Reagan years could be revived. Natural gas and electricity could replace oil, subsidized if necessary to ensure that the cost to the consumer would remain about the same.

The disasters at Three-Mile Island and Chernobyl have frightened people away from the further development of nuclear power, although it is clear that much, much safer plants are technically feasible. But there is another kind of nuclear power that would be infinitely safer—fusion.

Today's nuclear power plants depend on the principle of fission. The fuel is a natural isotope of uranium, U-235, or man-made plutonium 239, produced in a reactor when U-238, the more plentiful natural isotope, is bombarded with neutrons.

U-235 and plutonium are unstable, spontaneously breaking down and releasing neutrons in the process. If one of these neutrons strikes the nucleus of another atom of U-235 or plutonium, it, too, will split, releasing still more neutrons. If a certain amount of U-235 or plutonium is assembled in one mass—the so-called critical mass—a chain reaction will occur, resulting in the release of enormous amounts of energy. A nuclear power plant is simply a controlled chain reaction: Rather than exploding, it releases the energy in a steady flow.

After World War II the fusion bomb, or H-bomb, was developed, which worked on an entirely different principle. Fission occurs when a very heavy atom splits, releasing energy. Fusion occurs when the nuclei of two very light atoms are brought together and they fuse, making a heavier element and releasing even more enormous quantities of energy. In the fusion bombs and warheads so far tested, the light element used has been hydrogen—hence the more common name for a fusion bomb is the H-bomb. The by-product, helium, is not radioactive.

However, to accomplish fusion, very high temperatures are required—hence the alternative term to describe the bomb is thermonuclear. In a fusion bomb these temperatures are reached by exploding a U-235 or plutonium device as the first step of a two-step process. Although the fusion bomb, or H-bomb, itself does not produce radioactive by-products, its fission trigger does.

Research aimed at developing power plants based on fusion rather than fission has gone forward in both Russia and the United States. The problem is to find a bottle or container that could withstand the heat and pressure required to achieve fusion.

One approach, pioneered by the Soviet Union, is to use machines called tokamaks that create a sort of magnetic bottle to contain the hydrogen at the extremely high temperatures necessary. The other method is to use laser beams to hold and burn pellets of hydrogen.

The advantages of fusion as a source of energy are tremendous. First, as a practical matter there is no limit on the raw material; hydrogen is one of the most plentiful elements known, stored in the world's oceans, lakes, and rivers as water. Second, fusion power would be infinitely safer than nuclear reactors based on fission. The result of an accident in a fusion plant would not be an explosion or the release of radioactive materials; the plant would simply stop operating. A breakdown, unlike those at the fission plants at Three-Mile Island and Chernobyl, would produce only a negligible amount of radioactivity with a very short half-life, resulting from neutron bombardment of surrounding equipment.

Fusion research has been the poor cousin of science, beginning when President Carter cut the funds for it. The current budget calls for only $318 million per year. On September 28, 1990, a federal panel, the Fusion Policy Advisory Board, urged that the federal government double the amount budgeted for fusion research. Many scientists familiar with fusion power are convinced that if an all-out effort were launched similar to the World War II Manhattan Project, practical fusion plants could be built within a decade, or at most two. If they are right, the United States would become totally free of any need for foreign oil. Industry and office and home heating could be run by the electricity generated by fusion plants, while trucks and automobiles could be run on hydrogen safely carried in tanks containing hydrides.

Alternatives Open After Troop Deployment

Once Bush sent the troops to the Middle East, the critics shifted their ground.

Of course the measures necessary to free the United States from its dependence on foreign oil continued to be both feasible and urgent. The truth of the matter is that when the costs of the American military operations in the Middle East are added in, the price of foreign oil is closer to eighty dollars a barrel than twenty dollars. Announcing a dramatic plan to free the United States from foreign oil would give the American people hope for an end to the need for this kind of desperate adventure. It would inspire confidence in the Third World and among U.S. Allies. It would also make Saddam Hussein, Iraq, and the other Middle East oil states understand that they could no longer call the tune and would have to seek a compromise.

Once American military forces had been deployed in the Middle East and President Bush had demanded that Iraq withdraw from Kuwait without benefiting in any way from the invasion, it became much more difficult to turn over to the Arabs the problem of containing Saddam Hussein and Iraq and bringing the American troops home. Furthermore, since Bush was the architect of the intervention, he would have found it particularly difficult.

Bush's position, in fact, was similar to that of Saddam Hussein. Once Hussein had occupied Kuwait and proclaimed that its annexation was an "eternal merger," withdrawing and negotiating for something less was politically difficult. Similarly, once Bush had sent U.S. troops to Saudi Arabia and demanded that Iraq pull out of Kuwait without obtaining any benefits from the invasion, it was equally difficult for him to stop short of war and negotiate—much more difficult, a Washington wag remarked, than going back on a campaign slogan such as "Read my lips—no new taxes."

Although alternatives would have entailed some political cost, a number of critics argued that there were at least two alternatives to a U.S. invasion of Kuwait and Iraq.

The first alternative—which would have been the ideal solution—would have been for the U.N. to take over the entire Middle East military operation. The mission was still only to protect Saudi Arabia from invasion, and the American ground forces and land-based air forces could be replaced with contingents from the anti-Iraq Arab states and, possibly, from other Third World countries. The United States and the other developed Western countries could then have continued to furnish naval forces and sea-based air forces with relatively little political cost. Ideally, the entire force would have been commanded by an Arab general and flown the U.N. flag, as the Allied forces did in Korea.

The economic boycott would continue but be given even more force by being a U.N. rather than U.S. and Allied operation.

Realistically, however, it must be admitted that even if Bush had been willing to change his course, the chances would have been slim of getting the U.N. General Assembly to vote for such measures and of getting Arab and Third World countries to supply the troops.

A second alternative would have been for Bush to try to do what should have been done in the first place—let the Arab states take the lead and furnish the ground troops, while the United States and its Western Allies furnished economic and military aid and the naval and air backup forces. Senator George Aiken of Vermont once suggested that the way to end the Vietnam War was to announce that the United States had won and simply withdraw. Taking a leaf from Aiken's book, Bush could have announced that the American purpose had been to prevent an immediate takeover of Saudi Arabia. Since that purpose had been successfully achieved, the United States could begin a phased withdrawal of its forces, turning the positions over to Arab and Third World states. At the same time, Bush could have promised that the United States would provide both military and economic aid to support the replacement forces and the countries supplying them. He could have set the timetable for a complete American withdrawal from Saudi Arabia for, say, six months—although, as in the U.N. plan, U.S. naval forces and sea-based air forces could have been maintained for a much longer period.

Again, the economic boycott would continue. It would have less force than if it was run by the U.N. itself, but it would probably have had somewhat more credibility than a boycott sponsored mainly by the United States.

The goal of an economic boycott sponsored by the Arabs would not have been an Iraqi withdrawal from Kuwait "without conditions," as Bush wanted, but an Iraqi withdrawal from Kuwait coupled with an Arab-sponsored settlement of Iraq's grievances: the two islands blocking Iraq's access to the sea, the Kuwaiti pirating of Rumaila oil, Kuwaiti adherence to the OPEC quotas and a higher price for oil, and some sort of loan until Iraq could sell enough oil to pay its debts.

The Worst-Case Scenario

As discussed above, Hussein's ambition to be one of the principal leaders of the Arab world makes it unlikely that he would turn his back on a "brotherly" Arab solution. Suppose, however, that the Arab states were unwilling to take over. If so, Hussein might have waited until U.S. forces had withdrawn, then proceeded to invade and occupy Saudi

Arabia and the various sheikdoms. The result, admitted the advocates of this course of action, would not have been favorable. But, they argued, it would not have been a world-shaking tragedy. Hussein would then have controlled 21.5 percent of global oil production. He might also have controlled as much as 50 percent of the known reserves, although all figures on reserves are questionable. In the short run, the critics admitted, he could have forced a price increase. But the increase would have been limited—the oil would do Hussein no good if he could not sell it. What determines the price of oil is only partly what even a producer who controls as much as 50 percent of the world's production wants it to be. In the short run, an oil price increase is limited by the production costs of other producers, such as Canada, Venezuela, and Texas. In the long run, what determines the price is neither the desires of the large producers nor the production costs of competitors, but what economists call the "substitution price"—that is, the cost of substitutes for oil as a source of energy. It has been estimated that with oil at twenty-five dollars a barrel, Venezuela, Canada, and Texas could supply all the oil that Kuwait, Saudi Arabia, and Iraq supplied before the war. If the price goes only a few dollars higher than that, as noted previously, substitutes would begin to be competitive.

Also, if the United States and other developed nations had adopted a program similar to the one outlined above, Hussein's leverage would not have lasted long. With the kind of program outlined above, the world could last for many, many decades with the other 50 percent of the world's reserves—until, indeed, substitutes could be found that make oil unnecessary, a situation the world will face sooner or later in any event.

Had Hussein been able to forge his conquests into a single homogeneous nation, its population would be less than fifty million and its industrial capacity limited. Egypt and the rest of the Arab states would have been thoroughly alarmed and much more likely to take the major responsibility for containing any further Iraqi expansion.

Finally, as the critics argued throughout, unlike Hitler and Germany, Hussein and Iraq were no real threat to the rest of the world.

CHAPTER 6

Building the Coalition

On August 10 Iraq ordered the closing of embassies in Kuwait. It also informed the United States and other governments that, except for diplomats, their citizens would not be allowed to leave either Kuwait or Iraq. There were some 3,000 Americans in Kuwait and another 580 in Iraq. More than 300,000 non-Arab foreigners were working or living in Kuwait and Iraq, the majority being Egyptians, Indians, Bangladeshi, and Lebanese. The Soviet Union, Bulgaria, and Poland had more than 5,000 citizens in Iraq working as military advisers and technicians. Britain had about 3,000 in Kuwait and 2,000 more in Iraq. West Germany had about 900, Italy 500, France 400, Ireland 350, Spain 200, and Sweden 160. During the Iran-Iraq war, about 2,000,000 Egyptians worked in Iraq, but by the summer of 1990, this had gone down to about 1,000,000.

Also on August 10, President Bush repeated that the U.S. goals in the Middle East were to defend Saudi Arabia, to get Iraq out of Kuwait, and to make Saddam Hussein understand that aggression would not be successful. The strategy to achieve those goals, Bush said, was to impose economic sanctions. In response to questions from reporters, Bush set yet another goal. He said that the United States itself was not prepared to support the overthrow of Hussein, but that if Hussein did not change his spots, then he, Bush, hoped that the Iraqi people would do something about it—calling, in other words, on the Iraqi people to oust Hussein. In many countries, especially Arab and Third World, this call for Hussein's overthrow was viewed as a violation of international practice, if not law, since it constituted interference in the internal affairs of another state.

The Israeli government apparently thought that Bush's call for Hussein to withdraw from Kuwait was naive. Israeli intelligence reportedly believed

71

that if Hussein moved toward a peaceful settlement, he would be overthrown by an Iraqi military coup. They also apparently believed that if Bush's call for Hussein to be overthrown was acted on, the Iraqi military would put someone in his place who might well turn out to be worse than Hussein.

In response, on August 12 Saddam Hussein proposed that:

> . . . all cases of occupation, and those cases that have been portrayed as occupation, in the region be resolved simultaneously and on the same principles and basis that should be laid down by the Security Council, as follows:
>
> Preparations for an immediate and unconditional Israeli withdrawal from occupied Arab lands in Palestine, Syria, and Lebanon; a Syrian withdrawal from Lebanon; mutual withdrawals by Iraq and Iran and arrangement for the situation in Kuwait.

Hussein also called for the withdrawal of U.S. forces from the Middle East and their replacement by Arab forces.

Three days later, on August 15, Iraq sought peace with Iran, offering to withdraw all Iraqi troops remaining in Iranian territory, to return all POWs, and to divide the Shatt-al-Arab estuary equally between Iran and Iraq. Iran hailed the move but the next day said that it still backed the embargo.

Having dispatched the troops to the Middle East, Bush went on a long-planned twenty-five-day vacation to his family's retreat at Kennebunkport, Maine. He defended leaving Washington by saying that, as president, a complete modern communications system was available to him in Maine. In an oblique criticism of President Carter's action when the American embassy was occupied and its staff held prisoners Bush added that he did not want to be "held hostage in the White House."

Although his aides worried about the image he would project by taking a vacation at this time, a grim-faced Bush continued a frenetic round of golf, fishing, and driving his high-speed "cigarette boat." From Kennebunkport, he declared that the United States would not be intimidated by Iraq's decision to detain Americans and other foreigners. Breaking his vacation briefly to give a speech to the Veterans of Foreign Wars in Baltimore, Bush for the first time referred to the foreigners detained by Iraq as hostages—rather than using some other euphemism. Several times during the speech, he compared Hussein to Hitler.

Vexed by the press, however, Bush refused to answer questions. "I'm recreating," he snapped at them on one occasion. On another, a reporter shouted a question at him while he was jogging. In a peevish reference to his campaign promise of "Read my lips—no new taxes," the president shouted: "Read my hips!"

The public opinion polls were very much in Bush's favor. Polling experts, however, downplayed them to some extent, saying that, in a crisis, polls always reflected a "rally-round-the-flag" attitude. To support their contention, they cited the fact that John F. Kennedy's approval rating was highest at the time of his greatest failure, the Bay of Pigs fiasco. Nevertheless, it was clear that the American public was impressed by the skill and energy that Bush displayed in mobilizing not only American but world opinion and support.

A later poll, published on September 30, showed that the American people overwhelmingly supported Bush's goals in the Gulf, but that nine out of ten did not want the United States to go to war to achieve them.

The Allied Coalition

In addition to Saudi Arabia and the United States, Great Britain, France, and Egypt provided troops. Turkey joined the coalition and stationed troops along its common border with Iraq. Eventually, several other countries sent smaller troop contingents.

Syria also promised to send troops to Saudi Arabia, but urged the United States to seek a political and not a military solution to the problem.

Countries that offered support other than troops, such as financial aid, included West Germany, which furnished transport planes and ships. However, the United States estimated that the cost of the operation would far exceed $25 billion, and it was not satisfied with the financial support the effort was receiving. Accordingly, on August 30, Bush sent some of his top aides to Tokyo, Bonn, and various capitals of Middle Eastern countries in an effort to persuade them to share the cost of the military effort in the Gulf.

Fearful that any Israeli participation would cause the Arab members of the coalition to withdraw, the United States and the rest of the Allies urged Israel not to participate. Although the Israelis reserved judgment about what they would do in future contingencies, for the time being they agreed to comply.

The Soviet Union publicly ruled out any joint Soviet-American military operations against Iraq, but it joined in the call for a worldwide economic embargo against Iraq.

On August 24 Gorbachev sent a message to Hussein stating that Iraq would face additional economic sanctions if it did not withdraw its troops from Kuwait and release the foreign hostages. The Soviet Union, Gorbachev warned, was ready to back additional measures to toughen the economic sanctions against Iraq.

Gorbachev and Bush met in Helsinki, Finland, on September 9 and issued a statement that Iraq's aggression would not be tolerated, and that Iraq must carry out the terms of the U.N. resolution and withdraw from Kuwait. However, the statement fell short of what the United States was seeking. The press interpreted the statement as sending a signal that was "loud but unclear."

Countries Opposing U.S. Intervention

Remarkably few countries actively opposed the presence of U.S. troops in the Middle East or the U.N. resolutions condemning Iraq and calling for economic sanctions. The most significant was probably Jordan. King Hussein, of course, was in a difficult position. With Israel on one side, a very active and virulently anti-Israel Palestinian minority inside, and Iraq on the other side, King Hussein's problem was acute. Over the years he had succeeded in keeping on good terms with the United States, in spite of his country's peculiar situation, but he felt compelled to speak against the U.S. intervention. However, he made his protest as mild as possible, accusing the United States of creating an "explosive situation" in the Middle East.

Bush was annoyed. Recalling that during its war with Iran, Iraq had received most of its supplies from abroad through Jordan's port of Aqaba, Bush threatened to blockade the port if it was used to get supplies to Iraq.

Later, after a meeting between Bush and King Hussein, Hussein announced that, in spite of its sympathy for Iraq, Jordan would honor the embargo. Nevertheless, periodically throughout the crisis Jordan was wracked with pro-Iraq demonstrations.

Other states that supported Iraq politically and condemned the U.S. and U.N. intervention included Libya and Yemen, as well as the PLO.

On September 12, just one day after Iran and Iraq resumed diplomatic relations, Iran's supreme religious leader called on all Muslims to oppose the American troop deployment in Saudi Arabia. Iran also announced that it would take two hundred thousand barrels of oil a day from Iraq in exchange for food and medicine.

The Threat of Poison Gas and Germ Warfare

In the meantime, the press was full of speculation about Iraq's chemical and biological warfare capabilities. Articles in a number of papers pointed out that Iraq had ample stockpiles of chemical weapons, as well as germ warfare capabilities. The articles made a particular point about the difficulty of fighting in protective suits in 120-degree temperatures. An American soldier could wear full protective gear for only about an hour at a time in those conditions. Most of the articles also noted that Iraqi troops were the only ones in the world with experience in fighting in a chemical warfare environment. At about the same time as the articles appeared, the Iraqi ambassador in Athens said that if attacked his country would indeed use chemical weapons.

Most of the articles also made the point that if war came, chemical plants making new weapons would be easy targets, but added that the storage areas for the stockpiled weapons would not be.

On September 24 the press reported that American intelligence had discovered that the Iraqi forces had—ominously—prepared chemical decontamination sites in Iraq near the Kuwaiti border.

Reaction Among the American Public

Opinion polls during this period of the crisis showed that the American public did not place very much importance on the charges that Iraq was an aggressor or that its chemical and biological capabilities posed a serious threat to the United States. But the American public did take seriously the charge—which Bush played upon frequently—that Iraq would soon develop a stockpile of nuclear weapons. In November, however, fears were quieted when the International Atomic Energy Agency reported that inspectors had found Iraq's small stock of reactor fuel (highly enriched uranium) stored where it was supposed to be and that it had not been diverted to build a nuclear weapon.

Threats by Saddam Hussein

Following the announcement that foreigners remaining in Iraq and Kuwait were "restrictees" and would remain in Iraq, sharing the privations of the Iraqi people until the crisis was resolved, Hussein ordered some ten thousand American, British, and other foreign nationals to be scattered among Iraqi military bases, oil production sites, and industrial installations as virtual human shields. On August 23 a smiling Hussein appeared on TV with a group of grim-faced British hostages.

Less than a week later, following a storm of media protest, he announced that he would free foreign women and children.

By mid-September, there was evidence that the embargo had begun to pinch. On September 23 Hussein warned that if Iraq was "strangled" by the embargo, it would attack both Saudi Arabia and Israel. The United States immediately promised Israel that if Iraq did attack, the United States would respond "vigorously."

Refugees and the Rape of Kuwait

Indians, Bangladeshi, Lebanese, and others who had worked in Kuwait and Iraq poured into Jordan at the rate of ten thousand a day, creating a crisis in both food and housing. A similar flood of refugees, mainly Kurds, pounded on the doors of both Iran and Turkey.

These refugees painted a picture of Kuwait being plundered, with Iraqi troops pillaging the country, looting everything from TV sets to factory machinery. The Iraqi government itself had reportedly seized and sent to Iraq more than $3 billion in gold bullion.

President Bush, in his speeches around the country to build support for his policy toward Iraq, made much of these reports, most of which seem to have been true. But in one or two instances Bush seems to have gone overboard. One report that Bush used extensively, was made by a fifteen-year-old Kuwaiti girl who tearfully described to the shocked members of the Congressional Human Rights Caucus how she had watched Iraqi soldiers confiscate incubators in a Kuwaiti hospital, putting the babies who had been in them "on the cold floor to die." The joint chairmen of the Caucus, Tom Lantos, a Democrat from California, and John Edward Porter, an Illinois Republican, said that the identity of the girl, known to the public only by her first name, Nayirah, would be withheld to protect her family still in Kuwait. Seven senators who voted in favor of war against Iraq cited her testimony in their speeches justifying their vote, and the resolution passed by six votes.

No one bothered to check on the story at the time. However, after Kuwait was liberated, ABC's John Martin interviewed doctors in the hospital who charged that the story was without foundation.

What was even more significant, however, was that the girl was in fact the daughter of the Kuwaiti ambassador to Washington. The Kuwaiti ambassador issued a statement standing by his daughter's testimony, but no one explained how she could have been in Kuwait in August and September during the early part of the Iraqi occupation to witness the atrocity and yet been able to get out and to Washington in time to testify on October 10, 1990.

In January, 1992, Representative Lantos in a letter to the *New York Times* defended his decision to keep the identity of the young woman secret. He maintained that she had in fact been in Kuwait and later escaped. The American ambassador to Kuwait, Edward W. Gnehm, also angrily defended Nayirah's story. However, the director of Middle East Watch, Kenneth Roth, said that although his organization could not rule out the possibility of isolated cases in which infants had been removed from incubators, painstaking research had disproved reports of any widespread infanticide.

Peace Efforts

On August 21, through his foreign minister, Saddam Hussein proposed peace talks with the United States. At the same time, he delivered a slashing attack on Bush in an open letter. He threatened that if Bush did not talk he would bring on a "global disaster." The White House immediately rejected any talks unless Iraq first withdrew its troops from Kuwait.

Ten days later, General Schwarzkopf said that there would be no war unless Iraq struck first. His mission, he emphasized, was to defend Saudi Arabia.

At about the same time, the secretary-general of the United Nations, Javier Pérez de Cuéllar, held talks with Iraqi Foreign Minister Tariq Aziz. But the talks were broken off on September 1 as inconclusive, and the next day Pérez de Cuéllar said flatly that they had failed.

On September 4 the Soviets proposed an international conference on both Iraq's invasion of Kuwait and on the Israeli-Palestine issue, as well as other Middle East problems. Nothing came of the proposal.

That same day, Secretary of State James Baker announced that he anticipated a long stay for U.S. troops in the Middle East, even if Iraq voluntarily withdrew from Kuwait. The next day, Baker urged patience, saying that it would take at least a year for the embargo to do its work and cripple Iraq's economy.

Then the administration's mood seemed to change. In a speech to a joint session of Congress on September 11, Bush vowed to thwart Iraq despite fears for the hostages. His speech seemed intended to leave no doubt in Hussein's mind that the United States would use force, if necessary, to push Iraqi forces out of Kuwait. Bush repeated what was becoming a familiar refrain: "We will not let this aggression stand."

On September 19 Bush again hinted at war in a speech in San Francisco: "If Iraq does not meet these non-negotiable conditions [withdrawal from Kuwait and release of the hostages] then its isolation will not end. We are, as I have said before, prepared to take additional steps if sanctions and the quest for a political resolution do not work."

Shortly afterward, on September 25, the leaders of Iran and Syria issued a joint statement opposing Iraq's invasion of Kuwait. The statement also expressed opposition to the subsequent buildup of American and other foreign troops in the region.

On September 27 the House Foreign Affairs Committee backed Bush's Gulf policy but avoided endorsing actual war. The Senate passed a resolution on October 2 that also supported Bush's actions in the Gulf, but it, too, stopped short of endorsing the use of force.

The Bush administration, however, had apparently already decided that war might be necessary to accomplish its goals. On September 28, following a White House meeting between Bush and the ousted emir of Kuwait, Brent Scowcroft said that Bush's patience with Iraq was wearing thin. He suggested that the United States might seek another U.N. resolution, one that would authorize the use of military force against Iraq if it did not withdraw from Kuwait voluntarily.

Two days later, on September 30, senior Kuwaiti officials who had met with Bush said that they believed that the Bush administration doubted that the economic embargo would persuade Iraq to withdraw from Kuwait.

Then, on October 1, Bush addressed world political leaders assembled for the General Assembly meeting at the U.N. He made three points:

(1) Iraq and Kuwait could settle their differences through negotiations.
(2) New arrangements could be made for regional stability. By this, Bush was understood to mean the destruction of chemical and nuclear weapons by all the countries in the Gulf. Although he did not say so in so many words, it was also understood that he included Israel.
(3) The conflict dividing the Arabs and Israel needed to be resolved.

Although Bush was very harsh on Saddam Hussein in his speech, the Israelis were dismayed at his suggestion that the Arab-Israeli issue be linked to the Gulf crisis.

On October 2, presumably picking up on Bush's speech, Saudi Arabia's foreign minister urged Iraq to quit Kuwait in order to bolster Palestinian claims.

The following day, during a visit to Washington, Gen. Mikhail A. Moiseyev, chief of the Soviet General Staff, warned the United States not to attack in the Gulf. Economic sanctions, he argued, were working. In any case, military force should not be used without prior approval by the U.N.

On October 5 the Iraqi representative to the U.N. formally accused the United States of Western imperialism.

Yevgeny M. Primakov, the Soviet foreign minister, visited Iraq the next day. He reported that Hussein would be ready for a negotiated settlement, provided that the West did not issue ultimatums or threaten military intervention.

Then a number of Palestinians were killed during a demonstration in Israel. Hussein reacted by threatening to attack Israel with long-range missiles, implying that the missiles might be armed with chemical warheads.

In any case, the Israeli government had already begun issuing gas masks to its citizens, along with instructions on how to seal living quarters in case of chemical attack.

On October 13 the U.N. Security Council condemned Israel for killing Palestinian protesters. The vote was unanimous, that is, the United States joined in condemning Israel, which it had done only rarely in the past. At the same time, a number of delegates called for a U.N. role in the attempt to defuse the Middle East crisis. But Bush was firmly opposed.

Also on October 13, King Hassan II of Morocco said that there was "a moral link between the Iraqi invasion of Kuwait and the Arab-Israeli issue." His statement was interpreted as evidence of a growing rift within the anti-Iraq coalition.

Three days later, in Washington, Secretary of State Baker said that Hussein had indicated interest in a compromise in which Iraq would keep the two uninhabited islands blocking the Iraqi port and, perhaps, the disputed oil field. He stated that the United States rejected any compromise and insisted on an unconditional Iraqi withdrawal from Kuwait. Baker stated flatly that it was U.S. policy not to reward unprovoked aggression.

At some point during this period, Bush suggested that the Iraqi leaders would face "Nuremburg trials," referring to the post–World War II trials of Nazi leaders as war criminals.

CHAPTER 7

The Road to War

To recapitulate, at the beginning of the Gulf crisis, President Bush denied any intention of invading either Kuwait or Iraq. He said that the U.S. goals were to forestall an Iraqi invasion of Saudi Arabia and to put enough economic pressure on Saddam Hussein to force him to withdraw "unconditionally" from Kuwait. He said that the economic sanctions would be given time to do their work and that he was confident that the combination of economic pressure and world opinion would force Hussein to give in.

But, both inside and outside the administration, doubts gradually arose whether "a line drawn in the sand" of Saudi Arabia and an economic boycott would bring enough pressure on Hussein to accomplish such goals.

Are Boycotts Effective?

First, according to the argument against relying on the boycott, peacetime economic boycotts have never been very effective in the past. In time of war, blockades work better. During war, any ship crossing an arbitrary line can be sunk without the formality of boarding and inspection. What is more, combat on the battlefield consumes the enemy's supplies and bombing reduces his capacity to produce more.

The trouble is that boycotts leak, as the West discovered when it attempted to boycott Northern Rhodesia. In the case of Iraq, there were too many countries that would be tempted by bargain-basement oil prices and too many circuitous routes for oil to go out of Iraq and other goods to come in.

For example, King Hussein of Jordan had expressed sympathy for Saddam Hussein, and even though Jordan does not provide an easy route for oil to be sent out of Iraq, it could be used for getting some goods in.

Iran, on the other hand, out of hatred for the United States and hope for Islamic solidarity, was also supporting Iraq, in spite of their long and bloody war, and Iran provides a much easier route. Confirming these suspicions, on September 13, American and Arab oil executives reported that Iran and Iraq had made a deal for Iraqi oil to be sent to Iran.

Jordan and Iran were the most obvious ways for oil to go out of Iraq and other goods to come in, but they were not the only ways. Yassir Arafat and the Palestine Liberation Organization also expressed sympathy for Hussein, and the PLO had considerable experience in the game of getting weapons and supplies across Middle Eastern borders. The Kurds, who are scattered through the border areas of Iraq, Iran, Turkey, Syria, and areas of the present Russian Commonwealth, have been smuggling back and forth among these countries for generations.

As late as January 7, 1991, Western reporters in Iraq described shops brimming with goods produced both locally and abroad, although prices were higher than they were before the sanctions.[1]

Those hardest hit by the sanctions, ironically, were the people who remained in Kuwait. This was partly because of the widespread looting and partly because the Iraqi government made sure that Kuwait was at the bottom of the priority list.

For a time, Western diplomats believed that shortages would develop in the additives needed to purify water supplies and in the chemicals needed to produce jet fuel. However, a few days later a truckload of the water additives arrived by a secret route, and there seems to be no reason that the jet fuel chemicals could not have been brought in the same way. In any case, Iraq seemed to have stockpiled enough chemicals to last for some time.

If the boycott lasted long enough, however, even without actual warfare, Iraq might have eventually felt a pinch in replacing large equipment, such as pipeline pumps and generators, which are too bulky for easy smuggling.

The economic boycott was bound to have some effect, and the Iraqi people would have had to tighten their belts. Nevertheless, it would have been easier for Hussein to win popular support for belt tightening if the country exerting the pressure was the United States.

Remove Hussein?

As these doubts about the effectiveness of an economic boycott grew, leaks from inside the Bush administration made the point that even if Hussein did withdraw from Kuwait, he would still control a potent military force. The conclusion suggested by those leaking the information was that if Iraq merely withdrew from Kuwait, the threat Hussein posed would remain and, because of Iraq's nuclear potential, would actually increase over time. If so, they suggested, the only sensible way to accomplish American purposes in the Middle East would be to remove Saddam Hussein from power and to destroy Iraqi war potential—especially its chemical, biological, and nuclear war potential.

Public opinion polls conducted at about this same time indicated that the American people supported all of these goals, but that support dropped off sharply if achieving them would require the use of force. The one issue on which opinion wavered regarding the use of force was Iraq's longer-run potential to produce nuclear weapons.

Yet Iraq's potential nuclear threat was probably the weakest argument that the Bush administration put forward to support using force. Richard Rhodes, author of the authoritative history *The Making of the Atomic Bomb,* wrote an op-ed piece in the *New York Times* on November 27, 1990, pointing out why the argument was hollow. Israel, Rhodes wrote, is estimated to have one hundred to two hundred nuclear warheads mounted on rockets. Even if Iraq could develop two or three bombs over the coming decade, it would be insanely suicidal for it to bomb Israel. Israel's retaliation would be devastating.

The only possible use for Iraqi bombs would be to deter Israel from turning to its nuclear weapons in a conventional war that it was losing. However, Rhodes hastened to add, even though this sort of mutual deterrence may seem desirable, it would not necessarily increase stability in the Middle East because the danger of a misstep is real, and a misstep when both sides have nuclear weapons is very, very dangerous.

Although President Bush and his inner circle apparently had already decided on expelling Iraq from Kuwait by military force, as late as the first week in October General Powell felt that the combination of a deterrent force stationed in Saudi Arabia and economic sanctions was working. He was worried that the administration was moving too rapidly toward a decision to go to war and that to do something premature when there was still a chance that sanctions would accomplish the objectives would be a mistake.[2]

Powell went to Defense Secretary Cheney, arguing that the president should be briefed on the full slate of options. Cheney was noncommittal, so Powell then went to Secretary of State Baker. Baker was just as unhappy as Powell about the talk of developing an offensive capability. He wanted to rely first on diplomacy, and he intended to push for a full White House discussion of the strategy of containment.

But no such discussion followed. Powell then went to Scowcroft to present the case for continuing the containment policy. Finally, Powell was given a chance to present his view to the president, although in less than ideal circumstances. Powell argued that a force level of 230,000 troops, which the United States would reach by December 1, would box in Hussein and let sanctions work. It might take a year or even two, but containment would eventually grind him down.

Bush said that he did not think there was time "politically" for a strategy of containment.

A few days later, Bush asked for a briefing on what an offensive operation might entail. General Carl Vuono, the army chief of staff, flew to see General Schwarzkopf in Saudi Arabia. Schwarzkopf was furious. He had told the president that it would take seventeen weeks to put a defensive force in place. Only half that time had passed, and he was now being asked to plan an offensive.

A plan was hastily developed, however, and was presented to Bush on October 30. The briefing stressed that the defensive mission of protecting Saudi Arabia from an invasion had been accomplished, but that the number of American troops would have to be doubled—from 230,000 to almost 500,000—if an offensive to force Iraq out of Kuwait was envisioned. The president ordered the increase.

The Strategy: Bomb Iraq

As already related, air force chief of staff Gen. Michael J. Dugan had revealed that the administration believed that the only way to avoid a bloody land war was to rely on a massive air offensive.

In the meantime, Iraqi troops were devastating Kuwait, and the White House concluded that to wait would be self-defeating. On September 28, Brent Scowcroft, Bush's national security adviser, had raised the possibility of another U.N. Security Council resolution that would include specific mention of the use of military force against Iraq. President Bush himself suggested that the present stalemate could be allowed to continue only so long before "additional steps" would be taken.

Actually, it was really not surprising that the Bush administration began talking about offensive military action against Iraq. For Saddam Hussein to give up what he had proclaimed was the "eternal merger" of Iraq and Kuwait under pressure from the United States—the superpower that arouses more Arab suspicion and fear than any other—would be a degrading humiliation and most likely the end of both his reign and his life.

The U.N. Resolution Authorizing Force

Meanwhile, the Iraqi rape of Kuwait continued, and both Scowcroft and the president hinted that an attack would have to come sooner rather than later. In early October, leaks from the White House suggested, first, that the administration had decided that war was the only way to accomplish U.S. goals if Iraq did not withdraw from Kuwait promptly, and, second, that the timetable had to be stepped up.

Given the facts of how and why the Iraqi borders were created, the Reagan and Bush policy of tilting toward Iraq during the Iran-Iraq war, and the green light that Hussein had reason to believe he had been given by Ambassador Glaspie, there is probably nothing that Bush could have done to restore Kuwaiti independence short of an invasion.

For example, many of Bush's critics argue that sanctions should have been given time to work, even if it took a year or more. After the fact, of course, no one can ever be sure. But, as argued above, the Bush administration was probably right on the question of sanctions.

In late October there was another flurry of attempts at bringing the opposing parties to negotiate. On October 22, Saudi Arabia's defense minister, Prince Sultan Ibn Abdul-Aziz, hinted at a deal with Iraq. Specifically, he said that through considerations of Arab brotherhood, the Arab states might give Iraq the uninhabited islands, Warba and Bubiyan, that block Iraqi access to the Gulf. Bush rejected the overture the next day, saying that there would be no compromise on the Iraqi withdrawal from Kuwait and again comparing Hussein to Hitler.

Then, on October 25, Defense Secretary Cheney announced that the United States had decided to expand its forces in the Gulf and would send perhaps as many as 100,000 more personnel, which would bring

U.S. troop strength in the region to 340,000. In addition, Saudi Arabia had 60,000 troops stationed on the Iraq-Kuwait border, France had 13,000, Britain had 15,000, Syria had pledged 19,000, and Egypt 20,000. Several other countries had promised or had already sent smaller detachments or ships. But neither Germany nor Japan had provided even a token contribution.

The additional American deployment would give the coalition 467,000 troops when all were in place. Iraqi forces in Kuwait and southern Iraq, according to Pentagon estimates, totaled 430,000.

That same day, apparently in support of the moves toward military action, William Webster, the CIA director, said that the boycott might be hurting the Iraqi civilian economy, but that it was having little effect on the Iraqi military.

On the other side of the equation, Yemen's president criticized Saudi Arabia for forcing more than five hundred thousand Yemeni citizens working in Saudi Arabia to go home. He also criticized the Saudis for having invited the American forces into the Middle East.

On October 27, the Soviets asked the U.N. to postpone considering another resolution condemning Iraq to give time for one more try at negotiations. The next day, a Gorbachev aide departed for Baghdad. On October 29 the U.N. Security Council approved a resolution holding Iraq liable for damage in Kuwait, but the possible use of force was not mentioned.

Also on October 29, in separate but coordinated speeches in California, Bush and Baker underscored their resolve to roll back the Iraqi invasion with force if necessary. Bush, in particular, made a special point of talking about atrocities that the Iraqi troops were accused of committing, such as shooting Kuwaiti children and using zoo animals for target practice. He also repeated his slogan that this "aggression shall not stand." For his part, Baker said, "And let no one doubt: We will not rule out a possible use of force if Iraq continues to occupy Kuwait."

As if in response to these two speeches, Gorbachev said that there were signs that Hussein was willing to negotiate. "It's unacceptable," Gorbachev said, "to have a military solution to this question."

Replying to the Bush and Baker speeches, Hussein on October 30 warned his country to prepare for an attack. Three days later he vowed that if war began in the Gulf, it would be a long one.

That same day, a number of congressional leaders urged Bush to go slow on the decision for war.

Bush said that his patience was wearing thin over the one thousand Americans still held hostage in Iraq. The people in the embassy in Kuwait were being starved—they were not being resupplied. "Do you think I'm concerned about it?" he asked on October 30. "You're darn right I am. And what I'm [sic] going to do about it? Let's just wait and see. Because I've had it with that kind of treatment of Americans . . ."

At a news conference in Washington, the Iraqi ambassador, Mohammed al-Mashat, said, "We once more call for a negotiated solution, to have a political and a diplomatic solution. We seek to avoid bloodshed." He reiterated that Iraq was ready to negotiate if issues such as Israel's occupation of the Gaza Strip and the West Bank were included in the talks. "We seek a peaceful solution to all of these questions," he said. "All of them together. Now."

As the impression grew that the Bush administration had already decided to go to war, the press was filled with articles stressing the difficulties of the military task. These articles painted a picture of well dug-in Iraqi forces, underground command posts, hundreds of Soviet- and French-made surface-to-air missiles, extensive earthworks up to twenty-five feet high, and hidden, dug-in tanks, artillery, and antiarmor weapons. The Iraqi defenses, according to the stories, included intricate systems of minefields; deep ditches and earthen berms, intended to channel enemy armor into traps; pretargeted, dug-in artillery; interlocking fields of fire; and disbursed ammunition dumps to aid the Iraqi defenders. In addition, forward troops were supplied by well-constructed road networks that allowed for fast reinforcement of multiple positions by elite reserve armor and mobile infantry forces.

One specialist on the Iraqi military, David Segal, wrote in *Foreign Affairs* that the Iraqi defenders, particularly the elite Republican Guard, were so competent that the Iraqi army had won "nearly all its defensive battles between 1982–88." Frank Greve, of the Knight-Ridder syndicate, reported that Edward Luttwak, a Georgetown University strategist who appeared frequently on TV throughout the crisis, said that if the United States staged a frontal assault on Iraqi border positions, it would suffer thousands of casualties.

On November 7 Baker started on a swing through the Middle East. He found that the leaders of Saudi Arabia, Egypt, Kuwait, and Turkey were unanimous that the use of military force to expel Iraq must be approved by the U.N.

On November 8 Egyptian President Muhammad Hosni Mubarak called for a delay in any attack on Iraq, urging that sanctions be given two to three months to work before the Allies went to war.

Mubarak's plea was overshadowed by Bush's order to deploy more than 150,000 additional troops to the Middle East to provide "an adequate offensive military option." That same day Bush met with Soviet leaders, who said that they did not rule out the use of force but that any offensive must first be authorized by the U.N.

The Pentagon announced the following day that U.S. troops in the Middle East would not be rotated until the crisis was over. Senator Sam Nunn criticized the administration's "rush to war," assailing the decision to drop the troop rotation plan. The president, Nunn said, must explain why he was in such a hurry.

On November 11 King Hassan II of Morocco called for an emergency Arab summit meeting to avert war in the Gulf.

A number of press commentators picked up on the "rush-to-war" theme. On November 13, for example, columnist James Reston of the *New York Times* wrote that Americans don't like to differ with the president during a crisis. "But saying 'My President, right or wrong' in such circumstances is a little like saying, 'my driver, drunk or sober,' and not many passengers like to go that far."

The National Council of Churches followed up by unanimously approving a stinging rebuke of the administration's Gulf policy.

Seeking to counter all this criticism, high-level administration sources said that only the threat of early war could induce Saddam Hussein to withdraw from Kuwait. Secretary Baker also weighed in. As the *New York Times* put it on November 14, 1990: "With the domestic consensus for the Administration's policy on the Persian Gulf beginning to fracture, Secretary of State James A. Baker 3rd declared today [November 13] that a primary reason the United States must confront Iraq is to save American jobs." The U.S. economic lifeline, according to Baker, runs to the United States from the Gulf, and the United States cannot let a dictator sit astride that lifeline.

Alarmed at the course of events, senators from both parties urged Bush to call a special session of Congress to consider the Gulf crisis. Bush opposed the idea, but he assured congressional leaders that he would consult them before going to war. He stopped short of promising to seek congressional authorization in the face of a sudden provocation by Iraq, however.

Bowing to the insistence both at home and abroad that no offensive action be taken without U.N. approval, the United States announced that it was preparing to seek a U.N. resolution authorizing offensive military action against Iraq. Secretary Baker started a tour of capitals of members of the U.N. Security Council to obtain their support.

For their part, the Soviets called for a delay in introducing such a resolution and a new offer to Hussein that would give him a face-saving way out. Gorbachev said that he was convinced that war could be averted. Bush and Gorbachev met in Paris, but Bush failed to get Gorbachev to agree to the use of force.

Secretary Baker and Soviet Foreign Minister Eduard A. Shevardnadze met for three days, but Baker failed again to win Soviet approval of a U.N. resolution authorizing the use of force.

At the same time, Iraq announced that it was sending 250,000 more troops to bolster forces in Kuwait and southern Iraq.

Iraq, however, in what was interpreted as a move toward peace, announced that it would release Western hostages by late March, unless something took place that marred the atmosphere of peace. On November 20, Iraq agreed to free its German hostages, acknowledging that the move was an attempt to split the Gulf alliance.

That same day, forty-five congressmen filed a suit in an effort to keep Bush from resorting to force in the Gulf without congressional approval.

On November 23 Bush departed on a whirlwind tour of U.S. bases in the Saudi desert. He talked tough about Iraq, saying that there was an imminent threat that Iraq would acquire nuclear weapons.

Two days later, in separate appearances, Cheney and Scowcroft warned that Iraq's nuclear program was advancing despite the embargo and that Iraq might have a nuclear weapon within a year.

In response, a number of nuclear weapons experts issued a joint statement claiming that the administration was exaggerating. It was conceivable, they said, that Iraq might develop one unwieldy, untested nuclear device, but what could they do with it that would affect the situation?

Iraq called up its reserves on November 25. The same day, PLO head Yassir Arafat announced his support for Hussein's statement that an Iraqi withdrawal from Kuwait must be tied to an overall settlement of Middle East problems.

In testimony before a congressional committee on November 28, two former chairmen of the Joint Chiefs of Staff, Gen. David C. Jones and Adm. William J. Crowe, urged Bush to delay military action, asking that the embargo stay in place for a year. Former Secretary of State Henry A. Kissinger, however, argued that the United States could not afford to wait a year, because the presence of U.S. troops was "destabilizing" to the Middle East.

Then, on November 30, the U.N. Security Council passed a resolution giving Iraq until January 15 to withdraw from Kuwait or face a military attack. The vote was twelve to two, with China abstaining. The nay votes were cast by Yemen and Cuba. Saddam Hussein responded by saying that Iraq would fight.

Former defense secretaries Harold Brown, Robert McNamara, Frank C. Carlucci, Caspar W. Weinberger, and Elliot L. Richardson all advised patience in the Gulf. Only Donald Rumsfeld, defense secretary in the Ford administration and a longtime friend of Cheney, argued in favor of offensive action.

That same day, in a gesture toward peace, Iraq's troops in Kuwait delivered food supplies to the U.S. embassy.

Bush countered the Iraqi initiative, saying that he was "going the extra mile for peace" by offering to send Baker to Iraq at a mutually acceptable time between December 15 and January 15 and to meet himself with the Iraqi foreign minister in Washington during the latter part of the week of December 10. Iraq accepted the proposal but repeated that peace in the Middle East had to be linked to the Israeli occupation of Arab lands.

The next day, administration officials said in background interviews that the Baker mission was intended largely for U.S. domestic purposes, to convince Congress and the public that Bush was doing all he could for peace and to be responsive to Soviet urgings. They emphasized that Baker was not authorized to talk about anything but Iraq's withdrawal from Kuwait and the release of the hostages.

The United States also formally rejected the Iraqi effort to include Palestine in the discussions.

Attempting to build congressional support for the use of military force, Defense Secretary Cheney, in testimony before Congress on December 3, said that sanctions were not effective and argued that the Allies must act militarily and soon, that a long delay would damage the world economy and permit Iraq to improve its defenses.

That same day, in unrelated announcements, Moscow said that Iraq had agreed to release one thousand Soviet citizens still in Iraq; Iraq asserted that fourteen hundred children had died from lack of medicine due to the sanctions; and several of Israel's top leaders warned of their deep worry that the United States might find a peaceful solution to the Gulf crisis that would leave Iraq's military power intact.

On December 4 Democrats in the House of Representatives adopted a statement that Bush should not go to war without congressional approval. However, a few days later President Bush told the ambassadors of the twenty-eight countries forming the coalition that if he decided to go to war, he would do so whether or not Congress and the American people agreed.[3] Over a year later, in January 1992, a senior administration official bragged to reporters on background that in "going first to the U.N., we boxed the Democrats in nicely"—meaning that in the face of a U.N. vote in favor of using military force to drive Iraq out of Kuwait, members of Congress would find it difficult not to vote for war.[4]

The next day, CIA director Webster testified before Congress that Iraq could maintain its current combat readiness for only nine months under sanctions and its air force readiness for only three months.

Later that day, a number of prominent Democrats led by senior members of the Senate Foreign Relations Committee criticized the Bush administration for what they called "an indecent rush to war."

The *New York Times* published a news analysis on December 5 saying that an American war against Iraq would earn the undying enmity of Arabs. It quoted the Algerian foreign minister as saying, "So how do you think Algerians will react to thousands of Iraqi deaths once again at the hands of the West, this time the Americans aided by the French and a few Arabs for window dressing?" And a PLO official in Jordan said, "You can flatten Iraq. But no American plane will be safe in the sky, and you will need five bodyguards for every American in the Middle East."

On December 6 Hussein himself made another peaceful gesture, declaring that, to help the diplomatic efforts, he would free all the hostages. Bush welcomed the promised hostage release but said that Iraq must also give up Kuwait.

The next two weeks were relatively uneventful. Then, on December 19, the deputy U.S. commander in the Gulf said that American forces would not be ready to attack Iraq by the January 15 deadline. In

Washington, administration officials charged that the general had hurt their Gulf strategy.

President Bush, in a December 20 interview, said that Hussein needed to understand that "if we get into an armed situation, he's going to get his ass kicked."

On December 26 newspapers reported that the Pentagon planned to give soldiers in the Gulf injections to protect them from germ warfare.

The following day Hussein ordered Iraqi diplomats who had been called to Baghdad to confer to return to their posts and to work for a "serious dialogue." He then summoned Muslim leaders for a conference scheduled to begin on January 9.

On December 30 European foreign ministers announced plans for a special session on the Gulf crisis.

In the meantime, Baker's trip to Iraq to confer with Hussein remained on hold because the Bush administration thought that the date Hussein had suggested, January 12, would be too late—although Bush's original proposal was for any day between December 15 and January 15.

However, on January 2, 1991, in response to congressional and Allied pressure, the White House hinted that it might agree to talks if Iraq offered a new date.

The next day, Bush offered to send Baker to Geneva for talks with Iraqi officials. Baghdad accepted but pressed for the Palestine issue to be included in the agenda.

On January 4 the European Community offered to work to settle all disputes in the Middle East, including Palestine, if Iraq would pull out of Kuwait. Secretary Baker spurned the offer.

Bush followed up on January 5 with a warning that time was running out for Baghdad, that if the United States waited too long to attack after the January 15 deadline, Iraq would only strengthen its defenses, thus increasing the cost in U.S. lives.

That same day Iraq pressed again for talks between Baker and Hussein. The next day Hussein warned the Iraqi army to prepare itself for the "mother of all battles."

Bush made a formal request to Congress on January 8 seeking approval for the use of military force against Iraq if it did not pull out of Kuwait by the January 15 deadline.

On January 9 Baker met with Iraqi Foreign Minister Tariq Aziz. Baker reported that he found no sign of flexibility. For his part, Aziz said that if the United States attacked Iraq, Iraq would absolutely attack Israel.

Hussein told the Iraqi people that same day that American soldiers would "swim in their own blood."

On January 12, the leaders of Jordan, Yemen, Tunisia, and the PLO conducted a final push for peace, seeking mainly to reassure Israel, and the U.S. Senate approved Bush's request to use military force in the Gulf by a vote of fifty-two to forty-seven. Two Republicans joined the Democrats in opposing the use of force. Ten Democrats, mostly Southerners, joined the Republicans. However, Sen. Joseph Lieberman, a freshman Democrat from Connecticut, not only voted for the use of force but was one of its leading advocates.

In the House of Representatives, the vote was 250 in favor to 183 opposed. Those in favor of using military force included 164 Republicans and 86 Democrats. Those opposed included 179 Democrats, 3 Republicans, and one independent.*

Saddam Hussein and Iraq remained unmoved, and the January 15 deadline passed.

On January 16 the *New York Times* reported that the Pentagon had ordered a large number of body bags for immediate delivery. That same day, President Bush ordered an all-out air assault on Iraq and the Iraqi troops in Kuwait—just one day after the deadline. The war had begun.

---

*A number of commentators have noted that Senator Lieberman and Rep. Stephen J. Solarz of New York, who were among the more prominent Democrats who not only voted for the use of force but were leading advocates for the use of force, are both Jews and very active supporters of Israel. However, it should also be noted that more than half of the Jewish members of Congress voted against the resolution.

CHAPTER 8

Phase I: The Air War

The war—code-named Desert Storm—began at 2:30 A.M. on January 16, 1991, with an air attack on Baghdad and a large number of other targets in both Iraq and Kuwait. In a television appearance, President Bush said, "We have no choice but to force Saddam Hussein from Kuwait. We will not fail." He stressed that the goal was not just to liberate Kuwait but "to knock out Saddam Hussein's nuclear bomb potential. We will also destroy his chemical weapons facilities."

Bush repeated what he had said before—that this war would not be another Vietnam. By that he seemed to mean that he was determined to do whatever would be necessary, first, to win, and, second, to win quickly. American troops, the president said, would have the best possible support. In an apparent reference to the Vietnam War or possibly to both the Vietnam and the Korean wars, he said that American soldiers would not be asked to fight with one hand tied behind their back. He said that he was hopeful not only that the fighting would not go on for long but also that the casualties could be held to a minimum.

He continued:

This is an historic moment. We have in this past year made great progress in ending the long era of conflict and cold war. We have before us the opportunity to forge for ourselves and for future generations a new world order, an order in which a credible United Nations can use its peacekeeping role to fulfill the promise and vision of the U.N.'s founding fathers. We have no argument with the people of Iraq. Indeed, for the innocents caught in this conflict, I pray for their safety.

Our goal is not the conquest of Iraq. It is the liberation of Kuwait. It is my hope that somehow the Iraqi people can, even now, convince their dictator that he must lay down his arms, leave Kuwait, and let Iraq itself rejoin the family of peace-loving nations.

General Colin Powell remarked earlier that the lesson of Vietnam was not to escalate gradually but to begin with overwhelming force and apply it relentlessly. President Bush indicated that he agreed— that halfhearted, step-by-step efforts were self-defeating, that the United States should go all out from the beginning, defeat the enemy, and then quickly get out.

In line with this theory, the United States and its Allies had assembled one of the greatest air armadas in history, backed up by formidable ground and sea forces. About 690,000 Allied troops were stationed in Saudi Arabia and at sea in the Gulf—425,000 American and 265,000 Allied soldiers and sailors from twenty-seven other countries.

The primary mission assigned to these forces was to defend Saudi Arabia from an attack by the 545,000 Iraqi troops stationed in Kuwait and southern Iraq. The secondary mission—if it became necessary— was to attack and drive out the Iraqi forces occupying Kuwait.

High on the priority list of targets to be bombed in both Kuwait and Iraq, to repeat what was listed earlier, were command and control centers, antiaircraft defenses, airfields, and military installations of all kinds. Other prime targets included bridges, road and rail networks, communications facilities of all kinds (telephone, telegraph, radio, and television), factories, warehouses—in fact, Iraq's entire economic base. The number of aircraft involved, the intensity of the bombing, and the time to be devoted to it—which was intended to be several weeks at the least—demonstrated that this was to be among the largest air assaults in history.

More than one observer noted that the air campaign did not focus initially on liberating Kuwait or even on targets directly related to the task of liberating Kuwait. On the contrary, the primary targets were both Iraq's military and economic capabilities—not just command and control centers, bridges, communications facilities, and targets of direct military significance, but also the economic infrastructure that lay behind Iraq's military power. Part of the reason, the speculation ran, was that if the campaign had focused first on liberating Kuwait, the United States would have had difficulty persuading its Allies, especially the Arab allies, to agree to leveling Iraq's economic capabilities that could contribute to military capabilities in the future.

The first air attacks were hailed as a great success, and Allied casualties were remarkably light. To take full advantage of the American edge in night-fighting capabilities, most of the attacks were launched after dark. The first night, 159 targets were hit. Initial reports were that Allied casualties were one American plane lost, one Kuwaiti plane, and two British.

Within a few days a U.S. military spokesperson claimed that the Allies had established control of the air over Iraq. However, it turned out later that the claim had been premature.

The Iraqi Scud Missiles

On January 17 Iraq fired eight Scud missiles at Tel Aviv and Haifa. At about the same time, Scuds were also fired at Riyadh, the capital of Saudi Arabia. The missiles carried conventional, high-explosive warheads and did only slight damage. In Israel, seven people were slightly hurt by flying glass. No one was hurt in Saudi Arabia.

The Scud is a Soviet missile designed to attack targets beyond the range of artillery. It has a range of 186 miles, but the Iraqi version was reportedly altered to carry a smaller warhead and thus extend the range to 300 miles. Some Scud missiles are launched from fixed sites, others from eight-wheel mobile transporters. The Scud was designed to carry warheads of conventional explosives, which is what the Scuds usually carry. However, a Scud can be fitted with a chemical or even a nuclear warhead.

The United States had already deployed to the Gulf area an anti-aircraft missile, the Patriot. Although the Patriot was designed to be used against aircraft, the United States hoped that it would also be effective against the Scuds. In the first few days, Patriot missiles did succeed in shooting down several of the Scuds fired at Saudi Arabia.

The Scud missile is very inaccurate. At maximum range, its chances of hitting a target even as large as an urban area, such as Haifa, Tel Aviv, or Riyadh, are not great. So Scud missiles armed with conventional warheads are terror weapons with almost no military value.

However, Scuds fired at urban areas and armed with chemical or nuclear warheads could cause high civilian casualties. Although Iraq did not have any nuclear warheads, it did have a stockpile of chemical weapons that could presumably be fitted to the Scuds.

Predictably, the Palestinians and the mass of the people in Jordan, many of whom are actually Palestinians, were exuberantly delighted by the Scud attack on Israel. Israel threatened to retaliate, but Washington appealed for restraint. To retaliate, Israel would have had to fly over Jordanian territory, an act that might well have drawn Jordan into the war on Iraq's side.

What Washington feared even more, however, was the reaction of the Arab members of the coalition aligned against Iraq. If Israel retaliated, some Arab members would probably withdraw from the coalition. The Arab masses in other countries would surely riot and might even topple some of their governments. Clearly, the Iraqi motive for the Scud attack on Israel was to try to provoke Israel into an act of war. If Israel actually entered the conflict, the final result might well be a war with Iraq on one side; the United States, Israel, Britain, and perhaps France on the other; and all the other Arab states either neutral or siding with Iraq. Even Iran—non-Arab but Muslim—indicated at one point that it would not remain neutral if Israel entered the war.

So the United States urged Israel to refrain from retaliating and promised that the Scud launching sites would be given the highest priority in the coalition bombing campaign. Israel agreed to hold off but retained the right to respond in the future.

To reinforce its appeal, the United States sent two flights of F-15s based in Turkey to bomb the sites from which the missiles attacking Israel had been launched. In addition, high priority was given to seeking out and destroying both fixed and mobile Scud launchers all over Iraq.

On January 22 another Scud attack on Tel Aviv killed three people. To emphasize its plea for Israel to refrain from retaliating, the United States mounted a huge overnight airlift to deliver to Israel two Patriot missile battalions, manned by Americans, for defense against further Scud attacks.

In the meantime, Iraq also fired Scud missiles at the Saudi capital, Riyadh, but U.S. military authorities reported that Patriot missiles intercepted and knocked down most of them.

On January 25 seven Scud missiles aimed at Tel Aviv and Haifa were intercepted by Patriot missiles. Nevertheless, one person was killed and forty-two were injured. Two Scud missiles were fired at Riyadh, but these were also intercepted. Still, one person was killed, at least six were injured, and two office buildings were razed.

On January 27 American newspapers reported that in spite of these successes the Patriot missiles had showed serious flaws. Even when a Patriot hit an incoming Scud, the hit would often be on the body of the missile, leaving the warhead to continue on its course unharmed. In addition, the debris falling from the Patriot itself had caused casualties and damage.

By then, Iraq had fired fifty-one Scud missiles, twenty-six at targets in Saudi Arabia and twenty-five at targets in Israel, causing only slight damage. At the same time, Israeli intelligence sources said that even though the attacks on the Scud launching sites had gained a measure of success, many Scuds, especially the mobile ones, remained operational. What the Israelis obviously feared was that future Scud attacks might employ chemical warheads.

The Air War Continues

The United States claimed that the very highest priority targets had been destroyed, including Iraqi installations engaged in making chemical weapons and Iraqi nuclear research facilities. The Iraqi air force kept its planes in hardened bunkers, where relatively few had been damaged, but the Allies succeeded in cratering the runways of many airfields so badly that Iraqi planes presumably would have difficulty taking off.

General Schwarzkopf briefed the press on January 19. The Allies were flying two thousand sorties a day, and more than 80 percent of these succeeded in engaging their targets. In addition to the U.S. Air Force, air contingents from Saudi Arabia, Kuwait, the United Kingdom, Canada, France, and Italy had all taken part. Seven coalition aircraft had been lost.

During the briefing, Schwarzkopf showed films of laser-guided bombs hitting and cratering the middle of an airport runway, a direct hit on a storage bunker suspected of holding Scud missiles, a bomb descending directly into the air shaft of an Iraqi air defense headquarters, and a laser bomb scoring a direct hit on the Iraqi air force headquarters.

The laser bomb is a remarkable advance in accuracy. In World War II, targets that required pinpoint accuracy, such as bridges, were sometimes bombed a hundred or more times before a direct hit was scored. Not so with the laser bomb. The usual practice is to use a two-plane team, one with the laser and the other carrying the bomb. Using the so-called Pave Tack system, the laser-equipped plane uses its laser beam to navigate by identifying checkpoints, such as a bridge, and providing information on position and altitude. Once the pilot of the laser plane is within sight of the target, he fixes the cross hairs of his video display on the target and turns on the laser beam. Computers and stabilized sighting equipment keep the beam locked on the target, even though the plane engages in evasive maneuvers. Once the laser is locked onto the target, the pilot of the plane carrying the bomb can launch it while he is still several miles away. The bomb then follows the laser beam reflections bouncing off the target. It maintains its course to the target with its adjustable tail fins or, in some models, with its own propulsion system.

However, only about 15 to 20 percent of the bombs dropped on Iraq were "smart" laser bombs. The rest were "dumb" conventional bombs, lacking the laser's "surgical precision." This probably accounts for the fact that although the Allied forces maintained that everything possible was being done to minimize civilian casualties, refugees from Baghdad reported that many civilians were being killed and wounded. At about the same time, Cable News Network (CNN) reporter Peter Arnett, who had stayed in Baghdad, was shown a town north of Baghdad where twenty-four civilians had been killed by bombs, although the townspeople said that there were no military installations anywhere nearby.

By the end of the first week of bombing, more than ten thousand sorties had been flown, far surpassing the most intense bombing of World War II. The official assessment was that Iraq had been greatly weakened, but its capacity to wage war remained high. The damage to bridges, factories, and similar targets was extensive, but the Iraqi command and control system was still operating. The impact on Iraqi ground troops was at best uncertain. Probably as a consequence of this, General Powell announced that the United States was beginning to shift its air attacks to Iraqi ground forces.

At about the same time, seaborne U.S. Marine Corps forces began to practice landings.

Shortly afterward, Iraq set fire to oil refineries and storage facilities in Kuwait. The purpose was apparently to try to form a smoke screen to limit the vision of attacking planes. In addition, fire also confuses targeting systems that rely on infrared rays.

On January 29 Allied planes caught an Iraqi convoy exposed on a road and destroyed twenty-four tanks, armored personnel carriers, and supply vehicles. The next day, three Iraqi tank battalions attacked an abandoned Saudi Arabian port town of Khafji, just over the border from Kuwait. They were promptly driven back by U.S. Marines and Arab forces. Eleven Marines were killed in the fighting, but it was later reported that seven of them died from "friendly" aircraft fire. By February 1 the town had been recaptured.

On February 3 the Allies announced that any threat from Iraqi naval forces had been eliminated. Iraq had a fleet of mainly small patrol boats, twenty-four of which had been destroyed and thirty-one heavily damaged.

The Allies also announced that round-the-clock bombing had forced Iraq to abandon central control of its air defenses, giving the Allies unquestioned command of the air. After thirty thousand sorties, only nineteen Allied aircraft had been lost.

A U.S. spokesperson said that a total of twenty-nine Iraqi aircraft had been destroyed and that thirty-eight of forty-four airfields had suffered severe bomb damage, with nine of the thirty-eight no longer operational. Air attacks had destroyed more than seventy hardened aircraft shelters.

On the ground, 24 Iraqi army tanks and 52 belonging to the Republican Guard had been destroyed. The Guard had also lost 178 trucks and 55 artillery pieces. Because 25 out of 35 bridges on the major supply routes had been taken out, supply convoys jammed up and took heavy losses from air strikes.

The same day these announcements were made, however, a Soviet general said that some of the Scud missiles, tanks, and other vehicles that the United States claimed had been destroyed were, in fact, fakes. An Italian firm specializing in building fake but very realistic-looking planes, tanks, and other weapons had done a huge business with Iraq.

The Allied command announced also that the air war had shifted from bombing factories, bridges, and communications facilities to Iraqi military positions, including bunkers shielding aircraft. The command further reported that another sixty-eight Iraqi aircraft had been destroyed.

As for enemy personnel losses, the news media reported that the Pentagon and General Schwarzkopf's headquarters were vague in answering questions about casualties. The military in general believed that the emphasis on "body counts" during the Vietnam War had backfired. Schwarzkopf himself said that he was never again going to get into the "body count business."

Military spokespersons cited four reasons for their reluctance to offer even an estimate of Iraqi dead. First, they said that making accurate estimates was simply impossible. Second, the number of dead was not as important a measure of military success or failure as the number of hits against command centers, communications links, airfields, and major weapons systems such as tanks and artillery pieces. Third, officers who had fought in Vietnam thought that giving estimates of the dead was an invitation for criticism that they were either exaggerating or killing merely for the sake of favorable press treatment. Finally, in a coalition in which Arabs were a vital part, it was obviously politically imprudent to emphasize the blood shed by other Arabs. If it became known that large numbers of Iraqi soldiers and civilians were being killed, public opinion in both Arab and Western countries might be inflamed.

Iraqi Strategy

In background press briefings, U.S. officials described the strategy that Saddam Hussein and Iraq seemed to be following as "hunkering down." Iraqi planes were being kept in bunkers rather than being sent aloft to fight. By absorbing the blows rather than going out to meet the Allied forces, Iraq apparently hoped that sooner or later the coalition would be forced to launch a ground attack against Iraq's prepared positions. Well dug in, the Iraqi troops would be able to inflict heavy casualties on the attacking forces. The speculation in Washington was that Saddam Hussein assumed that the American public would not continue to support a war with very high casualties, especially a war in which Hussein saw the U.S. stake as being essentially access to cheap oil masked by a sanctimonious condemnation of "aggression." What Hussein seemed to be counting on was that high casualties would cause the American public to agitate for a negotiated settlement, as it had during both the Korean and Vietnam wars.

On January 25 Iraqi forces in Kuwait released millions of gallons of Kuwaiti crude oil into the Gulf. The Allied command speculated that Iraq was trying to impede an Allied amphibious landing and also to contaminate the desalinization plants that supply most of the drinking water for eastern Saudi Arabia. Whatever the motive, the fear in the rest of the world was that the oil would cause great ecological damage. President Bush termed the decision to spill the oil "sick."

Seeking to cut the flow of oil at its source, U.S. planes bombed the

Kuwaiti oil stations. By January 28 they had apparently succeeded in cutting off the flow of oil into the Gulf. However, the press speculated that the damage might already have been done. First, the oil slick had been moving rapidly toward vital Saudi Arabian desalinization sites. Second, since millions of gallons had already been released, the ecological damage might still be extremely severe, even if the flow of new oil had been stopped.

Iraqi Planes Flee to Iran

In the meantime, on January 26 a number of Iraq's most advanced jet warplanes inexplicably fled to Iranian airports. By January 28 more than eighty had done so. The evidence was not that the pilots were defecting but that they were actually obeying orders. Speculation in the West was either that Hussein had reached some sort of agreement with Iran that the planes could take shelter there until needed, or that Hussein planned some sort of peace agreement and hoped to keep the planes safe until better times. Some days later, Iran announced that the Iraqi planes would be held until the war was over.

Allied Plans

On January 27 the news media reported that U.S. intelligence officials had concluded that air strikes alone would not be able to force Iraqi troops out of Kuwait. A ground offensive would be needed. A ground war would probably be costly in terms of American lives, but doubts had grown that the U.S. and Allied goals could be accomplished without one. The military planners had hoped that bombing would reduce the effectiveness of the Republican Guard and its approximately four thousand tanks by 50 percent or, at the least, 30 percent before the Allies launched a ground attack. But the air attacks had apparently done only limited damage to the Guard, because its troops and equipment were so extremely well dug in.

Political Moves

In the meantime, both sides and a number of states not directly involved were busy with political and diplomatic moves.

Seven captured Allied pilots were interviewed on Iraqi TV. The faces of a number of pilots were bruised, sparking a flurry of debate about whether the bruises were the result of beatings or were the kind of injuries frequently sustained when pilots eject from damaged aircraft.

Whatever the case, Iraq announced that it would keep Allied pilots in areas likely to be bombed—a clear violation of the rules of war. President Bush said that the Iraqi leaders would be held accountable for any harm that came to Allied pilots.

In the waning days of January a number of countries that were not members of the coalition proposed a peace conference. President Bush responded that the United States would agree only if Iraq first pulled out of Kuwait. "There can be no pause now that Saddam has forced the world into war," he said. "We will stay the course and we will succeed—all the way."

Bush also began talking of toppling Hussein as one of the goals of the war. "No one," Bush said, "should weep for this tyrant when he is brought to justice." The *New York Times* interpreted these words to mean that Bush wanted to go on to Baghdad after expelling Iraq from Kuwait. To do this, the *Times* said, would mean a large increase in U.S. and Allied casualties. Various coalition officials said that adding the goal of occupying Iraq itself exceeded the U.N. mandate. They also felt that it would be unwise. Peace and stability in the Middle East, they argued, would not be served if Iraq were fragmented. Iraq was needed to counterbalance Iran and its Shiite fundamentalist rulers.

One of the most specific of these warnings came from Soviet Foreign Minister Aleksandr A. Bessmertnykh. He said that the Soviet Union was apprehensive of the indications that the United States was going beyond the U.N. mandate. He also said that the way the war was being conducted posed a growing danger to Iraqi civilians.

Uneasiness Among the Arab Masses

In the meantime, uneasiness continued to grow among the ordinary Arab people in the countries that had joined the coalition. The misgivings centered on the Allied bombing of Iraq and on Arabs joining the United States and other Western states in a war on fellow Arabs. On January 24 the *New York Times* reported that public sentiment in Egypt, which had supplied forty-five thousand soldiers to the Allied force, was shifting in Baghdad's favor. Egyptians, according to the reports, were shocked by the force and breadth of the Allied bombing of Iraq. In the first place, nearly a million Egyptians continued to live and work in Iraq. Second, reports in the Arab press played up the civilian casualties and the fact that they were Arabs. Stories about anti-Arab sentiment in the United States were also frequent. Many ordinary Egyptians, according to the Times, saw the Allied bombing attacks as demonstrating carelessness and indifference about the value of Arab lives.

In addition, ordinary Arabs had never had much sympathy for the way that the Kuwaitis, who had the highest per capita income of any country in the world, had lorded it over their fellow Arabs. During the Iraqi occupation a large number of Kuwaitis flaunted their wealth by living in luxurious Egyptian hotels and frequenting Egyptian discos. While King Fahd and other Arab leaders in the coalition had kept a low profile, Egypt's President Hosni Mubarak had been making public statements against both Hussein and Iraq. The same Muslim fundamentalists in Egypt who had opposed and eventually assassinated President Anwar as-Sadat for signing a peace treaty with Israel were now opposing Mubarak.

As a result of this growing pro-Iraqi sentiment, the Egyptian government extended the midyear university vacation out of fear of demonstrations if the students went back to the campuses. President Mubarak, in a speech to parliament, made a special point of defending his government's decision to join the coalition against Iraq. In justification, he cited both the U.N. mandate and the action of the Arab League.

Somewhat later, however, on January 27, the Egyptian government announced that it favored neither the destruction of Iraq nor the elimination of Saddam Hussein. Egypt, the statement said, was prepared to cooperate with Hussein in the future. Boutrous Ghali, one of Egypt's senior foreign policy decision makers, said that he had little doubt that once the war was over, "An Arab reconciliation of pro-Saddam and anti-Saddam forces will happen very quickly."

In Saudi Arabia, newspaper reports cited grudging respect for Hussein and enormous relief that he had not been totally crushed in the initial days of the war. One Saudi Arabian expressed a sentiment that was reported to be widespread: "In all of our wars, the Arabs were stopped, or ultimately spared by superpower intervention. But Mr. Hussein is steadfast against the world's only superpower and the 28 [sic] countries fighting alongside it."

A report in the New York Times said, "Apart from the relief expressed here [Riyadh, Saudi Arabia] that another Arab leader had not been humiliated at the hands of the West, there is a deep conviction in Riyadh, Cairo, and Damascus that Iraq must not be destroyed or dismembered in an effort to free Kuwait."[1] Many Saudis saw Baghdad as a bulwark against a resurgence of Iran and Shiite fundamentalism. Speaking of

Saddam Hussein, one Saudi official said, "This is a part of the world in which force and strength are respected, and even though we are opposed to him in this struggle, many here still admire, despite themselves, what they view as his steely resolve."

Doubts Among the Western Allies

In general, support in the Western countries that had joined the coalition against Iraq remained firmer than among the Arabs, and opposition was muted. However, the French foreign minister, Jean-Pierre Chevenement, resigned to protest that Allied goals in the Gulf War were going beyond those authorized by the U.N. But no other officials voiced any protests. As for the general public, there were demonstrations in France, England, and Italy against the Allied intervention, but nothing like those in, for example, Egypt.

Nevertheless, foreign policy specialists in Western Europe and members of the press expressed doubt. One of the more eloquent of these was Martin Walker, the Washington bureau chief of the *Manchester Guardian.* "American priorities," he wrote, "could hardly have been made more clear to the Soviet leaders." As far as the United States was concerned, *perestroika* could sink or swim. If the United States would be allowed to focus its attention on the "bully of the Gulf and his threat to the West's oil supply," then the Soviets would be left to their own devices.

"Under President Bush and Secretary of State Baker," Walker wrote, "the great opportunity in the East is being lost, while the blood and treasure of an international coalition is being poured out to defend one feudal Arab dynasty and to restore another. The U.S. and its allies are fighting not for the West's democratic ideals but almost in spite of them, lined up in a sad parade that reeks of neo-colonial interest and greed for oil."[2]

Third World Opinion

There was much uneasiness in the Third World about the Gulf War. In Delhi, the feeling was widespread that a U.S. victory in the Gulf would be a loss to the Third World, leading to a *pax Americana* that would exploit the rest of the world. Although informed people recognized that Hussein was a dictator and a tyrant, they had a surprising amount of sympathy for him.[3]

Throughout the rest of Asia, Muslim backing for Hussein and Iraq was solid. In China, however, Deng Xiaoping, still the leading figure, described the Gulf War as a fight between "big bullies" and "small bullies."

In his syndicated column published on January 30, Patrick J. Buchanan pointed out that in Algeria, Tunisia, and Jordan, pro-Iraq sentiment had forced the governments to virtually endorse Hussein. Petitions in favor of Hussein were circulating in Morocco and in Yemen. Similar reports of support and sympathy for Hussein had come from India, Pakistan, Indonesia, Malaysia, and Bangladesh. In Turkey there were resignations from the cabinet protesting Turkey's alliance with the United States. [At about the same time, Turkish fundamentalists called for Turkey to withdraw from the coalition, saying that the problem of Iraq and Kuwait should be settled by Muslim countries among themselves.] Buchanan also quoted Syria's foreign minister as saying, "All Arabs are delighted with missiles streaking toward Israel."

Doubts in the United States

A number of American observers also expressed doubts and opposition of various kinds.

Among the first of these, writing just days before the bombing began, were Paul H. Nitze and Michael F. Stafford.[4] Nitze, especially, had extensive experience in both foreign affairs and defense. He had headed the State Department's Policy Planning Staff in the Truman administration, played a prominent role in the Defense Department in the Kennedy administration, and had been one of the principal arms control negotiators in the Reagan administration.

Noting that General Schwarzkopf had said that it would take up to six months to win an all-out war and that even then such a war would require heavy reliance on ground forces, Nitze and Stafford urged giving economic sanctions a thorough trial. If, after six months, sanctions proved ineffective, the Allies could step up to a naval blockade and selective bombing that would minimize civilian casualties. If, after another several months, Iraq continued to refuse to withdraw from Kuwait, then the United States and its Allies could consider the wisdom of a ground attack.

Nitze and Stafford were particularly worried about the high probability of very large numbers of coalition casualties and the long-term consequences. "In sum," they concluded, "the all-out war option seems highly counterproductive in the long term and certainly not worth the thousands of lives it would cost."

In a January 20 op-ed piece in the *New York Times,* Efraim Karsh, the coauthor of the highly regarded book *Saddam Hussein: A Political Biography,* suggested that the reason Hussein had rejected all the face-saving formulas offered by third parties was that he thought war was inevitable and it offered him a better chance for political survival than giving in to Bush's demands. "Indeed," wrote Karsh, "a limited defeat would not only be acceptable but would enable him to emerge victorious." Hussein hoped that standing up to the West, even though he lost Kuwait, would lead the Arab masses to treat him as a new Nasser— an Arab leader who defied Western imperialism and survived. Karsh predicted that Hussein would try to provoke Israel into an act of war and induce the Allies into an early ground attack. As mentioned earlier, several observers remarked during this period that Hussein was apparently convinced that heavy casualties would turn the American people against the war and toward an early peace, thus permitting him to avoid a total defeat and the occupation of Iraq itself.

Still another commentator speculated that future historians might say that, to the American leaders, driving Iraqi forces out of Kuwait was less important than destroying Iraq's capacity to wage war. At the same time, if Iraq was reduced to impotence, who would counterbalance the Shiite fundamentalist regime in Iran? The United States, the argument concluded, was stuck either way.[5]

Some of the comment expressed disquiet over the possibility of large numbers of innocent civilians being killed by the bombing. Noting that B-52s had been striking targets all across both Iraq and Kuwait, a January 19 *New York Times* editorial said that students of the Vietnam War shuddered at the memory of B-52s dropping fifty tons of bombs each in "free-fire zones" and the indiscriminate havoc they had wrought. As if to confirm these worries, on January 25 Peter Arnett of CNN, who was still in Baghdad, transmitted TV footage via satellite showing considerable bomb damage to private houses, shops, and other civilian structures.

The *Times* editorial also pointed out that before very long the Gulf campaign was likely to include grueling ground fighting, with high casualties on both sides.

In this same vein of fear of high casualties, newspapers frequently speculated that Iraq was holding back potent weapons for use when the ground war started. One fear was that Iraq might use the so-called fuel-air bomb, in which a cloud of gasoline or other flammable liquid is ignited to form a huge fireball that creates overpressures of 240 to 350 pounds per square inch. Although Iraq did not use such a weapon, perhaps because it lacked the technology, the United States did use fuel-air bombs later in the war to make corridors through minefields and entrenchments by exploding or crushing mines and fortifications.

One particularly poignant point of doubt about the war was raised by American blacks. One of eight Americans is black, but among the soldiers sent to the Gulf, the ratio of blacks to whites was one to four.

On January 28 Saddam Hussein called in CNN's Peter Arnett for an interview and hinted that if the Allies pushed his back to the wall he would use all of the weapons available to him, including chemical and biological weapons. Picking up on this interview, Anthony Lewis, in his column in the *New York Times,* quoted a scientist as saying that if Hussein did in fact use such weapons, the casualties would be "massive." Lewis also quoted U.S. intelligence sources as saying that fifteen countries would have ballistic missiles by the year 2000 and that ten of those countries were reportedly working on chemical warheads for them.

In a separate story, the *Times* reported that the troops in the Gulf were well aware of the possibility that they might be attacked with both chemical and biological weapons and that they were understandably uneasy about it.

A few days later, General Schwarzkopf, while expressing confidence in victory for the Allies and considerable contempt for Iraqi military skills, said that he expected frontline forces to be subjected to attack by poison gas. He pointed out that the air offensive had destroyed the factories that made chemical weapons, but that it was easy for the enemy to conceal and protect stockpiles of chemical weapons that had already been made.

Everyone in the military, from the top commanders to the ordinary soldier, was also well aware of the possibility that ordinary conventional weapons could cause many casualties. The Pentagon kept its official casualty estimates secret. Privately, however, Pentagon officials did offer estimates—but only on background. The more pessimistic of these were for thirty thousand dead in the first month. A figure of forty thousand dead for the entire operation was the one most often cited. Before the ground attack began, this estimate was lowered to five thousand.

A newspaper story also appeared claiming that the Pentagon had ordered several thousand body bags and that the factory making them was working twenty-four hours a day to fill the order. Another story claimed that the total number of body bags ordered for the Gulf War was forty thousand.

As for aircraft losses, Gen. Merrill McPeak, the air force chief of staff, projected losses of "four or five aircraft a day." Afterward he said that "even in my . . . wildest dreams, I would not have said we would lose one aircraft every three days in this kind of operation."

Although the Pentagon would not reveal its official estimates for wounded, it acknowledged that enough blood supplies were in place to treat four thousand casualties a day. On February 1 press reports said that the U.S. military in the Gulf was set up to handle fifteen thousand wounded a day. First aid would be administered on the battlefield, and the wounded would then be transferred to one of thirty mobile hospital units. Backing these up were several larger hospitals ranging in size from five hundred beds to two hospital ships with a thousand beds each.

A big worry, however, was that, unlike Vietnam, where helicopters were able to get the wounded to a hospital in minutes, the desert would not permit the use of helicopters far enough forward for such rapid evacuation. The wounded would have to be transported on the ground to safe areas in the rear, then transferred to helicopters. Nothing can be done for a soldier who is killed instantly, but for one who is wounded, time is crucial. In World War I, when the wounded had to be carried to the rear and then transferred to an ambulance, 8.5 percent of the wounded died. In Vietnam, where the wounded were taken from the battlefield to a mobile hospital by helicopter, only 1.7 percent died.

Marines and helicopter pilots who fought at Khafji told reporters that although they were convinced of an eventual Allied victory, they had no doubt after the Khafji battle that the Iraqi ground troops would put up a fight. They thought that the coming land battle to drive Iraq out of Kuwait would go on for months, not weeks. As one Marine said, "The Iraqis are not as well organized as I expected, but they fight hard."[6]

After the war was over, General Powell told reporters that in January, just before the air assault began, he had estimated that U.S. forces would suffer several thousand casualties, although he did not specify how many would be killed and how many wounded.

The general public was equally uneasy about the prospect of casualties. A *Washington Post*/ABC poll conducted during the first week in January reported that support for the war dropped from 63 percent to 44 percent when respondents were asked if they would back a war in which a thousand American troops were lost. If the number of dead was increased to ten thousand, a figure often cited by military specialists, support for the war fell to 35 percent.

The Yellow Ribbons

One sign of the reaction of the American public was a spontaneous festooning of private homes, stores, and public buildings with yellow ribbons. Just how this phenomenon got started is somewhat of a mystery, for even though individuals were active in promoting the idea in a few towns, no national organization was behind it. Yellow was the color of the trim on the old U.S. cavalry dress uniform, and some historians cited evidence that during the nineteenth century cavalry campaigns against the Indians, the families left behind sometimes hung yellow ribbons on their doors. A favorite song among West Point cadets and throughout the army going back to before World War I concerned a yellow ribbon:

Around her hair, she wore a yellow ribbon,
She wore it in the springtime and the merry month of May,
And if you asked her why the hell she wore it,
She wore it for her soldier who was far, far away.

Far away, far away,
She wore it for her soldier who was far, far away.

The exact conclusion to be drawn from the yellow ribbon phenomenon was ambiguous. Some who displayed it said that it showed their support for the war. Yet people who opposed the war also displayed yellow ribbons, saying that they wanted to show they supported the troops, even though they did not support the war. Some of these said that their reason was to avoid what happened during the Vietnam War, when opponents sometimes blamed the soldiers who had to fight the war rather than the Washington politicians who had gotten the United States into it.

Refugees and Civilian Casualties

As the bombing continued, reports began to mount of civilian casualties and the plight of refugees. Jordan was so flooded with Sudanese, Indian, Yemeni, Syrian, Lebanese, and Jordanian refugees that the authorities could not properly take care of them.

The refugees reported that the road they had taken from Iraq to Jordan had been bombed heavily. The Allies apparently believed that the road was being used by Scud missile launchers. Inevitably, the refugees suffered casualties.

Up until this time, Iraq had played down civilian casualties, apparently to avoid morale problems. Previously, official Iraqi press releases had listed 650 civilians killed and 750 wounded. However, apparently sensing a propaganda advantage, Iraq said that, since the previous report, civilian casualties had been significant—that thousands more had been either killed or wounded.

Foreign reporters were shown damaged areas in Basra, and they reported much greater damage than in the Iran-Iraq war. On February 3 reporters were taken to a badly bombed village sixty miles from Baghdad that had no apparent military installations. News stories reported that many people who had left Baghdad were returning because outlying villages were no safer from bombing than Baghdad. One refugee was quoted as saying, "I thought I might as well be miserable in familiar surroundings, so I returned."

The negative reaction to the reports of civilian casualties in both the United States and the rest of the world prompted President Bush to hold a press conference on the question on February 5. He said that the Allies were doing all they could to limit "collateral damage," the military euphemism for civilian casualties. The real blame, he said, lay with Saddam Hussein, who was not only responsible for the original aggression but who was, Bush charged, relocating military headquarters to schools and other civilian installations.

On February 13 Iraq announced that during a predawn raid the United States had bombed a civilian air raid shelter in the Al-Amiriya residential district of Baghdad. United States military authorities claimed they had evidence that although the structure had been built as an air raid shelter during the Iran-Iraq war, it was being used as a military communications center. Western reporters on the scene during rescue operations confirmed that about three hundred women and children were killed, with only a handful of survivors. All over the world newspapers were filled with pictures of rescuers digging charred bodies from the ruins of the building while weeping families stood by and watched. On February 14 a headline in the *New York Times* read: "Carnage in Baghdad Erases Image of an Antiseptic War."

In answer to questions at a press conference, U.S. intelligence officials said that they could not explain why there were hundreds of civilians in the shelter, if it was indeed being used as a military communications center, except for the possibility that it was being used for military purposes during the daytime while continuing to be used as a civilian shelter at night.

The number of stories of civilian casualties increased considerably over the next few weeks. One report said that sixty Jordanian and Sudanese refugees fleeing from Iraq toward Jordan were killed when Allied planes attacked the buses in which they were riding. Another report stated that U.S. planes had bombed a plant that U.S. intelligence claimed was making biological weapons. However, Western visitors to the scene reported that signs around the factory identified the product as baby formula, although they also noted that the signs were in English rather than Farsi.

In Egypt and Saudi Arabia, the newspapers did not carry the story about the civilian shelter being bombed or the other incidents. Their governments were uneasy about how their people would react to the deaths of Arab civilians. But many other Arab and Muslim countries—Jordan, Yemen, the Sudan, Libya, and Tunisia, for example—declared a period of national mourning for civilian casualties in Baghdad.

In Jordan, however, refugees from Iraq told Western reporters that they did not believe that the bombing would break the Iraqi people's will. Rather, they reported "deep and widespread anger" at Bush and the United States for the bombing campaign. Spirits remained high, they said, and anger against the United States was nearly universal.

A *New York Times* editorial said that there had been too much bombing of targets in and near cities and that the bombing effort should be shifted to troops on the battlefield.

It was reported on February 15 that the Allies were reviewing their target plans to decrease still more the chance of civilian casualties. However, it was also reported that within the U.S. government the result of all the negative publicity was to increase pressure to step up the timing of the planned ground assault in an effort to bring the war to a speedy conclusion.

CHAPTER 9

Phase II: The Ground War

President Bush said on February 5 that he was skeptical that air power could do the job alone and that a ground offensive was required. He announced that he was sending Defense Secretary Cheney and General Powell to the Middle East to make that determination.

At about the same time, newspaper stories described the Iraqi defenses as formidable. Iraqi troops had laid more than half a million land mines in two belts north of the Saudi border, while holding another twenty million in their arsenals. These two belts of mines were part of multilayered fortifications that included twelve-foot-high sand walls (berms), oil-filled trenches that could be set on fire, and buried storage tanks filled with butane.

The Iraqi defense system, the stories continued, was designed to channel coalition forces into killing zones. There they would be met by the elite Republican Guard, eight divisions of about fourteen thousand men each consisting of three armored divisions, four infantry divisions, and one special operations division. They were equipped with Soviet T-72 tanks and powerful concentrations of artillery.

The Guard had been steadily bombed day and night, principally by B-52s based mainly in western Saudi Arabia, but also in England, Spain, and the Indian Ocean island of Diego Garcia. The B-52s flew high in sets of three planes carrying 1,900-pound bombs, with each plane's bomb load adding up to the equivalent of 60,000 pounds of TNT or 180,000 pounds for each flight of three planes. However, although the B-52s are formidable against area targets such as cities, U.S. military authorities said that they were not very effective against point targets such as dug-in tanks and artillery. On February 5 a Pentagon spokesperson said that the best of the Iraqi troops, meaning the Republican Guard, had not been badly hurt by the bombing. The Pentagon official did say that the Republican Guard had been damaged by the bombing but refused to be any more specific than to say that tank and artillery losses had been in only the low hundreds.

The Pentagon also reported that in spite of success in bombing bridges and communications routes, the bombing had not reduced Saddam Hussein's ability to supply forces in the field with their daily requirements. However, the Pentagon noted that requirements were low at that time since the troops were dug in and not actually fighting. As yet, the Iraqi troops had no need to start using stocks that they had stored in nearby supply depots that were dispersed and dug in and were thus safe from the bombing.

The *New York Times* said in a February 10 editorial that, to Bush, victory meant liberating Kuwait; disabling Iraq's aggressive army; eliminating its capacity to produce chemical, biological, and nuclear weapons; and getting rid of Saddam Hussein. There were well-informed people, according to the *Times,* who thought that these goals could be won at little cost in casualties. But there were equally well-informed people who thought that a ground war would be very costly indeed in terms of U.S. and Allied lives and treasure. The *Times* argued that there was no easy way to reconcile these views and asked, "What's the rush?" The strength of the United States, the *Times* argued, was in its air power. Iraq had fought an eight-year war against Iran on the ground. Why adopt a strategy that played to Hussein's strength?

President Bush, according to the *Times*, seemed readier to escalate than many in the U.S. military. To Bush, the lesson of Vietnam was to avoid gradualism, but the *Times* feared that a ground war would bring heavy casualties and that this would cause Americans to get angry and want further escalation. Iraq's sacrifices might end up boosting Hussein in the eyes of the Arab masses, demonstrating that Saddam Hussein "stood up to the invading infidels, their wealthy Arab backers and even Arab governments allied against him." In trying to humble Hussein, the editorial argued, Bush might end up jeopardizing friendly Arab governments.

On February 10 Defense Secretary Cheney and General Powell returned to Washington from their Middle East trip and recommended that the bombing be continued for the time being. Bush said the next day that he would postpone the decision about a ground offensive, and the coalition's forces stepped up the air offensive, focusing on Iraqi troops occupying Kuwait.

Peace Efforts Continue

On February 6 King Hussein of Jordan abandoned neutrality and aligned Jordan with Iraq. The Allied war effort, he said, was directed "against all Arabs and all Muslims and not against Iraq alone." The United States and its Allies, he said, intended to assert "foreign hegemony" in the Middle East, so the Iraqi forces were defending "us all." He ended by calling for a cease-fire. Bush rejected the proposal the next day.

That same day, Secretary of State Baker spoke about a five-point U.S. plan for the Middle East after the war:

(1) A new security arrangement for the region to prevent any one state from devouring its neighbors.
(2) An arms control agreement, at least among supplier countries, that would restrain Iraq from rebuilding its chemical, biological, and nuclear capabilities.
(3) A program of economic restructuring to reduce the spread between the "haves" of the Middle East and the "have-nots."
(4) A renewed effort to settle the conflicts between Israel and Palestine and between Israel and other Arab countries.
(5) A program to reduce U.S. dependence on Middle Eastern oil.

In addition, Baker made two other points. First, he said that the role the United States would have to play in the postwar era would require it to station some forces permanently in the Middle East. Second, he said that any aid to Iraq would depend on Saddam Hussein's removal.

On February 9 Gorbachev warned against exceeding the U.N. mandate in the Middle East and called for diplomacy. Iraq had been an important client state for the Soviet military, and the Soviet Union has a significant Muslim population, so Gorbachev had undoubtedly been under pressure to do what he could to prevent Iraq's destruction. Secretary Baker brushed aside Gorbachev's warning, but Sen. Robert Dole (R., Kansas) said that it must be taken seriously.

Gorbachev's statement was undoubtedly related to the fact that on February 6 he had sent a Soviet envoy, Yevgeny M. Primakov, to talk with Hussein about ending the war. Returning to Moscow on February 14, Primakov said that he saw a "glimmer" of hope for peace.

Undoubtedly related to the Soviet effort, Iraq announced the next day that it was willing to discuss complying with the U.N. resolutions to withdraw from Kuwait. However, it said that it had several conditions, although they were not detailed in the announcement.

Not surprisingly, the Soviet Union welcomed the statement. What was surprising was that there was jubilation in the streets of Baghdad. However, the jubilation ceased that night when the bombing continued.

When the full Iraqi statement was published, it included ten conditions. The most important were that Israel withdraw from the West Bank, the Golan Heights, and southern Lebanon; that the Allies declare an immediate cease-fire followed by the withdrawal of all U.S. and Allied military forces from the region within a month; and that a peace conference be convened that would include the topic of Palestine. The other conditions would exempt Iraq from eleven U.N. resolutions covering such matters as reparations.

The conditions were obviously unacceptable, but what was noted around the world was that for the first time Iraq had said that it was willing to withdraw from Kuwait.

The U.S. government swiftly rejected the Iraqi proposal, and a Pentagon statement insisted that Iraq must withdraw from Kuwait before there could be a cease-fire. In background briefings to the press, American officials said that the speed of the rejection was because the United States did not want to allow time for the proposal to sow division in the ranks of the coalition.

President Bush himself termed the Iraqi proposal a "cruel hoax." He then called for Saddam Hussein's overthrow. For the first time Bush made it explicit rather than implicit: "There's another way for the bloodshed to stop, and that is for the Iraqi military and the Iraqi people to take matters into their own hands, to force Saddam Hussein, the dictator, to step aside."

For its part, the Soviet Union assailed the conditions in the Iraqi proposal, but it continued to voice hope that Iraq's offer to withdraw would become the basis for talks.

Military Moves

On February 17 the U.S. Central Command announced that 30 percent of the Iraqi tanks, 28 percent of their armored personnel carriers, and

35 percent of their artillery had been destroyed. These figures were questioned by the CIA and other Washington intelligence agencies. Washington intelligence analysts based their figures on satellite reconnaissance; the Central Command included information derived from debriefing U.S. and Allied pilots. The CIA and other Washington-based agencies said that pilot reports were not very reliable. However, both Washington and the Central Command agreed that Iraq still had an effective fighting force.

Strategy of the Ground Offensive

That same day a number of newspapers ran stories about the strategy for a ground offensive, based on direct quotes from some of the top generals, such as Powell and Schwarzkopf, on analyses by nongovernmental military experts, and on background briefings from officers in the Pentagon and Schwarzkopf's headquarters.

The stories reported that the offensive would be based on the so-called "AirLand doctrine," which is designed to fight a quick war by relying first on overwhelming air attacks followed by large, swift thrusts by armored columns. The plans called for the massive use of ground forces, not just as a supplement to the air war, but a massive assault for which the air war had paved the way.

The U.S. troops involved would be the VII Corps, made up primarily of armor, and the XVIII Airborne Corps, which included both airborne and assault helicopter forces. The two corps were stationed in northern Saudi Arabia to the west of U.S. Marine Corps units. Also deployed in the north were British armored forces and troops from France, Syria, Egypt, Saudi Arabia, and the Gulf emirates.

General Powell himself was quoted as saying that the coalition forces had no intention of "stupidly" launching a frontal assault on the enemy's main defenses. The Allied ground forces, said Powell, would attack so as to draw the Republican Guard out of its dug-in positions and into the open where it would be vulnerable to air attack. Allied thrusts, Powell said, would first cut off the Iraqi army and then "kill it."

Consistent with these statements, outside military experts envisioned a ground assault that would drive into Iraq near its border with Kuwait, cutting off the Iraqi troops in Kuwait and in Iraq along the Kuwaiti border. Such a thrust would accomplish Powell's purpose of drawing the Republican Guard out into the open and at the same time preventing it from escaping north toward Baghdad. The outside experts speculated that at the same time, the Marine Corps force of seventeen thousand men stationed offshore would stage an amphibious assault to pin down the Iraqi forces in Kuwait or to inflict heavy casualties on them if they tried to retreat to the north.

If the Republican Guard refused to come out of its defensive positions, the Allies would have a number of options. One would be to stay south of Basra but thrust east, just north of the dug-in Republican Guard. The effect would be to box in the Guard between Iranian territory to the east, U.S. forces to the west and north, and the Marines landing in the south. The Iraqi forces would then have a choice of surrendering or trying to fight their way out to the north.

However, the Iraqi force would have a hard time fighting its way out because so many bridges on the route north had been destroyed and the roads so badly damaged that armor, artillery, and other heavy equipment would find the going very difficult.

Newspaper stories also reported that many Pentagon officers and members of Congress feared that a ground assault would bring a large number of American casualties.

On February 16 two U.S. planes were shot down over Kuwait and two British planes over Iraq. More Scud missiles were fired at both Israel and Saudi Arabia. Some Iraqi units seemed to be leaving the front in Kuwait, although it was not known whether they were withdrawing from Kuwait or merely pulling back to better defensive positions.

On another part of the border, Iraqi patrols clashed with U.S. troops. Two U.S. ships in the Gulf were badly damaged when they hit Iraqi mines. Every night during this period, Allied patrols crossed the border into Iraq, probing the Iraqi defenses.

A laser bomb dropped by the British missed the bridge that was its target and hit an apartment building and a marketplace, killing 130 civilians.

On February 21 newspaper stories told of an increasing number of raids into both Kuwait and Iraq. United States authorities issued a press release saying that the raids had destroyed many tanks and taken 450 captives. On one occasion, when Apache helicopters attacked Iraqi bunkers, Iraqi soldiers came out waving white flags.

Newspaper reports said that U.S. military officials believed that the bombing had reduced the Republican Guard's effectiveness by only

15 to 20 percent, well short of the 50 percent reduction preferred by military planners. The newspapers also reported that Allied troops were bracing themselves for a ground war, and that clashes with Iraqi troops along the Saudi Arabian border had increased. The *New York Times* ran a story with the headline "High U.S. Toll Is Feared If Iraq Uses Poison Gas."

Last-Minute Political Efforts for Peace

As the tension mounted, Moscow asked President Bush to hold off launching a ground offensive while the Soviets made a further attempt at negotiations. Bush agreed, but it was not clear whether his agreement was based on the hope that Moscow might succeed in its peace initiative or simply because the military was not yet ready to launch the planned ground offensive and preferred instead a few more days of bombing to soften the Iraqi defenses.

On February 17 Iraqi Foreign Minister Tariq Aziz arrived in Moscow for peace talks. On the eighteenth, Gorbachev offered a plan that called for Iraq to withdraw from Kuwait, a peace conference, and—in what appeared to be a new element—an offer of Soviet economic and political help to Iraq in the postwar period.

President Bush called the Soviet plan inadequate as a means to end the war. A Bush administration spokesperson said that there was nothing new in the Soviet proposal that would justify a delay in the planned ground offensive.

Thomas L. Friedman, writing in the *New York Times* on February 20, said that the Soviet peace initiative presented Bush with a painful choice: pushing for an all-out military victory or nurturing a diplomatic settlement that might get Iraq out of Kuwait but allow Saddam Hussein to save enough political face to preserve his government. As one U.S. official said, "If Saddam accepts this Soviet proposal we have a real problem."

Friedman reported that U.S. government officials had said on background that President Bush had been committed from the start to ending the Persian Gulf war by either defeating Hussein militarily and destroying Iraqi military capability or by humiliating Hussein politically and forcing him to withdraw from Kuwait without any "reward." Bush's objective, according to these officials, was not simply to get Iraq out of Kuwait, but to do so in a way that would ensure that Hussein had nothing to show to his people and the Arab world for his Kuwaiti adventure except the destruction of his army and his country. Aides said that Bush seemed to believe that the Soviet initiative, if accepted by Iraq, might prevent such a clear-cut outcome. Because Bush and his advisers had become convinced that they could crush the Iraqi army at a relatively low cost in Allied lives, Friedman continued, they were frustrated to have to deal with any solution that would save Hussein from a dramatic defeat, whether military or political. Bush, according to these officials, was determined to make sure that Hussein did not survive as Iraq's leader.

That same day, newspapers reported that Iran had said that Iraq was ready for an unconditional pullout from Kuwait and that Iraq would not link its withdrawal to an Israeli pullout from the occupied territories. However, there was no comment on the subject from Baghdad.

Also that same day, it was reported that Soviet officials were arguing with Washington against a ground offensive, saying that its only effect would be enormous human suffering and the destruction of Iraq.

Both the United States and Britain informed Moscow that the Soviet proposal must include a deadline. Iraq must withdraw very quickly, leaving behind its tanks and heavy equipment. They also insisted that Iraq pay reparations.

On February 21 the Soviets said that Iraq had agreed to pull out of Kuwait if the pullout was linked to a cease-fire and an end to sanctions. Notably absent was a link to an Israeli pullout from the occupied territories or the mention of Iraqi unwillingness to pay reparations.

President Bush rejected the offer. But his rejection had obviously been very carefully phrased. The reason was that Bush was apparently attempting to push Gorbachev to one side as gently as possible so as not to alienate the Soviet Union, and at the same time to prevent Moscow and Baghdad from reaching an accord that fell short of the unconditional victory that Bush sought.

In an extraordinary break with past practice in which Hussein decided every detail, Hussein gave Foreign Minister Aziz final authority to make whatever concessions were necessary to enable the Soviet proposal to succeed.

At the same time, it was reported that Iraq was setting fire to oil wells in Kuwait. President Bush accused Iraq of conducting a "scorched earth" policy in Kuwait.

President Bush issued an ultimatum on February 22 demanding that Iraq start pulling out of Kuwait that very day and complete the pullout within a week. In effect, Bush set a deadline of twenty-four hours for Iraq not only to agree to pull out of Kuwait but also to begin doing so.

In background briefings, administration officials told the press that there were two reasons behind the ultimatum. The first was the president's belief that a prolonged delay would give Hussein and his Soviet interlocutors more time to work out a withdrawal plan. The second was that such a withdrawal plan might split the anti-Iraq coalition and draw Washington into a protracted diplomatic process.

For its part, Iraq said that Bush's ultimatum was "shameful." It also made clear that it was pinning its hopes on the Soviet proposal. The only way to prevent war in the Gulf, an Iraqi spokesperson said, was for Washington to accept the Soviet peace proposals.

Most public statements from Congress approved of the Bush ultimatum. But Claiborne Pell, chairman of the Senate Foreign Relations Committee, and Thomas Foley, Speaker of the House of Representatives, said that differences between the Soviet proposal and the Bush demands were not very large and could be bridged.

On February 24 American newspapers reported that since Iraq had rebuffed the U.S. ultimatum and the deadline had passed, the Allied forces had been given the order to launch a ground offensive. Moscow blamed Baghdad for the "lost chance" for peace.

The newspapers also reported that bombing sorties against Iraqi troops in both Kuwait and Iraq were being launched at a record pace; that artillery fire against Iraqi positions was intense; and that Allied minesweepers had moved in to clear the way for an amphibious assault.

A broadcast from Baghdad told Iraqi soldiers to stand firm, that the "angels are at your shoulders."

Pentagon intelligence sources said that Iraqi soldiers had blown up or set fire to two hundred oil wells in Kuwait. They also said that Iraqi soldiers were rounding up and shooting Kuwaitis whom they suspected of being Allied agents.

In Saudi Arabia, the Central Command said that 1,685 Iraqi tanks had been destroyed out of a prewar total of 4,280, and 1,485 artillery pieces had been destroyed out of a total of 3,110. Since the beginning of the war, the Allies had flown 67,000 sorties over Iraq and Kuwait.

President Bush said that he regretted that Saddam Hussein had taken no action to comply with the U.N. resolutions before the deadline and that, as a result, the coalition forces had no alternative but to continue the war. "Military action," he said, "continues on schedule and according to plan."

Gorbachev made a series of phone calls to Bush and Allied leaders stressing that the two sides were not that far apart and that peace was still possible. He also stressed that Moscow did not want to be at odds with the United States. In public, Gorbachev said that he hoped that Iraq had the "guts" to retreat.

Just before the deadline, U.S. planes launched a huge air attack on Baghdad, including what was described as a "superbomb" of gigantic size. It was revealed that there were two such 4,700-pound laser-guided superbombs specially developed by the air force in just seventeen days and designed to destroy the two heavily reinforced bunkers that Saddam Hussein himself used as command centers. One of the bombs missed its target, but the other hit and killed a number of high-ranking Iraqi officers.

American vehicles specially equipped to detect poison gas roamed the front lines along the Iraqi and Kuwaiti borders. The *New York Times* ran a front-page story on the mood of the American troops who would lead the attack. The headline was "G.I.'s Poised on the Edge of the Unknown."

The Ground Offensive Begins

When the ground offensive began, there were 527,000 U.S. troops in the theater of operations. The army had 1,300 tanks, 1,420 armored personnel carriers, and 395 Apache helicopter gunships. The air force had 44 F-117A Stealth fighter-bombers, 38 F-111F strike bombers, 310 fighters, and more than 250 close air support, transport, and tanker aircraft. The Marine Corps had 500 to 700 tanks; 500 armored personnel carriers, and more than 300 aircraft and helicopters. The navy had more than 90 warships and submarines, including 6 aircraft carriers and 2 battleships, and more than 525 aircraft.

Other countries that provided significant forces, including armor and aircraft, were Great Britain, Egypt, France, Saudi Arabia, Kuwait, Syria, Morocco, Pakistan (which contributed planes), and the Gulf Cooperation Council (which included forces from Bahrain, Oman, Qatar, and the United Arab Emirates). New Zealand and South Korea contributed planes and medical teams.

Countries that contributed smaller forces included Afghanistan, Bangladesh, Niger, and Senegal.

Czechoslovakia contributed two hundred antichemical warfare specialists. Poland contributed two rescue ships. Hungary, India, the Philippines, Romania, Sierra Leone, Singapore, and Sweden contributed medical teams.

Naval forces, in addition to those from the United States, were contributed by Argentina, Australia, Belgium, Britain, Canada, Denmark, France, Greece, Italy, the Netherlands, Norway, Portugal, and Spain.

The total Allied troop deployment was approximately 750,000.

The Iraqi Forces

Iraq had an estimated 555,000 regular troops and 480,000 reserves. About 250,000 to 300,000 of these were stationed near the border with Turkey. More than 545,000 troops, including twelve armored divisions and thirty infantry and motorized divisions, were stationed in or near Kuwait when the ground war began.

Iraqi armor in or near Kuwait that had survived Allied air attacks included 2,595 tanks, 1,625 artillery pieces, and 1,945 armored personnel carriers.

As already mentioned, Iraqi naval forces, consisting mainly of patrol boats, had been eliminated.

The Allied Battle Plan

The actual battle plan differed in several respects from the plans hinted at by both the Pentagon and General Schwarzkopf's headquarters and from those that the outside experts had deduced. The actual plan consisted of seven thrusts, with no amphibious assault at all.

The first thrust was made by the U.S. 2d Marine Division, Kuwaiti ground troops, and Saudi Arabian armor. This column drove north along the coast toward Kuwait City into heavy Iraqi fortifications. The attacking soldiers wore chemical protection suits as a precautionary measure.

The second thrust, by the U.S. 1st Marine Division and Arab Allied forces, started from a position farther to the west and attacked northeast toward Kuwait City, also into heavy Iraqi fortifications.

American paratroopers dropped into central Kuwait, just west of Kuwait City, in front of these two columns.

A third and fourth thrust by smaller numbers of Egyptian and Syrian troops started from a point in Saudi Arabia still farther west and struck due north parallel to the Iraq-Kuwait border in a frontal assault on well-prepared Iraqi fortifications.

A fifth attack was launched by the U.S. 82d Airborne Division and 101st Airborne Division (Air Assault), which were parachuted or landed by helicopter deep inside Iraq itself.

The sixth and largest thrust was by the U.S. VII Corps, armored elements of the U.S. XVIII Airborne Corps, and the armored British "Desert Rats." This column attacked from positions still farther west in Saudi Arabia due north into Iraq itself. After making a deep penetration, the column was to wheel right and attack east against the Republican Guard in the area between Basra, Kuwait, and Iran.

A large helicopter-borne force landed fifty miles ahead of this column to set up what was described as "a giant, fortified gas station"—named Cobra Zone—embracing a defended circle twenty miles in diameter. As the Allies moved deeper into Iraq, this base would be moved farther forward.

Still farther west, just north of the town of Rafha in Saudi Arabia, a seventh, smaller column of French troops, including elements of the French Foreign Legion, also attacked due north into Iraq itself. Its mission was to screen the flank of the main thrust just described.

The Arab members of the coalition were apparently reluctant to do more than help evict Iraq from Kuwait, and accordingly there were no Arab forces with the columns that attacked into Iraq itself.

The first line of Iraqi defenses was manned by their poorest troops, reservists with the least training. The second layer of defenses was manned by slightly better troops, and the best troops, the Republican Guard, were held in reserve straddling the Iraq-Kuwait border due south of Basra.

All of the Allied thrusts made rapid progress. Resistance was light. A very large number of the first-line defenders offered no resistance but came out of their bunkers waving white flags. More than five thousand Iraqi soldiers surrendered the first day. On the few occasions when resistance was offered, it was light—presumably to cover withdrawal.

The Iraqi troops made no attempt to fill and ignite the trenches that had been prepared to form oil-fire barriers. Most importantly, the Iraqi army made no attempt whatsoever to use chemical weapons.

Everyone on the Allied side, including President Bush and General Schwarzkopf, expressed surprise at the light resistance, the high rate of surrender, and the low casualties among the Allied troops. However, many Allied military and civilian officials warned against euphoria, pointing out that the real test would come when the Allied forces came up against the elite Republican Guard.

As Iraqi troops retreated from Kuwait, they set fire to almost all of Kuwait's five hundred oil wells. The clouds of black smoke hampered Allied operations but did not prevent them.

On February 26 a Scud missile hit an American barracks housing support troops in Dhahran, Saudi Arabia. The missile killed twenty-eight Americans, including two women, and wounded more than a hundred. The missile had apparently broken up when it reentered the atmosphere, so it offered no coherent target for the Patriot missile defense. This single Scud missile caused more casualties than all of the seventy previous Scud attacks on Israel and Saudi Arabia combined.

The previous day, February 25, Baghdad radio announced that orders had been issued to the Iraqi armed forces to withdraw from Kuwait in an orderly manner and that this was "regarded as practical compliance with [U.N.] Resolution 660." The response from Washington was that the war would continue until Iraq complied with all the U.N. resolutions.

That same night, the Allies bombed Baghdad in what was described as "a sleepless night of horror."[1]

On February 26 doctors from the World Health Organization returning from Baghdad said that they feared the city would suffer a major epidemic of cholera and typhoid because of the destruction of water, sewage, and electrical facilities and the lack of food and medicines. Cases of severe diarrhea among children had quadrupled since the beginning of the war. Respiratory diseases among people of all ages had multiplied between three and four times.

Also on February 26, Les Aspin (D., Wisconsin), chairman of the House Armed Services Committee, after reviewing the Allied attack, said, "It is clear to me that the policy is to go out and destroy the Iraqi military as opposed to pushing them out of Kuwait. If all we wanted to do was push them out of Kuwait, we would have come in shallow and given them an escape route instead of moving to cut them off." On the same day, the Pentagon said that coalition forces had successfully disrupted Iraq's efforts to withdraw its troops from Kuwait. Fleeing Iraqi vehicles moving in close formation were being bombed by wave after wave of Allied planes.

That same day, Saddam Hussein made the public commitment that Bush had demanded—to withdraw from Kuwait. But Bush's response was that a mere promise was inadequate; he pressed for virtual sur-render, ordering Allied forces to continue attacking to break the Iraqi leader's "power and control in the Middle East." Saddam Hussein, Bush said, "is trying to save the remnants of power and control in the Middle East by every means possible and here, too, Saddam Hussein will fail." Bush said that to avoid being attacked, Iraqi troops must lay down their arms rather than simply retreat toward their homeland.

The *New York Times* commented that Bush's remarks pushed into the open the so-far unstated goal of American policy: to go beyond evicting Iraq from Kuwait, as the U.N. resolutions called for, and to smash Hussein's military capability while the opportunity was at hand.

Expressing his "outrage" at Hussein, Bush also said that the Iraqi leader could expect no quarter until he explicitly renounced his claims on Kuwait, returned all prisoners, and ordered his army to give up its weapons. Otherwise, Bush said, the coalition would "continue to prosecute the war with undiminished intensity."

As these political moves proceeded, the fighting continued. Before pulling out of Kuwait City, Iraqi troops destroyed a number of im-portant buildings with phosphorous artillery shells. United States Marines met stiff resistance from an Iraqi armored unit near the Kuwait City airport. The Egyptians, who were battling an Iraqi corps in western Kuwait, also had a tough fight.

In Iraq, two heavy U.S. infantry divisions met and engaged the most southerly of the Republican Guard divisions. This particular division had been heavily battered by the B-52 bombing attacks, but it was still able to offer stiff resistance. Although resistance was spotty in Ku-wait, other coalition forces also encountered pockets of stiff resistance here and there.

The retreating Iraqi forces suffered heavy casualties—as most re-treating forces do in war. For example, a column of more than fifteen hundred Iraqi tanks, trucks, and other vehicles, troops, and civilians and civilian vehicles twenty-five to thirty miles long was in retreat from Kuwait toward Basra, in places three abreast, along Highway 6. Ex-cept for a few surface-to-air missiles, the column was defenseless. According to an account in the *Washington Post,* "Navy, Air Force and Marine pilots trapped the long convoy by disabling vehicles at its front and rear, then pummeled the traffic jam for hours. Scores of Iraqis were blown apart or incinerated in their vehicles."[2]

According to one American pilot, the victims were "basically just sitting ducks." Another American pilot, who confessed he found the job distasteful, said that it was like a "turkey shoot." Another said that it was "like shooting fish in a barrel." Still another described the situation as "close to Armageddon."

As the reporters commented, the bombing demonstrated one grim irony of the ground war: "that a war undertaken to drive Iraqi forces from Kuwait ended with some Iraqi troops desperately trying to leave the emirate while U.S. forces held them in place and destroyed them."

Similar havoc was wreaked on other columns of Iraqi troops withdrawing from Kuwait, so much so that senior U.S. Central Command officers began to worry about the political repercussions. Saddam Hussein had announced a "withdrawal" from Kuwait. The Central Command called the Iraqi pullout a "retreat" rather than a withdrawal—a retreat being defined as pulling your forces back under military pressure. As the *Washington Post* article pointed out, however, tens of thousands of Iraqi troops had begun to pull out of Kuwait City more than thirty-six hours before any Allied troops reached it.

The End of the Fighting

On February 27 Bush went on TV from the Oval Office. He declared that Kuwait had been liberated and the Iraqi army defeated. He announced that as of midnight eastern standard time, exactly one hundred hours after the ground offensive had begun, all U.S. and coalition forces would suspend offensive combat operations.

For this suspension to become a permanent cease-fire, he said, Iraq must release all POWs, third-country nationals, all Kuwaiti detainees, and the remains of those who had fallen. Iraqi officials must inform Kuwaiti authorities of the location of land and sea mines. Iraq must also comply with all U.N. resolutions, including action to rescind the annexation of Kuwait and to accept the responsibility for paying compensation for losses and damage.

Shortly thereafter, General Schwarzkopf briefed the press. He said that the Allied forces were actually outnumbered by the Iraqi forces, whereas the usual military rule of thumb was that an attacker needed a three-to-one advantage to defeat a dug-in enemy. To overcome this disadvantage, the coalition had relied on air power to chew down the Iraqi forces and especially to isolate them in Kuwait and southern Iraq.

When air superiority had been achieved and the Iraqi planes had fled to Iran, the Iraqi army had been blinded. That made it possible for the Allies to move around without revealing their dispositions. The coalition forces kept up activity that made Iraq think that a main element of the attack would be a seaborne invasion. This pinned down large numbers of Iraqi troops along the Kuwaiti shoreline.

Then the coalition executed a maneuver that General Schwarzkopf compared to the so-called "Hail Mary" play in football. In the "Hail Mary" play, all the eligible receivers go way out to one end. When the play begins they all run like hell toward the goal. The quarterback takes the ball from the center and throws a forward pass to the receiver who is least effectively covered.

What the coalition did was to move its strongest forces west so that the main thrust would go into Iraq rather than Kuwait. Thus the assault was designed to cut off the routes of retreat for Iraqi forces in Kuwait and along the Iraq-Kuwait border.

The ground assault began with a feint as if a seaborne landing would be made in order to fix the Iraqi forces in position. The second element was a frontal assault by the U.S. Marines and Saudi Arabian and Kuwaiti forces against Iraq's main defensive positions in Kuwait. This is what the Iraqis had hoped the Allies would do, but its purpose was, again, to fix the Iraqi forces in Kuwait.

Schwarzkopf stressed that even though these attacks were essentially feints, they were made in sufficient strength to pin down the Iraqi forces and keep them from retreating into Iraq.

The main push was far to the west. One division had raced to the Euphrates River to block a Republican Guard escape route. After penetrating deep into Iraq, the U.S. XVIII Airborne Corps had then wheeled right toward Basra to attack the Republican Guard. Just south of the XVIII Airborne Corps was the U.S. VII Corps and the British 1st Armored Division. These forces had also penetrated deep into Iraq and then wheeled right to attack the Republican Guard.

The two corps met and engaged two Republican Guard armored divisions, behind which was a Republican Guard infantry division. As the war ended a major tank battle was in progress, with 800 Allied tanks and armored vehicles pitted against 250 to 300 Republican Guard tanks.

The battle was definitely going to the coalition forces, and if President Bush had not decided to call a halt and Iraq had failed to agree to the cease-fire terms, the Republican Guard divisions would have been destroyed within a very few days.

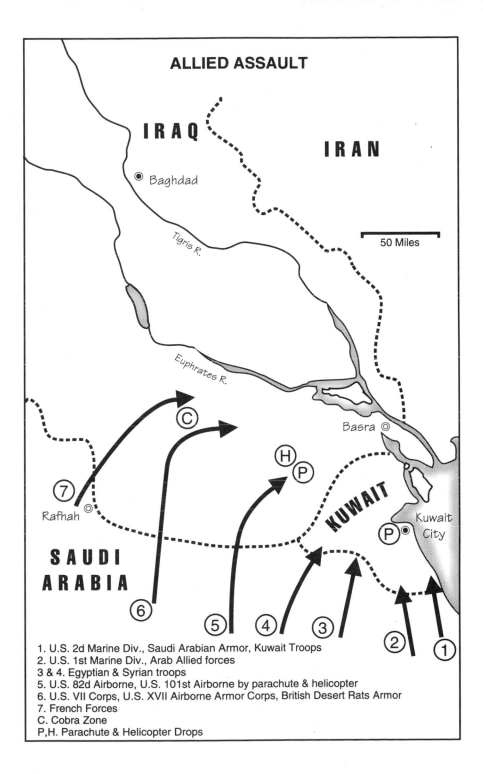

ALLIED ASSAULT

IRAQ

IRAN

⊙ Baghdad

Tigris R.

50 Miles

Euphrates R.

Ⓒ

⑦

Basra ◎

Ⓗ
Ⓟ

KUWAIT

Rafhah ◎

Ⓟ Kuwait City

SAUDI
ARABIA

⑥

⑤

④

③

②

①

1. U.S. 2d Marine Div., Saudi Arabian Armor, Kuwait Troops
2. U.S. 1st Marine Div., Arab Allied forces
3 & 4. Egyptian & Syrian troops
5. U.S. 82d Airborne, U.S. 101st Airborne by parachute & helicopter
6. U.S. VII Corps, U.S. XVII Airborne Armor Corps, British Desert Rats Armor
7. French Forces
C. Cobra Zone
P,H. Parachute & Helicopter Drops

CHAPTER 10

Rebellion in Iraq

President Bush hinted on several occasions that one of his goals was Saddam Hussein's removal. However, as already related, when Hussein made his February 15 peace proposal that included the statement that Iraq would consider withdrawing from Kuwait, Bush not only rejected the proposal as a "cruel hoax" but made an explicit call for Hussein's overthrow.

On February 17 the *New York Times* in both a news story and in Leslie Gelb's column reported that Bush decided to make his plea for Hussein's ouster after he watched TV pictures of jubilation in the streets of Baghdad over Hussein's peace proposal. Bush apparently decided on the basis of these TV pictures that the Iraqi people were ripe to overthrow Hussein, although the U.S. intelligence community had no information that would have supported such a conclusion. The *Times* commented that this "reflected the extent to which Mr. Hussein's downfall is a leading consideration in the Administration's strategy in the Persian Gulf war." Gelb's comment was that Bush's action went beyond the U.N. mandate and might well stiffen Iraqi resistance and prolong the war.

Bush's call clearly did not prolong the war, as Gelb feared, but it did reverberate among the Shiite and Kurdish people of Iraq. A clandestine radio station in Saudi Arabia had been calling for Hussein's overthrow since January. The station was purportedly run by Iraqi dissidents, but, as the world later learned, it was actually operated by the CIA.[1] When President Bush openly repeated his call for Hussein's overthrow, both the Shiites and the Kurds apparently concluded not only that the United States wanted them to rebel, but that the United States would support them if they did.

On March 4 U.S. newspapers reported that unrest in Iraq was spreading from Basra to three other cities and that a Shiite rebellion was possible. Heavy clashes in Basra were reported the next day between Shiites and the Republican Guard.

Hussein, apparently in response to this uprising, named a cousin as chief of internal security and expelled all foreign news reporters from Iraq, including those who had been in the country throughout the war.

The Iraqi government acknowledged on March 7 that it was facing an internal rebellion. At the same time, it claimed that Iraq had actually won a victory in the Gulf War since it had forced the United States to focus on the Arab-Israeli dispute.

It soon became clear that a substantial proportion of the Republican Guard had survived the war. These were not only the best of the Iraqi troops, but also the most loyal to Hussein. Hussein had created them. They had also done his bidding. Consequently, they would be the first target for revenge if he were overthrown. A substantial number of aircraft, especially helicopter gunships, had also survived, having been well protected in their bunkers.

The helicopters, especially, wreaked havoc among the rebelling Shiites, who in various ways pleaded for U.S. help against them. President Bush on March 13 said that Iraq's use of helicopters to suppress the rebellion violated the cease-fire. But he took no action, except to threaten that the Allies might delay their departure from Iraqi territory.

Apparently to emphasize the threat, the United States moved its troops in Iraq to a more forward position.

Despite the helicopters, however, the Shiites took control of Hilla, a town about a hundred miles south of Baghdad.

In the meantime, the Kurds also rebelled, and by March 14 they claimed control of wide areas in the north near the Turkish border, including five towns. A few days later the Kurds took Kirkuk, a major oil-producing center and the fourth largest city in Iraq.

On March 16 Hussein vowed to crush the rebels but at the same time promised major reform once he had done so, including a multiparty system and a written constitution.

The next day, Iraq asked the Allies for permission to move warplanes around inside Iraq. The United States and the Allies refused.

The Shiite rebels reported fierce fighting, that they were twelve miles from Baghdad, and that they planned to attack the city.

United States officials in Washington used background briefings to inform the press that the administration expected Hussein to be out by year's end. The United States would like to see the Baathist party out, too, but saw no immediate prospect. On the other hand, the U.S. government would *not* like to see control pass to the Shiites, since they would probably be dominated by Iran. As if to confirm this fear, Arab and foreign diplomats reported a few days later that Iran was organizing Hussein's foes, hoping that the Iraqi government would eventually be controlled by fellow Shiites. Iran immediately denied that it was giving arms to the rebels, asserting that the rebels had captured them from the Iraqi army.

Pentagon officials implied in a March 18 press briefing that U.S. warplanes would fire not only on Iraqi aircraft, but on helicopters being used to put down the rebellion. Almost immediately, a U.S. plane shot down an Iraqi fighter-bomber, and a second Iraqi fighter-bomber was shot down the next day.

Newspaper stories from Washington reported that the United States believed that Hussein was close to defeating the Shiite rebellion and that the Kurds might also eventually be beaten. The administration was engaged in an internal debate over whether to carry out its threat to attack helicopter gunships as well as fighter-bombers.

Newspapers reported on March 27 that Bush had decided to let Hussein put down the rebellions without interference from the United States rather than risk splintering Iraq. The administration also believed that both Arab and Western Allies would strongly oppose any U.S. intervention.

At about the same time, refugees from the disputed territories reported that the Iraqi army was putting down the rebellion ruthlessly and that atrocities were common. A leader of the Shiite rebellion in the south admitted that the rebellion had lost ground. For its part, the Iraqi government reported large gains against the Kurds. Iraqi forces, it said, had recaptured Kirkuk, which the rebels had held for about a week, as well as Dahuk and Erbil.

Newspapers also reported on March 27 a TV interview in which General Schwarzkopf said that the Iraqi general with whom he had been negotiating "suckered" him into allowing helicopter flights. The Iraqi general had said that the helicopters would be used for transporting key officials between cities, but it was clear now that they were being used as gunships to put down the rebellion.

Noting the failing rebellions, Iran charged that the United States had incited the rebels and then deserted them. On April 13 Iranian President Hashemi Rafsanjani blamed both the United States and Iraq for

Iraqi civilian deaths and for the refugee crisis. The United States, Rafsanjani said, "will eventually be put on trial."

President Bush stood firm on his policy toward the Iraqi civil war, however, repeating that the United States would not give the rebels any backing and would not interfere.

In an April 4 editorial, the *New York Times* supported Bush's decision. It was evident, the *Times* argued, that Iraq had used conscripts as fodder in the hundred-hour war and held back both its crack units and its armor to use against the rebels. That being so, the *Times* concluded, it was doubtful that the Allies could have saved the insurgents "with anything short of full-scale, and endless, intervention."

Others, however, believed that the decision not to help the rebels put the United States in an awkward position. These critics argued that the U.S. position was morally indefensible and, in the long run, would produce the very Middle East instability that the Gulf War was supposed to prevent. The result was self-determination for Kuwait but for no one else. Critics complained that it was Bush's call for the Iraqi people to topple Hussein that started the rebellions, but after having incited rebellion, Bush opted to leave them to their fate.[2]

Administration officials responded by telling reporters that they could not have it both ways. The policy decision was to let Hussein restore Baghdad's control of the country and then to use the arms embargo and economic sanctions that were built into the U.N. cease-fire resolution to encourage the Iraqis to replace Hussein.

On the other hand, many Middle East specialists argued that the approach was flawed and inconsistent. The United States, they pointed out, opposed Soviet repression in the Baltics, criticized Israel for its treatment of the Palestinians, and then accepted the annihilation of tens of thousands of Kurds and Shiites. One specialist complained that it seemed the United States had fought the Gulf War merely to maintain the status quo. The United States was standing by while the Kurds and Shiites were being slaughtered to keep Iraq from being broken up. Bush's "new world order," he concluded, was the status quo.

New York Times columnist A. M. Rosenthal, in his April 9 column, compared Bush's decision to the Soviets stopping on the Vistula River while the Nazis wiped out the Warsaw ghetto. "On March 28, 1991," he wrote, "United States troops in Iraq watched while Saddam Hussein's Soviet-built helicopters, left in his hands by American decision, strafed and shelled Iraqi civilians less than a mile away." The Americans had been ordered not to fire. Later, "grieving" American soldiers gave food and water to survivors who had managed to stumble to their positions across the fields.

At this point, the Shiite uprising in the south had been contained, and Hussein shifted the Republican Guard to the north against the Kurds. As the Kurdish irregulars fell back, hundreds of thousands of Kurds— men, women, and children—fled into the snow-covered mountains on the borders of Iraq, Turkey, and Iran. The refugees formed a solid column more than sixty miles long, and newspaper headlines around the world warned that deaths from starvation and disease would be "colossal."

Turkey stopped the refugees at the border. Iran, on the other hand, let them in. On April 2 Baghdad radio announced that the end of the insurgency in both the south and the north was at hand.

Sympathy for the Kurds was widespread throughout the world, including the United States. A typical newspaper story reported that as their uprising collapsed, the Kurdish rebels' praise for Bush turned to curses. Even the most worldly Kurds, the story said, "say they now are convinced that they were purposely betrayed by the United States"—even though it had called for Hussein's overthrow. They accused Bush of actively colluding with Hussein in what they called their "genocide," and they could "hardly contain their disgust for Bush, suddenly transformed, in one man's view, into 'a friend of Saddam.'"[3]

Another, vivid example of the Kurdish reaction came from a Kurdish woman who, with her husband and her son, walked for two weeks over the mountains into Iran. Who, she asked a Western reporter, was responsible for all this destruction? Her house had been destroyed and some of her family members killed. Answering her own question, she said, "Mr. George Bush is responsible for all this. He could destroy Saddam and his Army but he don't try. All this because he don't want Kurdish and Shia to be the leader in Iraq, to run Iraq." The Americans, she went on to say, saw all this, yet they did nothing. "Why?" she asked. "We are human, like you. Why?"[4]

On April 5, responding to the "uproar," President Bush ordered an airdrop of food and clothes to the Kurdish refugees camped in the mountains. A few days later, a U.N. report estimated that one million Kurds had become refugees and predicted that they would die in vast numbers without swift aid.

On April 10 the United States warned Iraq not to attack the Kurdish refugees, a warning that seemed to include the use of helicopters.

The plight of the Kurdish refugees worsened daily—it was like "living in hell"—and more than a thousand were dying each day. Secretary of State Baker visited the refugees. He was so shocked that he got on the phone to Bush and persuaded him that the United States had to do something more than airdrop relief supplies. As a result, U.S. military authorities were given the responsibility of providing relief for the Kurdish refugees, and plans were announced to feed seven hundred thousand people a day and to establish temporary shelters.

On April 17 the United States announced plans for providing medical and food supplies for one hundred thousand at each of five to six camps. However, a number of U.N. members expressed misgivings, believing that the United States might get ensnared in just the sort of tangle it had been trying to avoid. Some reaction in Washington was similar—that at best the refugee mission would be a "risky undertaking" and very possibly a "quagmire." A number of academic Middle East specialists also criticized the plan as leading to an indefinite military role for the United States in Iraq.

For its part, Iraq formally objected to the U.S. plans for refugee camps as an infringement of sovereignty, proposing instead that the U.N. accept the responsibility for aiding the refugees. The United States, however, after meeting with Iraqi representatives, decided to persist in the plan to establish camps.

On April 20 a U.S. Marine contingent landed in a deserted town in northern Iraq and began to set up refugee camps. Iraqi forces, complying with U.S. demands, began to pull back from the area where the camps were being established.

Two days later, U.S. authorities reported that they were having difficulty coaxing Kurds to return to Iraq and to the camps. However, some of the refugees were beginning to trickle back as disease and hunger began to overcome their fear of Hussein.

On April 23 Iraq again insisted that the U.N. must take over the refugee camps and again raised the issue of sovereignty. The next day, however, Kurdish leaders met with Hussein and reached a "broad new agreement" that they hoped would allow the Kurdish refugees to return to their homes in peace. By moving swiftly to make peace with the Kurds, Hussein was apparently trying to show that he could be accommodating—hoping that this would persuade the Allies to lift the economic sanctions. For its part, the United States said that it doubted Hussein's sincerity and that it would go ahead with the camps.

Within a few days, Kurds began to move out of the mountains to the Allied zone. President Bush announced that once the Kurds were safe, U.S. forces would leave Iraq. At that point the U.N. declared that it was ready to take over the United States' refugee role.

United Nations authorities said that the first step would be to seek an accord with Iraq on a U.N. police force to replace U.S. troops in northern Iraq. Iraq rejected the idea, and the United States indicated that this might delay the pullout of U.S. forces.

The problem was that if Iraq did not agree to a U.N. force, the only alternative would be to have the U.N. *impose* such a force on Iraq. This would have required the approval of the U.N. Security Council, in which both China and the Soviet Union, who were opposed to the idea, had a veto.

At the same time, the Allies extended the security zone for refugees seventy miles to the east and ordered Iraqi forces to pull back beyond that point. The purpose, U.S. authorities announced, was to give the Kurds the choice of going home or to the refugee camps.

Conditions among the refugees in the mountains were unimaginably difficult. Estimates were that between 900 and 1,600 Kurds were dying each day of disease, diarrhea, dehydration, and malnutrition—80 percent of them children.[5]

Those who attempted to return to their villages were also suffering. On the so-called Hamilton road, the main route for refugees returning from Iran to Iraq, mines were still in place that had been laid on both sides of the road during the Iran-Iraq war. A few days after the Kurds started returning, the only working hospital of "free Kurdistan" had treated four hundred Kurds for mine injuries. Hundreds were killed instantly or died of wounds before they could be helped. Most of the refugees avoided going off the road for any purpose. The result was that both sides of the road were one giant toilet—breeding disease.[6]

By the end of the first week in May, almost 200,000 Kurds had returned to Iraq on their own. As the refugees returned, a number of American soldiers engaged in helping them were pulled out. However, about 260,000 refugees remained in the mountains and would need help in returning to Iraq.

The United States succeeded in brokering a plan for the Kurdish refugees to return to the city of Dahuk, but the tribal leaders rejected it, insisting on an agreement with Baghdad first. On May 18 Kurdish leaders announced that they had reached an agreement with Baghdad that promised autonomy and democracy for the Kurds within the framework of a unified Iraq.

President Bush stated that he was willing to seek U.N. Security Council approval for a U.N. force to take the place of U.S. troops still in the Kurdish zone. Shortly thereafter, Iraqi troops in the north pulled back to make way for U.N. guards. The hope was to reassure the Kurdish refugees and so persuade them to return to their homes.

What the Refugees Feared

Throughout the Kurdish refugee crisis, relief workers among the refugees queried them about their motives for fleeing in the first place. On June 2, 1991, in a story on the *New York Times'* editorial page, "Why the Kurds Fled," Karl E. Meyer summed up the answers they got. The first answer was usually that the Kurds knew the Iraqis from long experience. The Iraqis, for example, had on several occasions used poison gas on Kurdish villages. But, on closer questioning, the relief workers found what they believed to be nearer the truth, that when President Bush reversed himself and ruled out the use of Allied air power to knock down Saddam Hussein's attacking helicopters, the Kurds felt wholly abandoned and they panicked.

In early May, Saddam Hussein—"newly confident" in the words of the *New York Times*—began again to make personal appearances, this time with a new public relations gimmick. After waving silently to the crowd from his podium, Hussein would take his pistol out of its holster and begin firing it in the air. The crowds, according to the *Times,* would go wild, chanting rhythmically a sort of slogan in Arabic: "Bush, Bush, listen carefully. We all love Saddam Hussein!"[7]

The Iraqis explained, the *Times* went on to say, that the gesture was one of defiance toward the United States and its allies, a reminder of Hussein's claim that he had resisted the "forces of imperialism and Zionism." Iraq's official line was that Iraq was the aggrieved victim rather than the aggressor. The assault on Kuwait was never mentioned; instead the war was portrayed as an American-led attack that Iraq had resisted, and Saddam Hussein was still in power—proof that the resistance was successful. The bomb damage that was there for everyone to see was presented as the worthwhile price for defending a just—and Arab—cause.

Saddam Hussein remained firmly in control. The Iraqi people were essentially unpolitical, according to the report, and wanted only for the government to provide them a tolerable life. Hussein had moved to do so. On his birthday in April, the gasoline ration was lifted. Electricity and clean water were gradually returning. Even the heavily bombed telephone system was beginning to work again. The pace of the recovery from the war damage astonished U.N. officials. The major reason the recovery was more rapid than expected was that Iraq had a policy of manufacturing at least part of the many sophisticated Western machines it imports, so it was able to make a lot of repairs even though sanctions remained in place. For the future, Hussein promised reforms to relax the social and political climate—a new era of democracy, personal freedom, and prosperity.

"Paradoxically," the *Times* story said, "President Bush may have helped consolidate Mr. Hussein's position, Iraqi officials say, when he called on the Iraqi people to remove their leader." When Iran attempted to exploit Bush's call by stirring up rebellion among the Shiites and the Kurds, the Sunni center of the population rallied to Hussein.

It seems probable, then, that rather than get rid of Saddam Hussein, as President Bush had so ardently desired, the Gulf War made Hussein's position stronger than ever.

CHAPTER 11

The Military vs. the Press

One of the negative aspects of the war was the feeling on the part of the press that it had been forced to operate under impossibly strict controls.

The rules governing the press in the Gulf War—and to which all correspondents had to agree before they were accredited by the Central Command—were as follows:

- All press travel outside of Dhahran and Riyadh was limited to assigned "press pools" of seven or eight reporters, each of whom was chosen by the military. What reporters in the pool wrote or filmed was then shared by those who remained back in the hotels in Dhahran and Riyadh.
- The press pools were accompanied by a military escort officer at all times.
- The military decided where the press pools could go and when.
- No officer or soldier could be interviewed without the approval of the escort officer and the interviewee's commanding officer. Unplanned interviews were barred.
- All news copy had to be submitted in advance of transmittal to military censors for "security review."
- Reporters were not allowed to live with military units but were rotated in and out with military escorts on a daily basis.*

*The one exception to this rule was the "Hometown News Program." In this program ninety-six journalists from generally small newspapers and television stations near a unit's home base, along with a handful from larger papers, including the *New York Times,* were flown to Saudi Arabia free on military aircraft and allowed to spend up

143

- Reporters going off on their own in an attempt to cover the war independently were detained and returned to the rear echelon. They also ran the risk of having their credentials lifted and being returned to the United States.
- Any violation of the rules was punishable by expulsion from the theater of operations.

In addition to these rules governing the press in the theater of operations itself, the Pentagon decided that there would be no solemn arrival ceremonies or press coverage for the dead whose bodies were returned to the Defense Department's military mortuary at Dover Air Force Base in Delaware. Wondering about the reason for this, reporters recalled that during Operation Just Cause, the U.S. invasion of Panama, a "triumphant" Bush was joshing with the press corps on TV when the networks unexpectedly split the screen to show the mournful arrival ceremonies at Dover for the soldiers killed in Panama. The president later complained bitterly, implying that the TV networks had done it deliberately in order to embarrass him.

Background of the Press Controls

The press controls in the Gulf War had their origins in the military's attitude toward the role of the press in Vietnam. It is widely understood that higher ranking military officers—including Generals Powell and Schwarzkopf—felt that the Vietnam War had taught at least two important lessons. The first was that rather than escalating the number of forces gradually, you should put everything you can muster into such a war at the very beginning. The second lesson was that the American press should be kept as far away from the action as possible.

At a meeting of the California Forum of the First Amendment Congress at Stanford University in early May 1991, a retired army colonel, Darryl Henderson, said that the reason the military usually gave for such strict control of the press was the need to protect military secrets, but it was

---

to four days with their hometown units. When asked why these reporters did not pose the problem the military thought other reporters posed, the answer was: "If they know that they're getting a free ride and they can't afford the $2,000 ticket, there's probably going to be a tendency to say, 'We'll do good stuff here.'" [The *New York Times* (May 5, 1991): 20.]

a "false" reason.[1] The real reason, he said, was a "Vietnam syndrome" within the military that blamed the press for the erosion of public support for the Vietnam War. Shortly after Vietnam, the military began to study techniques for "marketing" the military point of view, primarily to see that only "upbeat" reports went to the public. Then they trained public information officers in these techniques; Colonel Henderson himself had received such training. All this, Henderson said, paid off in the Gulf War.

At the same conference, Judith Coburn, who had covered wars in Central America, the Middle East, and Vietnam and who was at the time of the conference lecturing on mass communications at the University of California at Berkeley, disputed the idea that the press had been responsible for the erosion of public support for the Vietnam War. On the contrary, she said, the press followed the public, not the other way around. The press supported the war in Vietnam, and it was only after public support began to wane that the press, too, became disillusioned.

During the Vietnam War reporters were given freedom to go pretty much where they pleased, to interview pretty much whom they pleased, and to write pretty much what they pleased. They were given security guidelines but were not required to submit their copy before sending it out. If anyone violated the guidelines by sending out sensitive material, he or she was chided after the fact. But violations were extremely rare. What upset the military about the news coverage in Vietnam was not security violations, but stories that said the war was not going well or that contained complaints from soldiers or criticisms of the way military operations were handled. In other words, what the military brass were complaining about when they criticized the press was not security violations, but the fact that the stories tended to paint the military in a bad light.

In general, according to David E. Rosenbaum, the military came to believe that the free rein that journalists enjoyed in Vietnam damaged troop morale and turned the country against its own soldiers.[2] Many military leaders also believe that it is the nature of the journalism profession to concentrate on unfavorable information and to slight the favorable. In Vietnam, they contend, a victory would get a headline and a brief story, but if a battle went awry it would receive full treatment and analysis. The same was true of weapons and equipment. If weapons and equipment were good, a story was rare. But if they were faulty, everyone wrote about it. An example was the many stories about the fact that the M16 rifle tended to jam unless it was kept meticulously clean, a difficult task for men in combat in the jungle.

Another lesson the military drew from the press coverage in Vietnam was that if the public learned how gruesome the fighting really was, it would turn against the war.

Patrick J. Sloyan traced the press policy in the Gulf War to what the military thought it had learned from Vietnam, Grenada, and Panama.[3] When it came to the invasion of Grenada, during the Reagan administration, the Pentagon policy was to allow no reporters or photographers whatsoever. Operations were covered by military personnel whose reports and pictures were screened and then turned over to the press. Several enterprising reporters rented motorboats to try to cover the story themselves, but they were seized and imprisoned by the U.S. Navy for two days.

When the December 1989 invasion of Panama—Operation Just Cause—was being planned by the Bush administration, the Pentagon in effect offered the press a choice between the Grenada policy of permitting no press at all to accompany the troops or a "press pool" of about ten reporters representing the wire services, the newspapers, TV, radio, and photograph agencies. Pool members would deploy with U.S. troops and their reports would be made available to all the news media. Reluctantly, the press agreed to the pool.

But the pool system turned out to be a fiasco. Pool members arrived in Panama several hours after the fighting had ended at two of the battle sites, and at the third, where fighting was still going on, the pool was barred. Members of the pool got their information by listening to CNN broadcasts of Pentagon briefings in Washington.

The Pentagon's idea of a press pool, according to Sloyan, proved to be a "trap" for the press. The Bush administration portrayed the Panama invasion as a "flawless, almost bloodless conflict." In fact, 23 soldiers were killed and 265 wounded or seriously injured in three battles the first day. Not a single photo, filmstrip, or eyewitness account was published about the fighting.

Lieutenant General Tom Kelly, director of operations for the Joint Chiefs of Staff, told reporters that he knew of "no casualties" in Panama. Even before he spoke, however, injured paratroopers from Panama were arriving at the military hospital in San Antonio, Texas. One doctor there called it an "orthopedic nightmare." It was only later that the army conceded that eighty-six soldiers had been hurt in the airdrop.

What galled the press even more about the Panama invasion was that its requests for film footage made by military photographers were largely rejected. As a result, the press complained, the American public still did not know the extent of Panamanian civilian casualties.

However, it would be wrong to suggest that the military and the military alone was responsible for the controls that so limited the press in the Gulf War. The *New York Times* conducted a six-week review of interviews and documents dealing with press policy in the Gulf War, which showed that President Bush and his "inner circle" were determined from the start "to manage the information flow" so that it would support their political goals. "They punctuated that determination on the war's eve with a Pentagon rule limiting all press coverage of combat to officially escorted pools."[4]

Press Complaints

The basic complaint that journalists had about the rules governing them in the Gulf War was that more than a thousand journalists were accredited to cover the war, but only 126 were assigned to pools— 126 to cover a war in which more than a half million Americans served. The rest of the journalists never got out of their hotels in Dhahran and Riyadh except to attend official military briefings.

What was worse, according to the press, was that many of the 126 were photographers, TV camera operators, technicians, and sound men. Only twenty-five to thirty pool slots existed for newspaper, magazine, radio, and television correspondents. The wire services and large newspapers complained that even the few places they were allotted had to be shared with journalists from small town newspapers or those with very narrow special interests. One example was *Mirabella,* a monthly women's magazine. Another was *Stars and Stripes,* the newspaper run by and for the military.

In fact, several of the pools never actually got to the field. They, too, sat around hotels in Dhahran and Riyadh. Other pools visited nothing more spectacular than air bases far behind the lines or ships in the Persian Gulf. When a Scud missile killed twenty-eight soldiers in a barracks in Dhahran, a "quick reaction" pool of reporters was only a few miles away, but it was not allowed to go to the scene. Official information came from Riyadh, 150 miles away.

In another example, the pool formed to cover the attack on Khafji was not brought to the battle area until a full day after the fighting there was over.

Although the press was led to believe that the pools would be permitted to accompany the troops into battle, in practice no pool was allowed near any battlefield.

At the height of the bombing campaign the members of one pool pressed hard to be allowed to interview some of the pilots. Instead they were sent to a military motor pool whose commanding officer had complained that his "unsung heroes" had not been receiving the publicity they deserved.

James LeMoyne of the *New York Times,* expressing the frustration of most reporters, said that under the Pentagon's press rules, the military decided which units the press could visit, how long the visit would last, which reporters would make the visit, and, to some extent, what the soldiers could say, what the TV cameras could film, and what the reporters could write.[5]

Reporters who asked hard questions, according to LeMoyne, were warned by press officers that they were seen as "antimilitary" and that their requests for interviews with senior officers would be in jeopardy—all of which dampened critical reporting.

At times events were actually staged for the TV cameras. At other times cameras were stopped because military escorts did not like what was being filmed.

LeMoyne had a standing request for more than two months to interview General Schwarzkopf. While his request was pending, he got a running account of which of his stories the general liked and which he did not like. On the occasions when the general did not like his story, it was suggested that his request for an interview was being jeopardized. Finally, LeMoyne published an article in which some of the soldiers he interviewed criticized President Bush and questioned the purpose of the war. His long-standing request for an interview was canceled.

Later one of the men whom LeMoyne had interviewed told him that when the story came out all "hell broke loose." The commanding officer demanded that those interviewed explain why they had expressed critical views. For the next six weeks almost all print journalists were denied permission to visit army units. However, sports announcer O. J. Simpson and weatherman Willard Scott were escorted to several units. When asked why these two were allowed to visit and regular reporters were not, army authorities explained that Simpson and Scott did not "cause problems."

On another occasion, General Schwarzkopf himself called the commanding officer of a soldier who had expressed critical views to demand an explanation.[6]

Over the course of the war more than two dozen reporters were stopped and held for up to eight hours for trying to cover the war on their own. A photographer from *Time* magazine was seized, spread-eagled, and searched.

The press reported a number of occasions when officers tried to intimidate soldiers who answered questions about the war with a negative tone. Some officers put their hands over the lenses of TV cameras to prevent pictures from being taken. Reporters who refused to allow their stories to be doctored to conform to what the military wanted often found that the transmission of their stories was delayed—in a number of cases until the war was over.

The Pentagon press guidelines said that escort officers would not suppress material "for its potential to express criticism or cause embarrassment." Reporters found the situation to be otherwise. For example, when the Associated Press reported that navy pilots were watching pornographic films before leaving on missions, a military escort officer deleted the item.[7]

Another example concerned pictures of the bombing. Only the laser bombs had cameras in their noses, and the military briefers obviously delighted in showing film of a bomb going right down the smokestack of its target. Some of the laser bombs missed, but no picture of a miss was ever shown. The British, however, did show their press such a picture. The American press heard about it, and asked to see pictures from errant bombs. The American briefers used "the same reasonable tone that worked to their advantage throughout the conflict, avoiding a flat No." The briefers said they would "look into it," but nothing ever came of it and when asked, "officials adopted a tone of innocent forgetfulness."[8]

The military refused to make film clips taken by helicopter gunships available at all. However, John Balzar of the *Los Angeles Times* saw one by accident. Balzar said that the tape showed Iraqi soldiers as big as football players on a TV screen. "A guy was hit," Balzar said, "and you could see him drop and he struggled up. They fired again and the body next to him exploded." Balzar was never again allowed near a helicopter unit.

During the Gulf War, in the words of one reporter, the pool system was used "not to facilitate news coverage but to control it." The pool system resulted in "taking the most basic journalistic decisions out of the hands of correspondents and giving them to commanders."

In general journalists felt that neither they nor their readers had the information they needed to "assess how the war is going, information that reporters and editors believe could be provided without compromising security."[9]

Although the military insisted that the purpose of the rules was military security, out of 1,351 pool reports filed, only four went to the Pentagon to be reviewed for security reasons and only one of these was changed. "Clearly, most of the pressure brought to bear on reporters was motivated not out of concern for security, but public relations."[10]

This point was not lost on even small town papers. *The Day,* a daily newspaper published in New London, Connecticut, in an editorial entitled "From watchdog to lapdog" criticized the press for becoming a "lapdog" but was even harsher on the military's "blatant censorship." The military censors, it said, were motivated more by concern for their image than military security.[11]

The final result of the military system for handling the press was that the vast majority of the reporting on the Gulf War was just a rehash of the daily press briefings. Reporters had no choice but to write the stories the military gave them. This meant that the stories that made the United States and its Allies look good were played up and the stories that made them look bad were ignored or played down. All stories were always given a rosy tint. Reporters could not gather news on their own or exercise their own judgment about what was news but instead were forced to write up the handouts and briefings in their own words. As Malcolm E. Browne, who won the Pulitzer Prize for his reporting of the Vietnam War, put the case, a correspondent became "an unpaid employee of the Department of Defense, on whose behalf he or she prepares the news of the war for the outer world."[12]

The American public, two reporters charged, knew little of what was really going on in the Gulf War. "Because of the restrictions placed on the news media by the Pentagon," they wrote, "rarely have so many labored so hard to convey so little." Reporters, they went on to say, became puppets of the military, simply reciting what official handouts said. The effect was that the public saw film of Patriot missiles knocking down Scuds and film from the nose of a laser bomb hitting dead on its target, but nothing about the political and military execution of the war or the political results in the Middle East.[13]

However, the sheer length and frequency of the TV briefings made the public think it was getting more information than it was, although most of the information consisted of long lists of innocuous statistics, such as the number of missions flown, which added little real knowledge of what was going on. "As one admiring White House official put it, the briefings made the Pentagon seem to be making public 'much more information than it was.' "[14]

Press Analysis of the Military's Motives

As the war drew to a close an impressive number of reporters attempted to explain the reasons why the military had been so determined to exercise such tight control. Almost all cited the point mentioned above, that the military thought that the press in Vietnam had eroded support at home by its negative reporting. Some, however, believed that it was not just the way correspondents reported but that war itself was hell and that the public should be shielded from stories that pictured the horrors of war. Patrick J. Sloyan, for example, wrote that the real reason for the censorship was that the administration feared that reports and pictures of combat would have a bad effect on American public opinion.[15] Sloyan quotes air force doctor William Burner (who was borrowing from Bismarck): "Two things people should not watch are the making of sausage and the making of war. All that front-page blood and gore hurts the military. We're guilty by association."

Over and over again, reporters noted that they were not allowed to take pictures of dead or wounded soldiers, whether American or Iraqi. It was only when they got back to the United States and were free from their military censors that some journalists reported what some of the shocked American soldiers said who had "inspected the dismembered and incinerated bodies of the trapped and panicked Iraqi soldiers fleeing Kuwait."[16] As Rick Du Brow, a *Los Angeles Times* television reporter, said, "It became clear that attempts to withhold the ugliness from home viewers were part and parcel of policy."

Sloyan recalled a picture from Vietnam of bleeding and dead American Marines sprawled on a tank retreating from the battle of Hue. Senator Eugene McCarthy, who ran for president on a platform opposing the Vietnam War, later said that when he saw that picture he knew support for the war had reached a "turning point."

To this fear that the public would turn against the war if they knew how gruesome it really was, there was added another, very special fear: If the Arab publics knew how many Arabs were being killed and the details of the carnage, they would—out of horror—withdraw from the alliance.

Formal Protests by the Press

The press was fully aware that it was being used, and sixteen smaller publications and individual writers filed suit seeking to have the pool system abolished. However, the courts held in favor of the Pentagon and, to make matters worse so far as the people involved were concerned, the Pentagon forbade any military or civilian employee from appearing on any TV program that included any of the sixteen newspeople who filed the suit.

None of the major news organizations joined in the suit, but some time later the editors of fifteen major American news organizations wrote a letter to Defense Secretary Cheney and then paid him a formal call to protest that the Pentagon had exercised "virtual total control" over the press during the Gulf War. "Virtually all major news organizations agree," the letter said, "that the flow of information to the public was blocked, impeded or diminished by the policies and practices of the Department of Defense." They said that they would press for more open coverage of military operations in the future. The conditions laid down by the Pentagon, they said, "meant we could not tell the public the full story of those who fought the nation's battle."

"Pools did not work," the letter went on to say. "Stories and pictures were late or lost. Access to the men and women in the field was interfered with by a needless system of military escorts and copy review. The pool system was used in the Persian Gulf war not to facilitate news coverage but to control it."

Pentagon Defense of the Press Policy

The military's defense of its press policy in the Gulf War was that hordes of journalists would interfere with the conduct of the war and that journalists would end up being killed. After the war, they suggested that what happened to Bob Simon of CBS News proved their point. Simon and three TV crew members had gone off on their own and fell into the hands of the enemy. Simon and his crew were not released until the end of the war.

Not only was there much hostility between the press and the military, it was also mutual. A senior air force officer began his first press briefing by saying, "Let me say up front that I don't like the press.

Your presence here can't possibly do me any good, and it can hurt me and my people. That's just so you'll know where we stand with each other."[17] Marvin Kalb, a veteran TV war correspondent who served in Vietnam and is now director of the Shorenstein Barone Center on the Press, Politics, and Public Policy at Harvard, said, "Given the record of significant deception [in Vietnam], reporters and the American people are entitled to skepticism."[18]

The Peter Arnett Story

Peter Arnett's story is different. Arnett was an Associated Press reporter in Vietnam, where he served longer than anyone else. Arnett was one of the few correspondents who stayed in Saigon to report its fall, and he holds the record for having covered more wars than any other reporter of his generation. Some time before the Gulf War, Arnett joined CNN, and at the beginning of the war found himself in Baghdad. When the rest of the Western press corps was told to leave, Arnett stayed on. He simply refused to go and the Iraqi authorities allowed him to stay because of his reputation for "impartiality." When the United States and its Allies bombed Baghdad, Arnett refused to go to the hotel bomb shelter. Leaning out of the window of his room, he reported live via a telephone link to the entire world. General Schwarzkopf angrily said that Arnett was "aiding and abetting the enemy," but most of the senior officials in both Washington and the Central Command listened to his broadcasts avidly.

Arnett was, of course, closely watched by the Iraqi censors, and he was careful. But it is difficult to censor a live broadcast, and he got away with a lot. For example, when the United States bombed what Iraqi officials claimed was a baby formula factory, the White House angrily said that Arnett had been duped and the factory was really making chemical weapons. It does not prove whether the factory was involved with baby formula or chemical warfare, but what the White House overlooked was that Arnett had carefully pointed out in his broadcast that the factory's "baby formula" signs were printed in English.

Arnett came under considerable criticism for staying in Baghdad, but the sharpest attack of all came from Sen. Alan K. Simpson (R., Wyoming), a longtime close friend of President Bush. The senator said that Arnett "is what we used to call in my day a sympathizer." Arnett, the senator went on, "was active in the Vietnam war and he won a Pulitzer Prize largely because of his anti-Government material, and he was married to a Vietnamese whose brother was active in the Vietcong. I called that sympathizer in my early days in the Second World War."[19]

Criticism of the Press

But the criticism of Arnett for staying in Baghdad under Iraqi censorship was not really as bad as the criticism of the rest of the press for becoming the "lapdogs" of the U.S. military and submitting so meekly to its censorship. As is usually the case, the sternest critics of the press were other members of the press. Some of this criticism has been described above, but the most withering and detailed criticism was by Lewis H. Lapham, editor of *Harper's* magazine, in an article entitled "Notebook: Trained seals and sitting ducks."[20]

Within a matter of hours after the bombardment of Baghdad began, Lapham wrote, newspaper and television correspondents "abandoned any claim or pretension to the power of independent thought." They seemed to have enlisted in an "elite regiment, sworn to protect and defend whatever they were told to protect and defend by the generals who presented them with their morning film clips and their three or four paragraphs of yesterday's news."

Reciting the rules controlling the press described above, Lapham says that the media acted grateful that they were being allowed to attend "what everybody was pleased to call a war—rather than the destruction of Iraq and the slaughter of an unknown number of Iraqis. . . ." Actually the "war" would have been "more precisely described as a police raid, as the violent suppression of a mob, as an exemplary lesson in the uses of major-league terrorism." Although the Iraqi army had been advertised as cruel, evil, and "battle-hardened," with a huge arsenal of "demonic weapons," it quickly proved to "consist of half-starved recruits, as scared as they were poorly armed, only too glad to give up their weapons for a cup of rainwater."

"The Pentagon," Lapham wrote, "produced and directed the war as a television miniseries based loosely on Richard Wagner's *Götterdämmerung* with a script that borrowed elements of *Monday Night Football, The A Team,* and *Revenge of the Nerds.*" Television defined the war as a game, and the military was careful to "approve only those bits and pieces of film that sustained the illusion of a playing field (safe, bloodless, and abstract) on which American soldier-athletes performed feats of matchless daring and skill."

The evidence, according to Lapham, suggests that Bush resolved to make the Iraqi invasion of Kuwait an excuse for a war that could be quickly and easily won—thereby keeping the price of oil low, reviving the American military budget, and diverting attention from the troubled U.S. economy. But none of this could be accomplished unless a "credulous and jingoistic press" could be enlisted to help convince the American people that Hussein was as evil as Hitler, that the Iraqi army was almost invincible, and that the fate of nations and of mankind "trembled in the balance." "It wouldn't do," Lapham wrote, "to send the grand armada to the Persian Gulf if the American people thought that the heavy guns were being wheeled into line to blow away a small-time thug.

"The trick," Lapham concluded, "was to make the sitting duck look like the 6,000 pound gorilla. . . ."

CHAPTER 12

Postmortem on the War

Looking back on the war, opinion worldwide was unanimous that the U.S. and Allied military operations were superb. More than a half million troops and several thousand tanks, armored personnel carriers, artillery pieces, Patriot missiles, aircraft, trucks, and other kinds of military equipment were transported thousands of miles to the Gulf without a major hitch. The flow of food, petroleum products, ammunition, and other essential supplies was ample, steady, and unimpeded.

The tanks and other mechanized equipment worked better in the harsh desert environment than anyone had dared to hope.

The laser-guided precision bombs performed far beyond anyone's expectations. During World War II and the Korean and Vietnam wars, bombers sometimes made a hundred sorties before scoring a direct hit on a pinpoint target such as a bridge. Although the laser bombs made up only 7 to 10 percent of the bombs dropped—about 6,520 tons out of 88,500 tons—they hit their targets 80 percent of the time.

The U.S. and Allied air forces gained complete command of the air. This made it possible to knock out enough bridges and highways to impede enemy troop movements. Round-the-clock bombing of the enemy troops destroyed or damaged a significant number of their tanks, artillery, and other heavy equipment and eroded the troops' morale. Control of the air also blinded the enemy, making it possible to move the U.S. and Allied forces who made the main assault into position for the ground offensive with complete secrecy. The deception plans that feinted a seaborne landing in Kuwait pinned down a substantial number of Iraqi troops. The "Hail Mary" end run caught the enemy by surprise and struck his main forces in the flank and rear.

On the negative side, scientists testified to Congress that the Patriot missile was very successful against aircraft, for which it was designed, but that employing it against Scud missiles did more harm than good. They asserted that more damage was done by debris from the Patriots than if the missile had not been used at all. Dr. Theodore A. Postol, a physicist and professor of national security policy at the Massachusetts Institute of Technology and one-time Pentagon science adviser, went even further in an article in the January 1992 issue of *International Security,* a journal published by Harvard University. Dr. Postol wrote that the Patriot experienced "an almost total failure to intercept quite primitive attacking missiles." However, both the Pentagon and Raytheon, which makes the Patriot, disputed his charges.

Unlike the laser bombs, conventional bombs were not very accurate. According to official air force figures, 74 percent of the conventional bombs missed their targets. For the B-52s, the percentage of misses must have been much, much higher. B-52s flying at high altitude are effective against area targets, such as cities, but hardly effective at all against pinpoint targets, such as bridges or dug-in troops. In the Gulf War, B-52s were used mainly against dug-in troops, tanks, and other equipment, and they seem to have had very little effect at all.

An important disappointment was that much more Iraqi armor survived than U.S. intelligence had estimated—armor that was used to suppress the Kurdish and Shiite revolts. Inside the U.S. government, questions were raised about the wisdom of President Bush's decision to declare a cease-fire at the time he did rather than to continue the war for a few more days. Later estimates were that about 700 of Iraq's more advanced Soviet-built T-72 tanks survived, as did 1,430 of Iraq's 2,880 armored personnel carriers. However, only 340 of Iraq's 3,257 artillery pieces were believed to have survived. In addition to those that escaped, Iraq had more than 1,200 tanks stationed throughout the country outside the battle zones, including 100 T-72s on its border with Turkey.

On a March 27 TV program, General Schwarzkopf said that he had recommended to President Bush that U.S. forces continue the attack into Iraq to annihilate Iraq's forces, but because of Bush's cease-fire order, "significant elements" of both the Iraqi army and the Republican Guard escaped into Basra. If the war had been allowed to go on for another twenty-four hours, Schwarzkopf said, the United States could

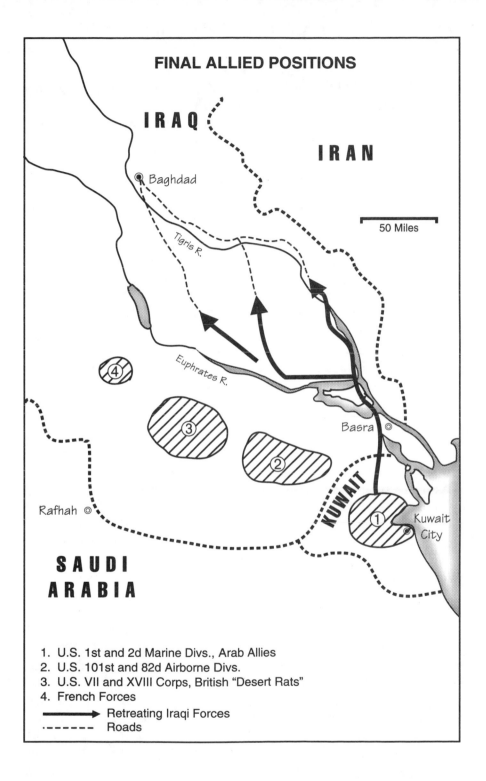

FINAL ALLIED POSITIONS

IRAQ

IRAN

Baghdad

50 Miles

Tigris R.

Euphrates R.

④

③

②

Basra

Rafhah

KUWAIT

①

Kuwait City

SAUDI ARABIA

1. U.S. 1st and 2d Marine Divs., Arab Allies
2. U.S. 101st and 82d Airborne Divs.
3. U.S. VII and XVIII Corps, British "Desert Rats"
4. French Forces

→ Retreating Iraqi Forces
- - - - - - - Roads

have inflicted terrible damage on the Republican Guard, which was the mainstay in putting down the Kurdish and Shiite rebellions.

The White House wasted no time "sternly" disputing Schwarzkopf's account of the decision to end the war. It issued a rebuttal the next day of the general's assertion that he wanted to continue the war and maintained that Schwarzkopf had fully agreed with the decision to end it at that time.

A year later newspaper and magazine reports told a somewhat different story. However, it should be stressed that the issue was not whether or not the U.S. and Allied forces should have continued on to Baghdad—with the implication that if they had done so, they might also have been able to end Saddam Hussein's rule. Going on to Baghdad would have exceeded the U.N. mandate and would also have been vehemently resisted by Arab and other U.S. allies. The issue was whether or not the war should have been continued for one, two, or three more days in order to complete the encirclement and destruction of the Iraqi forces that later put down the Shiite and Kurdish rebellions and that were committed to maintaining Saddam Hussein in power.

As mentioned earlier, the main route the Iraqi forces used in retreating from Kuwait was Highway 6, the so-called "Highway of Death." Allied bombers destroyed both the head and the rear of the column, preventing it from either advancing or retreating, and then proceeded to demolish the main body. The retreating Iraqi forces were able to offer almost no resistance, and a number of U.S. and Allied pilots were variously quoted as saying the experience was "sickening," a "turkey shoot," a "senseless slaughter," and describing the Iraqi retreat as a "panicked, desperate flight." A "senior military source" reportedly said that the attacks were "militarily irrelevant." As these descriptions came in to Washington, General Powell and the White House became increasingly concerned about how world and Arab opinion would react. In addition, both Saudi Arabia and Egypt had pressed the United States to stop the fighting. Finally, the forward units had run out of fuel, and it might take two or three additional days for their resupply. General Powell took the lead in recommending that the war be ended, and no one at the meeting disagreed.

Schwarzkopf's statement on TV that he had wanted to continue the war was apparently made deliberately, to get it into the record. But Pentagon sources claimed Schwarzkopf had two distinct opportunities to urge Bush not to stop the war immediately, yet said nothing.[1]

The Costs

The Pentagon reported to Congress that 148 American soldiers, airmen, Marines, and sailors were killed in action and 467 wounded. Another 156 were killed in accidents of various kinds. Among the Allies, 24 British soldiers were killed in combat, 23 died in accidents, and 44 Saudis were killed in combat. Although detailed figures on casualties among the rest of the Allies have not been published, they were somewhat less because fewer of their troops were involved.

After further study, the Pentagon reported that 35 of the 148 Americans killed were actually killed by "friendly fire"—that is, by fire from other Americans. Of the 467 wounded, friendly fire was responsible for 72. Among the Allies, 9 British soldiers were killed by American A-10 warplanes. On another occasion, 2 more British soldiers were also killed by friendly fire. There is no information on friendly fire casualties among the other Allies.

A 1986 U.S. Army study of earlier wars concluded that in all the wars from World War I through Vietnam, the casualties from friendly fire were less than 2 percent. In the Gulf War, friendly fire was responsible for 23 percent of those killed and 15 percent of the wounded.

All the M1A1 tank casualties were caused by friendly fire. The American forces used armor-piercing ammunition made of depleted uranium—which is two and one-half times as dense as steel. These shells leave a small but detectable trace of radioactivity, and all the U.S. tanks knocked out showed this telltale trace. Actually, probably none of the conventional armor-piercing ammunition used by the Iraqi forces would have been capable of piercing the extremely thick and hard armor on the M1A1s.

There was a total of twenty-eight friendly fire incidents. United States ground forces attacked other U.S. ground forces sixteen times, killing 24 Americans and wounding 57. United States airplanes attacked U.S. ground forces nine times, with 11 killed and 154 wounded. One U.S. ship attacked another U.S. ship, but there were no casualties. One U.S. ground force unit attacked a U.S. Navy jet, but again there were no casualties.

One explanation for the high casualties from friendly fire is that the technology for killing at a distance has been more highly developed than the technology for distinguishing between friend and foe.

Another reason was offered by Col. Roy Alcala, an aide to Gen. Carl Vuono, then army chief of staff. Colonel Alcala pointed out that the percentages in the Gulf War were skewed because "in previous wars a lot of people died from things that didn't happen in this war—the other side fighting back."[2] If the other side does not fight back, he observed, the only casualties tend to be those inflicted by your own forces, so the *percentage* of total casualties caused by friendly fire is much higher.

The Dollar Costs

In dollar terms, the cost of the war is very difficult to determine. Press reports put the cost at something between $80 and $100 billion. The Pentagon request to Congress for additional funds to make up for those spent on the war was for $80 billion. However, the Congressional Budget Office argued that the correct figure was more like $30 billion. So much depends on how the different expenses are allocated that a figure any more exact than this range of $30 to $80 billion may be very difficult to determine. Perhaps the most informative way to express the dollar costs is to repeat a Pentagon wisecrack about the savings expected from the ending of the cold war: "If you're looking for the peace dividend, it just left for Saudi Arabia."

Events in Kuwait

As described earlier, President Bush announced the liberation of Kuwait on February 27. Several days later Western newspapers carried stories that the Kuwaiti people were puzzled and confused by the failure of the emir or any other member of the Kuwaiti royal family to return.

When the Kuwaiti authorities did return from Saudi Arabia, they rounded up about two thousand people. Most of these were foreigners suspected of collaborating with Iraq, but some were Kuwaiti citizens who advocated political reform and democracy. Dozens of those rounded up were killed. Others were taken to the Iraqi border and dumped in the desert without water, food, shoes, or documents. Refugees from Kuwait reported that all foreigners suspected of aiding the Iraqi occupying forces or cooperating with them were being tortured. In addition, "goon squads" made up of younger members of the royal Sabah family were abducting, beating, and killing suspects. Ordinary Kuwaitis also attacked foreigners, especially Palestinians, who had formed a large proportion of the work force before the war. The motive was apparently to take revenge for the fact that the PLO had sided with Iraq in the war.

United States military and diplomatic officials pressed Kuwaiti authorities to halt the attacks on foreigners, but the Kuwaiti officials paid little attention. When Secretary of State Baker visited Kuwait, an opposition group attempted to put on a demonstration to protest the newly appointed cabinet as just a rearrangement of members of the Sabah family. The government promptly put it down.

United States officials also pressed Kuwaiti authorities to take steps toward reforming the political system. Newspaper reports, however, said that President Bush himself was not pressing Kuwait on reform. The president was said to believe that he could not force democracy on Kuwait. The White House, however, was aware that the situation in Kuwait could become one of the tests by which Bush's "new world order" would be judged.

Finally, on March 15, the emir, tired and tearful, returned to Kuwait. His welcome seems to have been disappointing, however; many of the Kuwaiti people who had remained during the occupation were bitter toward those who had fled to Saudi Arabia and sat out the war in luxury hotels.

Western newspapers began to run uncomplimentary stories about the emir, questioning by implication whether the lives of American soldiers should have been put at risk to restore him to his throne. Kuwait was hardly a democracy, the stories pointed out, noting that most governmental positions were held by members of the emir's family.

Some delved deeply into the emir's background. On March 27, for example, the *New York Times* ran a story pointing out that since he became emir in 1977, Shaikh Jabir's "interest in statecraft appears to have waned, it is widely said, in favor of concentrating his energies on his frequent, although brief marriages." The story went on to say that almost every Thursday, the eve of the Islamic sabbath, the emir would marry a young woman and then divorce her on Friday.

On May 9 Kuwait began trying suspected collaborators. Lawyers for their defense said that many of the charges were trumped up and that confessions had been extracted by torture. Most of those being tried were Palestinians. Of the approximately 320,000 Palestinians who worked in Kuwait before the war, 170,000 fled and were not allowed to return. Of the 150,000 who remained in Kuwait, according to Kuwaiti authorities, most would probably be expelled.

On May 15 Kuwaiti authorities jailed five people for putting up posters welcoming opposition figures returning home from abroad.

The trials of the people rounded up earlier opened on May 20. The procedure was as follows. First, the accused was charged. No evidence was presented and no witnesses for either the prosecution or defense were permitted. After hearing the charges, the judge pronounced the sentence; each trial took about five minutes.

The Western press reported that the mood was vengeance, not justice. One of the accused, for example, was sentenced to fifteen years in prison for wearing a T-shirt with Saddam Hussein's picture on it. The U.S. government protested, but Kuwaiti authorities denied any wrongdoing. Two days later another twenty-two persons accused of aiding Iraq were tried and sentenced in the same procedure.

Kuwait announced on June 3 that parliamentary elections would be held in October 1992, a year later than opposition leaders had advocated. A June 16 *New York Times* editorial noted the announcement scheduling elections under the headline "The Long Wait in Kuwait." Criticizing the delay, the *Times* went on to point out that martial law persisted in Kuwait, the press was muzzled, and opposition meetings were banned. The ruling family, the editorial continued, which had been restored to power by an immense international effort, seemed chiefly concerned with reestablishing its old prerogatives.

The Kuwaiti government, the *Times* continued, had shrugged off the protests and forcibly expelled Iraqi POWs, in violation of the understanding with its coalition partners. The Kuwaiti government had also continued to carry out vengeful executions of suspected collaborators, dumping their unidentified bodies in mass graves. Nobody was being held accountable. Little wonder, the editorial continued, that the two hundred thousand Kuwaitis who did not flee were unhappy. What the ordinary Kuwaiti wanted was a free press, minimal accountability by the government for its actions, and the vote for women. The ruling Sabah family said that it would think about all this, and maybe it might eventually make some concessions.

Most people concluded that any concessions would be nothing more than a crumb or two. In 1962, for example, Kuwait became the only Arab state in the Gulf to adopt a constitution and allow an elected parliament, although the right to vote was restricted to one-tenth of the male population. However, protests from Saudi Arabia prompted the emir to suspend parliament in 1976.

Progress in Arab states is blocked by the stubborn mind-set of the sheiks who see their countries as family businesses. A growing middle class, the *Times* concluded, rightly wonders why.

On June 16 Kuwait sentenced to death six journalists who had worked for a newspaper sponsored by the Iraqi army of occupation; the total death sentences handed down by the military courts eventually reached twenty-nine. A few days later seven entertainers, mostly Iraqi citizens who had been living in Kuwait, were sentenced to life imprisonment. Others, mainly musicians, were given long jail sentences. In dozens of other cases, severe jail sentences were handed down. The U.N. secretary-general protested, citing evidence that the confessions had been obtained by torture, that normal trial procedures had been lacking, that no witnesses had been permitted to testify, and that the judicial bodies had been nothing more than kangaroo courts.

On June 21 another *Times* editorial pointed out that the proceedings were marred by the stench of vengeance and denial of rudimentary safeguards. Living under an army of occupation, the editorial argued, was hard. In such circumstances it is difficult to refuse the occupiers what they want. And it was particularly unseemly, the editorial concluded, for such severe penalties to be handed down by members of a ruling family who spent the war living in luxury hotels in Egypt and were contemptuous of world opinion.

Kuwait announced that martial law would end on June 26. The major change that the end of martial law would bring was that cases pending before military courts would be transferred to civilian ones. Security forces would change from military to police uniforms. The next day Kuwait commuted the twenty-nine death sentences handed down by the military courts to life imprisonment. All the other sentences—those for life and for long prison terms—were confirmed.

=CHAPTER 13=

Peace with Iraq

At the truce talks between the Allies and Iraq, the Allies presented the Iraqi generals with five terms, ranging from the standard ones for any truce to some that were exceptionally stiff. The first was for prompt release of all POWs. The second was for help in finding the land mines laid down by the Iraqi forces. The third was for an arrangement to separate the Allied and Iraqi forces to avoid further skirmishes. The fourth was for Iraq to accept responsibility to pay for war damages. The fifth was for Iraq to accept the terms of the various U.N. resolutions passed since the Iraqi invasion of Kuwait. The Allied position was that only when all these terms were met would the U.S. and Allied forces withdraw from southern Iraq. The Iraqi generals accepted the terms, although reluctantly.

In its formal letter of acceptance Iraq said that the terms were "unfair and vindictive." The letter argued that the terms were not the result of the "events of August 2nd"—the Iraqi euphemism for their invasion of Kuwait. On the contrary, the Iraqi letter argued, the terms were motivated by "the fact that Iraq has not accepted the unfair situation which was imposed on the Arab nation and the regional states many decades ago and which made Israel the dominant aggressive power in the region with the most modern and destructive conventional weapons and the weapons of mass destruction it possesses, including nuclear weapons." But, the letter concluded, Iraq found itself with only one alternative: to accept the terms of the truce, although under protest.

Shortly thereafter, Iraq freed thirty-five POWs, saying that thirty-five was all they had. On April 4 the United States withdrew twenty thousand troops from southern Iraq, including two major armored units.

In the meantime, the U.N. Security Council voted stern conditions for a formal end to the war. Iraq would be required to renounce terrorism; to pay billions of dollars in compensation; to accept the borders with Kuwait that it had agreed to in 1963 but renounced just prior to the invasion; and to destroy all of its chemical and biological weapons, its nuclear facilities with the potential for making nuclear weapons, and its stockpile of Scud and other missiles, and to pledge never to acquire such arms again. The terms eased sanctions on food and emergency civilian goods, but the bulk of sanctions would not be lifted until all the conditions had been met.

Referring to the fact that sanctions had been eased on food and emergency civilian goods, Iraq asked the U.N. for permission to sell oil to pay for food imports, but permission was denied. Iraq complained bitterly that sanctions on food and emergency civilian goods had been lifted but that the country was being denied the only way it had to get the money to buy them.

The U.N. called for Iraq to give up 25 percent of the revenues received from any future oil sales to pay reparations. Since the prewar revenue from oil had been $20 billion per year, this meant that $5 billion per year would go for reparations—just about what Iraq spent to buy foreign arms in the period before the war. The total reparations would probably run in the neighborhood of $50 billion.

In response, Baghdad assailed the U.N. conditions as an effort by the United States to control the world. But it gave no hint as to whether or not Iraq would ultimately accept.

Nevertheless, the main U.S. forces began their withdrawal from Iraq. The plan called for the remaining troops to pull out over the following several weeks—to be replaced by U.N. observer forces and representatives of international relief organizations. On April 25, in a symbolic move, control in southern Iraq was formally passed to the U.N. The last of the U.S. forces left Iraq on May 6. A demilitarized zone was established six miles inside Iraq and three miles inside Kuwait. No troops from either side would be permitted inside this zone. United Nations observers would be stationed in the zone to monitor compliance, but jurisdiction and police functions reverted to Iraq and Kuwait within their respective territories.

The Question of Sanctions

One of the two most troubling questions surrounding the peace settlement with Iraq was the question of when economic sanctions should be lifted and what Iraq should be required to do in exchange for the lifting of sanctions.

The U.N. report mentioned earlier said that the Allied bombing had deprived 90 percent of the Iraqi labor force of both work and income. Iraq's "sole laboratory" for producing veterinary vaccines was destroyed by bombing. So were all "seed warehouses" and all stocks of potatoes and vegetable seeds. Almost all of Iraq's modern communications facilities had been destroyed, as were most of its electrically operated installations. Since these included water purification plants, the population was forced to rely on contaminated drinking water.

American newspapers reported that economic hardship was widespread in Iraq and that the people blamed the United States. Their feeling was that President Bush was punishing the Iraqi people for what Hussein had done. The destruction of Iraq's electrical and telephone systems, according to these reports, particularly upset them, since much of both served only local needs. Other troubles blamed on the bombing were the lack of medicine and soaring food prices. The ordinary Iraqi, according to reporters, argued that the bombing campaign had served no military purpose, but was designed to demoralize the Iraqi people as a way of undermining Hussein and the Iraqi government. Naji al-Hadithi, an undersecretary at the Iraqi Ministry of Information, on May 11, 1991, said, "It is ironic that the civilized world should try to return a developing country to underdevelopment."[1]

On May 9, 1991, the *New York Times* ran a story headlined "Sanctions on Iraq Exact a High Price from Poor." Sanctions, the story said, had helped to force Baghdad to make a deal with the Kurds, to promise a kind of democracy for the Iraqi people, and to show its readiness to comply with U.N. demands that Iraq destroy its chemical and biological weapons and its potential for making nuclear weapons. But sanctions were having no effect on Hussein's power and position. So, according to the *Times,* the question was, would the sanctions persuade the elite to do something about Hussein? "Or will the sanctions do what they have done so far—bring yet more hardship to the poor while causing only modest inconvenience to the rich and powerful?"

The rationing system, the story continued, gave the poor a minimum of life's necessities. But the private market was supplied by trucks from Jordan and by smugglers from Turkey, Iran, and Syria. The prices of goods coming into Iraq by these routes were sky-high, but people who had the money could get whatever they wanted.

Sanctions had been formally lifted on food and medicines. But, as already mentioned, since the U.N. committee monitoring sanctions had denied Iraq's request to export $1 billion worth of oil, and since Western governments, including the United States, Britain, and Switzerland, had refused to unfreeze Iraqi assets, Iraq did not have the money to buy food and medicine, even though these items were no longer sanctioned.

The position taken by the United States and its Western allies was that before Iraq would be allowed to sell oil or sanctions would be fully lifted, Iraq must meet two conditions. First, it must dismantle its chemical and biological weapons, its ballistic missiles, and its facilities intended eventually to produce nuclear weapons. Second, Iraq must agree to pay 30 percent of its future oil revenues to Kuwait in war reparations—which upped the percentage previously proposed. For its part, Iraq said that it was willing to cooperate with the military demands but it balked at paying 30 percent of its oil revenues as reparations. In any event, Iraqi officials argued, how could Iraq pay reparations when it was not allowed to export its oil?

The Iraqi information minister pointed out that Iraq normally imported three-fourths of its food, of which wheat made up a large proportion. "The war is over," he said. "We are meeting the allies' demands. So why make our children starve and die in hospitals with no medicine?" Ominously, he then went on to say that he thought that Allied policy was not going to break the determination of the Iraqi people, but rather would stiffen their resolve.

On May 20 President Bush said that the United States would oppose lifting sanctions until Hussein was forced out of power. Since the United States has a veto over any action taken by the U.N. Security Council, sanctions could not be lifted unless the United States agreed. If it was true that sanctions hurt the Iraqi people but did not weaken Hussein's grip on power, then the inevitable result would be a stalemate.

In mid-July, Iraq made another effort to have the sanctions eased. The basic ration, mentioned above, provided only 55 percent of the calories most people need. The other 45 percent had to be purchased and, because of the sanctions, the price of basic foodstuffs had risen 2,000 to 3,000 percent. Trade Minister Mohammed Mehdi Saleh told a news conference that Iraq had already signed a contract with Australia for $1 billion worth of grain, but could not take delivery because it did not have the money and had no way of getting it unless the U.N. Security Council permitted it to sell oil.

On the free market in Iraq, flour was 2,037 percent higher than what the government charged for rationed flour. Baby formula was 2,500 times the cost of the single can per week on the government ration. Elliot Richardson, former U.S. attorney general, who was a member of the U.N. team, reported that he had met a woman who had to sell 1,500 dinars' worth of gold jewelry to buy milk for her child because the ration was not sufficient. Trade Minister Saleh charged that the Allies were trying to starve the Iraqi people into a revolt against Saddam Hussein by refusing to let Iraq sell oil to buy food. "The decision of the U.S., France and Britain is," he said, "that all the Iraqi people should die."

However, in mid-July 1991 a Western medical team visiting Iraq reported that there was no widespread famine. But they did say that conditions were bad, especially for children. The cost of basic foods had risen to twenty times what they had been before the war. A can of milk that had cost fifty cents now cost ten dollars. Half of the 680 children up to the age of five that the team examined suffered from chronic malnutrition. The malnutrition was severe in 8 percent of the children over one year old. The cause was the lack of infant formula and the fact that malnutrition among nursing mothers had caused a large-scale failure of breast feeding.

Nearly half of the children examined showed severe stunting. A nine-year-old Iraqi child, for example, was about the same height as a well-nourished six-year-old elsewhere in the Middle East. As many as 30 to 40 percent of the children examined showed severe wasting. The team noted, however, that the stunting and wasting among children had begun with the hardships of the war with Iran and that the effect of the Gulf War had been to aggravate the condition, although rather severely.

Water, sewage, and electrical power systems had been severely damaged by bombing but there were no materials to repair them or money to import the materials. Crops that required irrigation had failed, and the country was in a crisis of typhus, cholera, and a whole range of gastrointestinal diseases.

By late October 1991 the situation still had not improved. A team of American experts from Harvard University submitted a report stating that child mortality in Iraq had tripled or perhaps quadrupled as a result of the war. It estimated that as many as 170,000 more children would die in 1991 than had in the previous year. The causes were the shortage of baby formula, powdered milk, and essential medicines, and the rise in the price of food. Children under the age of five were receiving enough food to avoid acute starvation, but an estimated 29 percent—about one million children—were severely malnourished.[2]

In the population as a whole, millions of Iraqis were going hungry for two-thirds of each month. The bombing had caused breakdowns in irrigation systems and shortages of electricity, fertilizers, pesticides, and seeds. The result was that the output of Iraq's farms was down 75 to 80 percent. Herds of cattle, sheep, and goats—the principal sources of high-protein meat in Iraq—had shrunk by 50 to 60 percent. The teams surveying the drinking water of 156 households found that 105 were still drinking water that was contaminated by sewage, and estimated that the total number of Iraqis drinking contaminated water was in the millions. The country's hospital system remained devastated, with shortages of medicine, food, and staff. The electrical generating system had come back to 68 percent of prewar production, but the supply of spare parts would soon be exhausted and when it was electrical output would go down.

In late July 1991 the U.S. State Department drafted a plan that would permit Baghdad to sell oil so it could buy food. The U.N. would maintain sanctions but would permit Iraq to sell a total of $1.6 billion worth of oil. The money would go into an escrow account controlled solely by the U.N.

Iraq rejected the draft for two reasons. First, the plan did not provide the financial resources for the needs of the Iraqi people for food and medicine even at a minimal level. Second, it would deny Iraq sovereignty over its natural resources and put them under the control of other countries.

However, the U.N. Security Council adopted the resolution as drafted, permitting Iraq to sell oil worth $1.6 billion, the money going to an escrow account controlled by the U.N., with one-third of the total being set aside for reparations.

Iraq's response was that it would not sell its oil under such conditions.

By November 1991 the U.N. had $4 million worth of food stored in warehouses in Jordan and Baghdad. The U.N. said that the food would be released only if the U.N. itself could distribute it. Iraq, on the other hand, insisted that the food be distributed through Iraqi channels. They argued that distribution by the U.N. would not only be a violation of Iraqi sovereignty, but they feared that if the U.N. distributed the food, riots would quickly follow.

Again Iraq asked that $1.4 billion in Iraqi funds frozen in American and other banks be released for the purchase of food and medicine. The request was denied.

Stories in the Western press played up the human tragedy. One story, for example, was headlined "How Bad is War? It depends on the TV pictures," and quoted a bitter Iraqi doctor who said, "I know of no Iraqi baby who invaded Kuwait, so how could the Iraqi babies be punished?"[3]

In the meantime, Iraq passed a law permitting opposition parties, but it allowed only the Baath party to operate in the military establishment. At about the same time, Hussein dismissed most of the officials of the interim government whom he had installed just after Iraq's defeat—including the premier, who had advocated permitting rival political parties. Talk in Iraq of democratic change was no longer heard.

CHAPTER 14

Iraq's Nuclear Potential

The second most troubling question surrounding the peace settlement with Iraq was the question of Iraq's potential for building nuclear weapons. Iraq informed the U.N. on April 19 that a substantial chemical arsenal survived the war but denied that it had any nuclear arms, weapons-grade nuclear material, or biological weapons.

On May 17 Iraq accepted the U.N. proposal for a rigorous system of inspections for nuclear weapons. The U.N. observers said that they were very pleased with how forthcoming the Iraqi letter had been: It contained what the U.N. observers described as a detailed account of the Iraqi uranium stockpile and where it was stored.

However, on May 31, the U.S. government announced that Iraq still had enough uranium to make at least one bomb. The main purpose for bombing Iraqi nuclear facilities, the statement said, had been to destroy Iraq's uranium stockpiles. But the uranium had been moved, and thus the bombing had failed.

Some time later, U.N. aides also said that Iraq might be concealing nuclear materials. For seventy-two hours, U.N. inspectors were denied access to a barracks that U.S. intelligence believed was being used to hide machines designed to enrich uranium to weapons-grade quality. When they were finally allowed to continue their inspection, the suspected machinery was gone.

In a second incident, Iraqi troops actually fired warning shots over the heads of U.N. inspectors to prevent them from entering a military compound to inspect a convoy of trucks parked there—a convoy suspected of carrying the equipment taken from the barracks.

About the same time, an Iraqi defector claimed that Iraq had eight primary sites for nuclear research and development. The Allies had known about and bombed only three of those sites. The defector said that Iraq had succeeded in enriching about ninety pounds of uranium to weapons-grade material. Although the defector suggested that this would be enough for two crude atomic bombs, Western scientists said that it took about fifty-five pounds of such material to produce one bomb.

On the other hand, no one suggested that Iraq had developed or had the capacity to develop the means to *deliver* an atomic weapon to a target, whether by long-range aircraft or by missile. In fact, nuclear scientists said that even though Iraq might be able to develop a nuclear device within a few years, the Iraqis lacked the capacity to miniaturize the device sufficiently to make it a practical weapon. The director of the Defense Nuclear Agency, Gen. Gerald G. Watson, said that if Iraq did succeed in building a nuclear device, it "would weigh five tons and have to be carried on a flatbed trailer"—hardly a practical weapon of war.

The Iraqi defector also said that Iraq was using a very primitive method for extracting weapons-grade uranium, a method that the United States had tried in World War II and abandoned. Even so, the Allied powers took Iraq's effort to evade U.N. inspection seriously. On June 26 the United States showed members of the U.N. Security Council reconnaissance photos of the machinery used to enrich uranium being moved by Iraqi trucks or buried to evade detection by U.N. inspectors. The next day, Secretary Baker said that Iraq's actions were "extraordinarily serious," and reporters were given background briefings suggesting that the United States might renew its bombing—this time to concentrate on the suspected nuclear sites.

In response to protests about the incident in which warning shots were fired over the heads of the U.N. inspection team, the Iraqi government announced that Saddam Hussein had ordered that the U.N. teams be allowed to inspect whatever they wished. However, President Bush accused Hussein of lying to conceal a nuclear weapons program, and he threatened an air strike.

On July 8 Iraq admitted that it had been running three clandestine programs designed to produce weapons-grade enriched uranium, in violation of the nuclear nonproliferation treaty that Iraq had signed.

At the same time it submitted a new list of nuclear sites and material that had not been included in previous reports to the U.N. Iraq admitted to producing one pound of slightly enriched uranium, although it claimed that the uranium was not enriched sufficiently to be suitable for a bomb. The U.S. government, however, said that it believed that Iraq actually had enough material to build at least one nuclear bomb.

Then on July 17, 1991, U.N. inspectors announced that Iraq had "deluged" them with new information over the past few days and that they had concluded that Allied bombing had probably destroyed Iraq's uranium enrichment installations before the Iraqis had succeeded in producing any weapons-grade material. The U.N. report said that the only highly enriched uranium in Iraq—about ninety pounds—was and continued to be under the International Atomic Energy Agency's safeguards. The report appeared to support Iraq's claim that it was not hiding any nuclear installations. Iraq maintained that it had only about one pound of low-enriched uranium, which would not be suitable for a bomb; the U.N. team said that it was inclined to believe Iraq's claim. In any case, the U.N. team did not believe the defector's claim that Iraq had produced ninety pounds of fully enriched uranium.

The next day, Iraq gave the U.N. a formal pledge that it had no more clandestine nuclear plants and that it had revealed all of its nuclear secrets. United Nations officials, however, said that they continued to be suspicious and would send another U.N. team to Iraq later in the summer.

Although Washington continued to threaten to bomb suspected Iraqi nuclear sites, Pentagon officials admitted that bombing was unlikely to be effective. During the war, bombing had failed to destroy the sites and the concealed uranium, and there was no reason to believe that bombing would be any more effective against such targets now. Bombing, a Pentagon official said, could be used to punish Hussein or to scare him. But after the bombing he would still have some nuclear materials left, plus the experts who had run the Iraqi nuclear program.

Nevertheless, President Bush threatened that the United States would solve the problem of Iraq's nuclear potential "one way or the other." He accused Iraq of "cheating and lying and hiding" nuclear materials, adding that he believed that the authority already existed for using military force against any suspected nuclear installations in Iraq. Bush approved a list of twenty targets if Iraq failed to comply with

U.N. and Allied demands, then he began to lobby U.S. Allies to obtain their agreement to renew the bombing. President François Mitterrand of France agreed; Prime Minister John Major of Great Britain said only that Iraq was clearly in violation of the U.N. resolutions but not that he necessarily favored renewed bombing.

On July 28 American newspapers carried a story that the Pentagon had briefed Allied governments on plans to bomb suspected nuclear facilities in Iraq. Egypt voiced strong objections to more bombing. Saudi Arabia said that it would not agree to more bombing unless it was given more Patriot missiles to protect its airfields and cities from Iraqi retaliation. Turkey indicated that it would not permit its bases to be used in such an attack. "I rule it out," Prime Minister Mesut Yilmaz said flatly. Israel asked for seventy-two hours' notice of any such attack to give it time to prepare for retaliation.

In briefing French and British officials, Pentagon officers said that the plans included bombing not just nuclear facilities but also "leadership targets," specifically Saddam Hussein himself if his whereabouts could be determined. France reserved its position. British officials, on the other hand, apparently agreed to support a bombing attack if diplomatic pressure failed.

The Soviet Union for its part said that air strikes could have "negative consequences" that would be greater than the immediate goal of bombing Iraq's nuclear potential.

President Mubarak of Egypt said that the Arab world thought that between Hussein and the Allied bombing, the Iraqi people had suffered enough. Aides to President Bush, however, leaned toward bombing. The exception was Gen. Colin Powell, who argued that they would just end up bombing the U.N. inspectors.

Nevertheless, the U.S. Senate voted to back the use of "all necessary means" to eliminate Iraq's ability to produce nuclear, chemical, or biological weapons. Bush administration officials said that the United States was prepared to bomb Iraq's nuclear facilities "almost immediately" after President Bush gave the order.

However, only a few days later the news media reported that George Ullrich, the deputy director of the Defense Nuclear Agency, said that bombs and missiles could not succeed in wiping out hidden nuclear material. "You could put it in a suitcase," he said, "or hide it under a bed."

During the period that followed, Iraq and the U.N. inspectors played something of a cat-and-mouse game with Iraq's nuclear facilities. The

U.N. issued a formal complaint setting a July 25 deadline for Iraq to make a full disclosure.

Then, on July 30, the U.N. team reported to the Security Council that it had found four times as many chemical weapons as the Iraqi government had reported. Although most of the weapons contained relatively harmless tear gas, a few were warheads for missiles, such as the Scud, containing the very powerful nerve gas Sarin. The team also said that Iraq's failure to report some of its nuclear facilities was not just a technical matter but "an attempt to conceal a major program for the enrichment of uranium."

On August 1 the International Atomic Energy Agency submitted a tough, very comprehensive plan to oversee Iraq's nuclear installations that would give the agency an unlimited right to move about Iraq and inspect its facilities. Diplomats described it as the most stringent inspection requirements in the history of the U.N.

Nevertheless, the cat-and-mouse game continued. On September 10 U.N. inspectors complained that Iraq was refusing to let them use their own helicopters in making inspections. Iraq argued that using U.N. helicopters was an infringement of Iraqi sovereignty and insisted that Iraqi helicopters be used. The trouble, of course, was that there were often delays before the Iraqi helicopters were made available. The next day the head of the U.N. Special Commission officially charged that Iraq was deliberately delaying and obstructing the U.N. inspection teams. However, the U.N. official also said that the inspectors had found 46,000 pieces of chemical ordnance and already destroyed 8,000 of them. They had also destroyed forty-six "major items" related to Iraq's ballistic missile programs.

Then, on September 23, in a building in Baghdad, a U.N. inspection team found some secret Iraqi plans for making nuclear weapons. But Iraqi guards forced them to leave the building without the documents.

The next day the U.N. team found more apparently incriminating documents in the personnel files of Iraqi scientists. About fifty Iraqi soldiers detained the forty-four-member U.N. team in their buses in a parking lot.

In talking to the U.N. secretary-general, Iraqi Foreign Minister Ahmed Hussein said that if the personnel files were taken and Israeli intelligence—the Mossad—learned the names of Iraqi nuclear scientists, the scientists would be assassinated—just as artillery designer Gerald Bull had been assassinated.

The Iraqi fears were given some credence when Rolf Ekeus of Sweden, the executive chairman of the Special Commission set up by the U.N. Security Council, discovered that the team was sending the information it found straight to the U.S. State Department. Ordering the practice to cease, Ekeus said that sending reports directly to the State Department tended to bolster the Iraqi charges that the American head of the team, David Kay, was really a CIA spy. Thereafter, the team's reports went to the U.N. Special Commission and the U.N. International Atomic Energy Agency based in Vienna.

Shortly after the U.N. team was confined to the parking lot in Iraq, President Bush said that he was "plenty fed up" with Iraq's behavior and announced that he had ordered American warplanes to prepare to escort U.N. helicopters should that measure be required. He also ordered two battalions of Patriot missiles to Saudi Arabia as a prelude to the deployment of about fifty combat aircraft to escort U.N. inspection teams and their helicopters.

After detaining the U.N. team in the parking lot for two days, Iraq agreed to release both the team and the documents, but only if Iraq was given a list of the documents being taken. The U.N. Security Council agreed to this compromise.

At the same time, Iraq also agreed to permit the U.N. inspectors to use unarmed German helicopters while making their inspection trips around the country. In response, the United States canceled the decision to send helicopters and escort aircraft to Saudi Arabia.

As time went on, the U.N. inspection teams discovered installations that were not known to U.S. and Allied intelligence. One was a complex of buildings—Al Atheer, about forty miles south of Baghdad—that was apparently the nerve center of the Iraqi nuclear program. United States and Allied intelligence had not learned just how important the complex was, and it had been only slightly damaged in the bombing. Another plant—at Furat, just outside Baghdad, where Iraq was secretly building a uranium-enrichment plant—was not recognized for what it was until after the war, when U.N. inspectors found it.

In November, a U.N. team found traces of uranium enriched to 93 percent, which made it weapons-grade, at the Twaitha nuclear installation 40 miles southwest of Baghdad (Twaitha was the nuclear installation that the Israelis had bombed in 1981). The U.N. inspectors said they had found no evidence that the machinery that Iraq planned to use to enrich uranium was yet operational, so they suspected that the enriched uranium had been supplied by a foreign government, either the Soviet Union or China. If so, it might well be that Iraq still had some enriched uranium hidden at some secret site. The trace of enriched uranium the U.N. team found was contaminated by U-236, suggesting that it had first been used as reactor fuel, reprocessed to separate the plutonium, and then enriched to weapons-grade levels.

The Emerging Picture of the Iraqi Nuclear Program

The information gathered by the U.N. teams gradually built up a picture of an Iraqi nuclear program that was both larger and more sophisticated than anyone in the West had suspected.

In order to ensure that at least one method worked for making the enriched uranium needed for a bomb, Iraq had sought to make the uranium by three completely different methods. One was based on chemical separation, another on a technique known as electromagnetic separation, and a third on centrifuges to separate the uranium isotopes.

United Nations officials suspect that a fourth method was also being used—the so-called "nozzle" technique developed by two German companies and currently used in South Africa in two uranium-enrichment plants that it operates. The nozzle technique separates lighter isotopes by forcing uranium gas through a jet. This kind of plant would be relatively easy to conceal. If such a plant was found, the U.N. inspectors would look into the possibility that South Africa had aided Iraq with the knowledge and equipment.

The Iraqi nuclear program employed more than ten thousand scientists and technical workers and cost at least $10 billion. United States and Allied bombing had destroyed a lot of the brick-and-mortar installations, but many key materials and much equipment had survived. More importantly, Iraq's formidable corps of scientists, technicians, and weapons experts were unharmed and could be put back to work as soon as inspections and sanctions ended. Iraq, in fact, had the largest technical base in the Middle East, although Israel's was qualitatively better.

The Iraqi nuclear program had received substantial help from foreign companies and governments. Although the U.N. did not make the names of these companies and governments public at first, U.N. authorities did say that they included a number in Western Europe. The help included highly sensitive and restricted technologies, such as carbon-fiber rotors that are used in high-speed uranium gas centrifuges and extremely hard maraging steel of the type used both in centrifuges and in actual bombs.

Asked about help from American and European firms, a U.N. representative told the press that European firms were certainly involved, but he was unsure about American firms. However, the press reported that West German firms supplied centrifuge technology, Finnish firms supplied copper coil, British firms supplied precision machine tools, and Swiss firms supplied metal castings and special high-strength steel. The reports admitted that all of this equipment could be used for purposes other than developing a nuclear capacity, but they argued that imports of this kind should have raised suspicions. In fact, some foreign companies supplying the equipment were owned by their governments, so in those cases the government should have had at least an inkling of Iraq's nuclear program. Later, the U.N. inspectors identified two American firms that supplied products that Iraq used in its nuclear weapons program: Du Pont and the Pennsylvania subsidiary of a German company.

Some of the technology in the centrifuge machines resembled that developed by Britain, Germany, and the Netherlands in their joint Dutch-based Urenco commercial reactor. It has been widely reported that Pakistan acquired Urenco know-how for its own nuclear program from a Pakistani scientist who had worked in the plant, so the suspicion also arose that Iraq may have acquired some of the information through Pakistan.

Early on, Iraq acknowledged trying to produce highly enriched uranium at plants in Tarmiya and Ash Sharqat by the electromagnetic separation technique, which the United States had used in producing its first atomic bomb. This was not cause for much alarm, however, since the U.N. commission estimated that each plant could have produced no more than about thirty pounds of enriched uranium a year, less than is needed for one bomb.

However, in January 1992 Iraq admitted that some German firms had sold it enough special magnets and housings to build up to ten thousand uranium gas centrifuges, which is by far the most efficient technology for producing enriched uranium. United Nations inspectors found a plant designed to make about a thousand centrifuges a year. The German government announced that it is investigating the sale to determine if the firms could be prosecuted.

Centrifuge machines work by spinning uranium gas at very high speeds, thus separating out the fissionable U-235 from the more common

U-238. Arranged in a cascade system, each centrifuge enriches the gas, and then passes it on to the next centrifuge. The uranium becomes suitable for weapons when 93 percent of the gas is composed of U-235. Experts say Iraq would have started with a small experimental cascade of about a hundred or so centrifuges before proceeding to full-scale production. But no trace of any such pilot plant has been found.

It takes about two thousand centrifuges to produce enough U-235 for one bomb—about fifty pounds. So once it had ten thousand machines in operation, Iraq could have produced enriched uranium for three to five bombs a year.

Iraqi officials claim that all of the components for the centrifuges were destroyed immediately after the cease-fire. They showed U.N. officials piles of metal debris that they said were all that was left of the equipment. United Nations inspectors took samples, but withheld judgment.

After completing its investigation, the German government gave the U.N. inspectors a list of the centrifuge equipment that German firms had sold to Iraq, and in January 1992 the U.N. inspectors reported that they had located and destroyed everything on the list. However, they also said that they could not exclude the possibility that Iraq had built and successfully concealed a centrifuge pilot plant.

An Iraqi H-Bomb?

The evidence gathered by the U.N. teams not only suggested that Iraq could have tested a fission bomb within a year, but that it was also developing the capacity to build an H-bomb. Iraq had a stock of deuterium oxide, so-called heavy water, that it had purchased some years earlier. Hans Blix, head of the International Atomic Energy Agency, said that his inspectors had found documentary evidence that Iraq was planning to produce lithium 6, whose only known use is in H-bombs. When deuterium oxide and lithium 6 are combined, the product is lithium 6 deuteride, the main component of an H-bomb. The bottom line is that with these materials a crude atomic bomb can be transformed into a hydrogen warhead small enough to fit on top of a missile.

Nuclear Weapons Design

Iraq had apparently not made much progress in weapons design. It was frequently stymied because the complicated machinery needed was not available commercially. However, Iraq did have a weapons development program, and it was in the process of designing a device to detonate nuclear weapons. United Nations officials disclosed that Iraq had tested a missile that would be able to carry a warhead of the size needed for a hydrogen bomb. Similar warheads carried by U.S. missiles have the explosive power of three hundred kilotons of TNT, as compared to the fourteen kilotons of the Hiroshima bomb.

Based on the information described above, experts estimated that if it had not been for the Gulf War, Iraq could have tested a reasonably sophisticated nuclear weapon by 1993 or 1994 and an H-bomb several years later.

The Intelligence Failure

What is clear is that U.S. and Allied intelligence underestimated the size of the Iraqi nuclear program and overestimated the damage that the bombing had done to it. On January 23, for example, President Bush said, "Our pinpoint attacks have put Saddam out of the nuclear bomb-building business for a long time." On different occasions in late January, General Schwarzkopf said that the bombing attacks "had destroyed all their nuclear-reactor facilities" and "neutralized their nuclear manufacturing capability."

After the war, high-ranking Pentagon officials admitted to the press that the intelligence community's failure to assess accurately Iraq's nuclear program raised serious concerns about how much the United States could learn about the nuclear programs of other potentially hostile countries such as Libya and North Korea.

In fact, the same could be said of Iraq in the future. Rolf Ekeus, head of the U.N. group charged with destroying Iraq's nuclear, biological, and chemical capabilities, presented a plan to carry out the mission, but Tariq Aziz, Iraq's deputy prime minister, said that Iraq would not permit the U.N. to push it back to a preindustrial age. Ekeus predicted that Iraq would claim that everything the U.N. wanted to destroy could be used for peaceful purposes—that it had a "dual use" and as such was exempt from destruction. Other U.N. officials pointed out that what the U.N. inspectors had discovered in Iraq demonstrated that the nuclear nonproliferation treaties contained both flaws and loopholes that tended to nullify their effectiveness.

But even though the Iraqi nuclear potential was greater than anyone had suspected, Gen. Colin Powell told the press that Saddam Hussein's ability to develop nuclear weapons was not any real threat—either in the short term or even the medium term. In addition, even if Iraq did succeed in developing the capacity to produce a few small nuclear weapons a year, it would for many years lack the means to deliver them anywhere except in its immediate neighborhood.

Iraq's Motivation to Build Nuclear Weapons

Marshall Wiley, ambassador to Iraq during the Carter administration, pointed out on television that it was understandable that Iraq felt driven to try to build a nuclear capability.[1] Iraq, with eighteen million people, felt threatened from the east by Iran, with a population of fifty-five million controlled by a militant Shiite priesthood hostile to Sunni Muslims, and from the west by Israel, with a stockpile of some two hundred nuclear warheads and the missiles to deliver them. Ambassador Wiley argued that whether it was Saddam Hussein who was the leader of Iraq or some military junta that replaced him, the Iraqis would feel that it was essential for their national security that they have some kind of "high-tech weapons capability." Referring to President Bush's speech before the U.N. on September 23, 1991, vowing that there would be no compromise on eliminating Iraq's potential for building nuclear weapons, Wiley said that the Bush administration was making an open-ended commitment that would be extremely difficult to carry out unless it was approached on a regional basis, rather than directed at a particular country, such as Iraq. No matter how hard the United States pushed on this, as soon as it stopped pushing, Iraq—no matter who was its head—would resume some kind of nuclear program. The director of the CIA, testifying before Congress in January 1992, said that Iraq could rebuild its nuclear, chemical, and biological weapons within a very few years. The surviving cadre of nuclear scientists and engineers, he said, could reconstitute the dormant Iraqi program very rapidly.

Asked what in practical terms President Bush or the U.N. could do to back up Bush's very adamant stand, Wiley said that the only way the United States could be sure that it had removed all the high-tech weapons from Iraq would be to occupy the country with perhaps a million men and keep them there for a period of years—at a cost that he did not believe the American people were willing to pay. The Bush administration seemed to be focused on removing Saddam Hussein and eradicating Iraq's high-tech weapons, but it was not really looking beyond to what all this would mean to the future stability of the area.

One of the great ironies in these worries about Iraq's potential for nuclear weapons, according to newspaper reports, was that *because* Iraq was being denuded of its potential for building nuclear weapons, a number of Arab countries were considering acquiring their own. If Iraq had succeeded in building a few nuclear weapons and the capacity to deliver them, the reasoning goes, it would have deterred Israel from actually using its own nuclear weapons in some future crisis. With Iraq no longer able to supply the deterrent, other Arab states are likely to feel that it is necessary for them to fill the void. More than one observer recalled that after the Israeli bombing of the Iraqi nuclear reactor in 1981, Saddam Hussein called on all "peace-loving nations" to help not just Iraq but all the Arab world "in one way or another to obtain the nuclear bomb in order to confront Israel's existing bombs."

The crux of the problem is that Iraq is not the only country to pose a nuclear threat to its neighbors. If the United States undertook to remove all of these potential threats unilaterally with American military force, a number of observers argued, it would be very, very busy for a long time to come. In ancient Rome the Temple of Mars was closed only during time of peace, and for one period it remained open for two hundred years. If the United States undertook the role of nuclear policeman to the world, the American equivalent of the Temple of Mars might be open for several times as long. The only hope for a long-term solution to such threats, the argument concluded, was not unilateral action by the United States but some sort of international action.

Israel's Nuclear Arsenal

Almost as if it were timed to support Wiley's contention that when Israel developed nuclear weapons and missiles, Iraq and the other Arab states felt compelled to follow, correspondent Seymour Hersh came out with a book detailing the development of the Israeli nuclear program. The title of the book is *The Samson Option,* referring to Samson's act of desperation in pulling down the temple, killing both his enemies and himself.[2]

As Hersh relates the story, President Kennedy pressed David Ben-Gurion repeatedly to give the United States assurances that Israel was not building nuclear weapons. Finally, Israel agreed to permit an inpection of its Dimona plant once each year. According to Hersh, Israel built a fake control room and convinced the inspectors that the purpose of the plant was peaceful. President Johnson, however, lost interest in the subject, and the plant began to produce nuclear weapons in 1968. The Nixon administration, Hersh continues, did not press Israel on the issue because Henry Kissinger was sympathetic to the idea that Israel should have nuclear weapons. As a result, Israel had stockpiled hundreds of nuclear warheads, including more than a hundred nuclear artillery shells and a large number of neutron warheads that kill people with minimal property destruction. Hersh says that Israel has gone on a full nuclear alert on three separate occasions, twice during the 1973 war and once in the Gulf War when it was attacked by Scud missiles.

Other Countries With a Nuclear Potential

The debate about the Iraqi nuclear program quickly brought worries about other countries to the fore. The United States, the former Soviet Union, the United Kingdom, France, Israel, China, and India all have proven nuclear stockpiles. In addition, U.S. intelligence believes that between fifteen and twenty other countries are trying to develop nuclear weapons.

Among the most worrisome was North Korea. The North Koreans signed the nonproliferation treaty, but refused to initial the nuclear safeguards accord requiring inspections of nuclear sites that went along with it. Since then North Korea has continued to refuse access for U.N. inspectors. Then, in the fall of 1991, announcements from Washington, Tokyo, and Seoul asserted that there was a growing body of evidence that the North Korean nuclear complex at Yongbyon was intended to produce nuclear weapons.

At about the same time, in a move clearly designed to put pressure on North Korea to permit inspectors, President Bush announced that the United States would withdraw all of its nuclear weapons based in Korea. The president of South Korea also declared that the United States would no longer be allowed to keep nuclear weapons in South Korea.

The government of North Korea—and independent observers in other countries—immediately pointed out that both moves were hollow gestures, since U.S. submarines armed with nuclear missiles continued to patrol Asian waters and U.S. long-range bombers were based in nearby Okinawa. In any case, five days after Bush's announcement, North Korea laid down two new conditions before it would permit inspection. First, South Korea must renounce protection of any kind by U.S. nuclear weapons, including the protection of American long-range bombers based outside Korea and missiles launched by submarines. Second, U.S. planes carrying nuclear weapons should be prohibited from flying over the Korean peninsula and ships carrying them prohibited from docking at Korean ports.

At the same time, China succeeded in stalling the international effort to press North Korea to accept inspectors on the grounds that dialogue was more proper than pressure.

During the preceding few years, the United States had reduced its troops stationed in South Korea to about 39,000 men, and another 3,000-man reduction had already been scheduled. But Defense Secretary Cheney, visiting Korea in late 1991, announced that the next reduction of 6,000, which was to begin at the end of 1992, would be delayed as a result of North Korea's unwillingness to accept inspectors.

In December 1991, North and South Korea signed a nonaggression treaty and at least opened the way for travel and commerce between the two. However, discussions on the question of nuclear weapons were postponed. Skeptics pointed out that reaching an agreement on the nuclear issue would be difficult while the North continued to refuse to permit international inspection and continued to work on building a reprocessing plant designed to produce weapons-grade plutonium.

Finally, North Korea did promise to sign the safeguards agreement and to permit inspection. However, many experts were skeptical. North Korea had built and was nearly ready to start up a giant plant to produce plutonium. Some specialists believe that the plant had already been operating at low levels in a testing program, and in the process may have produced—and hidden away—enough plutonium to produce several bombs.

Even more ominous was the fact that North Korea could easily freeze its nuclear program in return for benefits from the United States and the West and then unfreeze it at any time in the future that it pleased.

The North Korea experience also suggests still another ominous note. The evidence is, first, that North Korea got some help from the Soviet Union early on but that it ceased long ago; and, second, that it got no help at all from China. If so, North Korea was able to get to its rather advanced nuclear stage almost entirely on its own. If North Korea could do it, so can many other underdeveloped countries.

Pakistan and India

India successfully tested a nuclear weapon in 1974 and it is generally agreed that Pakistan has an advanced nuclear weapons building program. In early 1992 Western newspapers reported that India was stubbornly going ahead with building a nuclear arsenal. Indian officials refused to discuss the subject on the record, but off the record they argued that Pakistan had developed a nuclear and missile stockpile, that Pakistan continued to be aggressive toward India, and that since Pakistan has a smaller population and army than India, India must assume that in any war between the two Pakistan would use its nuclear weapons. India also pointed out that its neighbor to the north, China, had a significant stockpile of both nuclear warheads and the missiles to deliver them and refused to even discuss the matter. India concluded that it had no choice but to build a nuclear deterrent of its own. Pakistan, for its part, kept repeating that it was willing to talk to India about nuclear arms control anytime India wanted to—although many observers around the world were skeptical that Pakistan would actually agree to a nuclear ban.

Iran, Algeria, South Africa, Syria, and Libya

In early 1992, American newspapers also reported that U.S. intelligence had concluded that Iran intended to launch a program to develop nuclear weapons and that it had made a deal with China to purchase the necessary technology and equipment. Iran admitted that it had bought nuclear technology from China but insisted that it was for peaceful purposes.

Concern about Algeria's nuclear potential also burgeoned. It was well known in the West that the Chinese had supplied Algeria with a nuclear reactor some three years earlier. Many U.S. and other officials suspected that it was intended not for peaceful purposes but for research on nuclear weapons and eventually their production.

Many Western experts also believe that South Africa has secret installations designed to manufacture nuclear weapons.

Syria is also a worry. Like North Korea, Syria signed the nuclear nonproliferation treaty but did not sign the safeguards agreement providing for inspections. Although there is no concrete evidence that Syria is working on nuclear weapons, the possibility is clearly there.

There have been no reports that Libya has made any move toward building nuclear weapons, but it does have a large chemical weapons facility at Rabta. United States intelligence has reported that Libya is not only making chemical weapons—as much as one hundred tons, according to the CIA director—but that it is in the process of dispersing both weapons and equipment to hidden sites, with a strong possibility that a second, secret chemical weapons plant is already in operation.

Western newspapers reported that after watching the U.S. bombing of Iraq, Libyan officials voiced fears that Libya might also be subject to bombing. The officials also indicated that Libya intended to allay Western fears by inviting an inspection of the Rabta plant, although the press speculated that the invitation would probably come only after the equipment for making chemical weapons had been moved.

The Established Nuclear Powers

Finally there remains the question of what humankind would do about the countries that have long since developed both nuclear stockpiles and the missiles and bombers to deliver them—the United States, the Soviet Union, Great Britain, France, and China.

One problem is what happens to the vast nuclear complex operated by the former Soviet Union, especially the scientific and engineering personnel it employed. The Soviets had ten secret complexes devoted to the design and production of nuclear weapons. The American counterpart employs 100,000 people and costs $11 billion a year. No one knows what the Soviet effort cost, but estimates are that the complexes employed 900,000 people—including workers and guards as well as scientists and engineers. As many as 2,000 of these people know how to make nuclear weapons, and it is feared in the West that if some way cannot be found to use their talents for peaceful purposes, they might well be lured away by countries like Iraq, who want nuclear weapons of their own. Dr. William G. Sutcliffe of the Lawrence Livermore National Laboratory believes that $10 million a year would finance the work of 10,000 nuclear experts in the Russian commonwealth—work that could begin with cleaning up Russia's mountain of nuclear waste.[3] But most scientists are skeptical that the U.S. government can rid itself of its wariness of its former enemy or look that far into the future. So far the only step in this direction has been that the U.S. Congress authorized the administration to take $400 million out of the military budget to help the Soviet successor states destroy short-range nuclear missiles.

An especially puzzling problem was what the successor states will do with their longer-range missiles and warheads, including those capable of reaching the United States. Several of the Soviet republics that had joined the new commonwealth midwifed by Boris Yeltsin expressed doubts about permitting Russia to have sole control over the former Soviet Union's nuclear arsenal, and one, Kazakhstan, stated flatly that so long as Russia retained nuclear weapons, Kazakhstan would also do so. Apparently 104 SS-18 heavy intercontinental missiles are stationed in Kazakhstan, as well as long-range bombers.

As already mentioned, the United States and the Soviet Union agreed to eliminate their short-range nuclear missiles in Europe. In addition, the United States also plans substantial cuts in its nuclear weapons plants.

CHAPTER 15

The Search for Middle East Peace

Even more important than a satisfactory end to the war with Iraq was an overall peace for the Middle East—a peace that would end the Arab-Israeli struggle, the hostility between Iran and the Arab states, and the hostility among rival Arab states, such as that between Syria and Iraq.

On March 6, 1991, President Bush called for just such a wider peace, one for the whole of the Middle East that included a settlement between Israel and the Arabs.

Whether or not the two were connected, that same day the United States agreed to give Israel $650 million in aid, the amount that the Israelis claimed the war had cost them, including the damage inflicted by the Scud missiles.

To help enforce an overall peace in the Middle East, President Bush also proposed a continued U.S. military presence in the region. To implement the idea, Defense Secretary Cheney sought Arab permission to store arms in their countries and to station troops there. The plans called for storing the equipment for a full division in the area, for stationing an unspecified number of troops there permanently, and for bringing in other forces periodically to conduct maneuvers. On May 10 Cheney announced that his negotiations had been successful. But the conclusion turned out to be premature, and Saudi Arabia continued to voice objections to the idea of prepositioning equipment on its territory.

Also at about the same time, several American newspapers reported that the U.S. government was weighing a plan to ban some types of arms in the Middle East. The Israeli nuclear arsenal would be frozen at its existing level, the Arab states would be required to give up chemical weapons, and all Middle East states would be required to give up ballistic missiles with a range of more than ninety miles.

Within a few days, eight Arab countries endorsed Bush's proposals for seeking an overall Middle East peace, but at the same time they refused to ease their traditional anti-Israel stand.

For its part, Israel was reluctant. Finally, on March 28, the Bush administration offered a plan for talks that would be jointly sponsored by the United States and the Soviet Union. In response, Israel said that it would agree to a jointly sponsored conference if it was limited to a single session. However, the questions of when the conference would be held, the agenda, and whether or not Arab countries would be asked to participate were still unresolved.

Continuing his search for an overall peace, Secretary of State Baker visited both Israel and the various Arab countries. American newspapers reported that the Israelis did not like what they heard. Among the Arab countries, Saudi Arabia announced that it would not attend the proposed conference. On April 26 Secretary Baker accused Israel of failing to provide the needed response.

However, Saudi Arabia and five other Arab states announced on May 11 that they had agreed to participate in a peace conference with Israel. In addition, apparently as a result of U.S. pressure, Egypt, Saudi Arabia, Lebanon, and Jordan offered to end their boycott of Israel. The offers, however, were clearly linked to an end of Israel's building Jewish settlements in the occupied territories.

Then in mid-July Syria, in a letter to President Bush, signaled that it was willing to take part in direct negotiations with Israel as part of a regional peace conference. Although details of the letter were not revealed, Bush called it a "breakthrough." Some Middle East specialists speculated that Syria's sudden amiability was related to the turmoil in the Soviet Union. The Soviet Union had been Syria's major supporter, but Syria now stood alone.

Israel, however, announced that it would not offer any concessions to match those made by Syria. What Israel wanted was direct, bilateral negotiations, not a conference. The United States, on the other hand, wanted not only a conference with as many of the various players in the Middle East struggle as possible, but also a U.N. observer and an agreement that the conference would reconvene periodically. Israel feared that the United States might have made a secret deal with Syria about the Golan Heights—or, at the least, that the United States had fallen into a Syrian trap. The Israelis insisted that no Palestinians from East Jerusalem or with any connection to the PLO be allowed to attend. Prime Minister Yitzhak Shamir also made it clear that Israel would make no territorial concessions whatsoever.

In the wake of these announcements, newspaper reports said that the United States had assured Syria that it had not recognized the legality of the Israeli occupation of the Golan Heights and that it had assured Israel that it would support Israel's position on excluding the PLO from any talks.

In any case, on August 1 Israel gave the United States a "conditional yes" on the talks. The conditions principally concerned the exclusion of the PLO, Palestinians living in East Jerusalem, which Israel claimed as its own, and Palestinians living outside the territories occupied by Israel; that is, Israel would not agree to let any Palestinians attend the conference who were not citizens of Israel or living in Israeli-occupied territory.

For its part, the PLO seemed willing to compromise; for example, a PLO spokesperson said that the PLO would be represented by Palestinians in the Jordanian delegation who were citizens of Jordan. The very next day, however, another PLO representative backed off, saying that the compromise suggested was a personal opinion and not that of the PLO. A few days later, Yassir Arafat, the PLO chairman, said that the PLO would insist on naming the Palestinian delegates and that it would also insist that Israel agree in advance to trade land for peace.

In the meantime, Israel had asked the United States for $10 billion in housing loan guarantees to help resettle Jewish immigrants from the Soviet Union. Since 1967, United States aid had totaled $77 billion, of which about three-quarters had been outright grants and one-quarter loans. This $10 billion would be a loan.

In what Israel and Americans supporting Israel regarded as a bid to intimidate Israel during the peace conference, the Bush administration asked Congress to postpone considering the request until *after* the conference, which was planned for October. Bush threatened a veto if his request was not honored, and he complained bitterly that "powerful political forces" were working against him, including "something like a thousand lobbyists." "I've worn out the telephone," he said, and described himself as "one lonely little guy down here" facing a hostile horde. What the Israelis forget, Bush said, is that "American men and women in uniform risked their lives to defend Israelis in the face of Iraqi Scud missiles." In any case, Congress agreed to postpone the loan.

The Israelis reacted angrily. One Israeli spokesperson called linking the peace conference to humanitarian aid to help resettlement "a dangerous precedent." The Israelis were particularly outraged by Bush's comment about Americans risking their lives to defend Israel from the Scud attacks. What Bush conveniently forgot, they said, was that Israel absorbed missile attacks without retaliating in order to keep the coalition from breaking apart. "Look how cynical he is and how he pays us back," Eliakim Haetzni, a member of the Israeli parliament, said to American reporters. Another member of parliament called Bush an "anti-Semite and a liar" and accused him of "cheap demagoguery."

Some of the trouble between Israel and the United States stemmed from the difficult personal relations between Shamir and Bush. This difficulty, according to the critics, stemmed in turn from Bush's reliance on his personal relations with foreign leaders rather than on the State Department and the corps of U.S. ambassadors as the basis of the administration's foreign policy. During their very first meeting in April 1989, when Bush complained about the settlements in the occupied territories, Shamir replied that the settlements would not be a problem. Shamir apparently meant that if Israel really had an Arab partner for peace talks, the settlements would not be an obstacle. But Bush thought Shamir meant that he would stop or slow down the settlements immediately. When Shamir returned to Israel, however, the rate of establishing settlements was actually stepped up, and "the seeds of Mr. Bush's personal wrath with Mr. Shamir were firmly planted."[1]

For his part Shamir, in "a defiant gesture," vowed to continue to build more settlements in the occupied territories.

On September 17 the Bush administration made explicit what everyone had assumed: that the $10 billion loan for housing Soviet Jewish immigrants would not be granted unless Israel agreed to a freeze on Jewish settlements in the occupied territories. The problem—for both Israel and the Arab states—was that about 350,000 Soviet Jews, many from the Baltic states, had come to Israel in the preceding two years, and as many as a million more were expected in the next few years. The American government had long disapproved of settlements in the occupied territories, but this was the first administration to link the issue to American aid.

Then, on September 23, in an apparent attempt to offer Israel some sort of olive branch, Bush made a speech to the U.N. calling for the repeal of the 1975 U.N. resolution that described Zionism as "a form of racism and racial discrimination." On December 16, 1991, the U.N. did in fact do so.

In any case, Secretary of State Baker came to an agreement with the Israeli government to put to one side for a time the problem about the loan. Apparently, the American Jewish lobby convinced the Israeli government that the opposition on Capitol Hill to a loan at this particular time was just too great and that the issue should be postponed for a period of four months, as Bush wanted.

At about the same time, Israeli jets flew a spy mission over Iraq. Fearful that such flights would jeopardize its appeal for a peace conference, the United States expressed its annoyance, pointing out that such acts imperiled the good relations between Israel and the United States.

Demonstrating that the Israeli people were far from united on a hard-line stance, Shimon Peres, the leader of the Labour party, urged a halt to settling Soviet Jews on the West Bank. He also argued that there could be no long-lasting peace in the Middle East unless Israel gave up some of the lands it had seized in the 1967 war.

Structure of the Peace Conference

Secretary of State Baker proposed that the peace conference be comprised of three separate sets of talks. The first would be a short opening session chaired by the United States and the Soviet Union. It would be short and largely ceremonial, designed to satisfy the Arab desire that the talks take place under a wide international umbrella. The second set of talks would be bilateral and direct between Israel and Syria, Israel and Lebanon, and Israel and a joint Jordanian-Palestinian delegation. The third set of talks would again be multilateral, to discuss regional problems, such as water rights, economic development, and arms control. Just as the first set of talks was bait for the Arab states, these regional talks were designed as bait for Israel, which had never had diplomatic relations with some of the Arab states, such as Saudi Arabia.

Syria, however, announced that it would not attend the third set of talks unless Israel promised in advance to return the Golan Heights, captured by Israel in the 1967 war and occupied by the Israelis ever since. Throughout the negotiations, the return of the Golan Heights remained Syria's first and foremost goal.

In an attempt to put pressure on Israel to agree to the talks, Boris D. Pankin, the Soviet foreign minister, met with Israeli officials. However, Pankin did not offer what Israel wanted most from the Soviets: the restoration of diplomatic relations that had been broken during the 1967 war.

Secretary of State Baker also met with Israeli officials at about the same time—and also failed to end their doubts about attending the talks. What Israel feared most was that it would end up negotiating directly with the PLO, which would constitute de facto recognition.

Baker's negotiations were conducted in what was a sort of diplomatic charade. He would talk to Palestinians from the West Bank and the Gaza Strip who had no formal links to the PLO. These were the Palestinians whom Israel wanted him to talk with, since they were under Israeli control. But before these Palestinians would agree to anything, they would talk to the leaders of the PLO—Arafat and the others. Only after having obtained the PLO's concurrence would these Palestinians agree to any of Baker's proposals.

As the Western press reported, all this meant that, as a practical matter, Shamir had two choices. One was to turn a blind eye to the fact that Israel was in fact negotiating with the PLO, if only tacitly. The second was to abandon the entire process, and the opportunity of opening negotiations with the Arab states, which Israel had so long sought. An important element for the Israelis was that such negotiations would be a tacit recognition of the state of Israel.

The United States and the Soviet Union then seized the initiative by inviting Israel and the Arab states to a peace conference to be held in Madrid on October 30.

As further bait for Israel, the Soviet Union offered to restore full diplomatic relations, which had been broken off twenty-four years earlier. Israel promptly agreed.

On October 20 the Israeli cabinet voted to accept the invitation to the conference in Madrid.

Some forty-eight hours later, the Palestinians named their fourteen delegates. All met the Israeli criteria: None of the delegates were from Jerusalem and none had any formal ties to the PLO. Still the Israelis criticized the choices, saying that the Palestinian team had a "blatant PLO cast" to it.

For his part, Arafat said that since any Palestinian anywhere shared the aims of the PLO, it was true that the Palestinian team spoke for the PLO. Arafat went on to say that because of this unity among Palestinians, the PLO's leadership would not interfere in the negotiations at Madrid. Arafat's position was widely interpreted as an attempt to avoid giving Israel an excuse for pulling out of the talks.

At the same time, the PLO named a "liaison group" consisting of six PLO members. Although none of this PLO group would attend the meetings, they would be present in Madrid to act as advisers to the Palestinians who did attend. Predictably, Israel was most unhappy at the surprise announcement.

In spite of this development, Prime Minister Shamir took an optimistic line in his public statements, saying that the Madrid talks offered hope for a significant change in the Middle East. At the same time, the Israeli delegation was top-heavy with hard-liners. Shamir also announced that he would lead the Israeli delegation himself —an announcement that many observers interpreted as a sign that Israel was taking care that the conference would be hobbled.

For its part, the United States announced that it hoped that the Madrid conference would create a new atmosphere in the Middle East. Accordingly, the United States would not push a plan of its own but would remain on the sidelines.

The principal anxiety of the Israeli government was clearly to avoid the blame if the conference failed—a result that the Israeli government feared one day and ardently desired the next. The right wing in the Israeli government hoped that the Madrid conference would collapse. The rest of the government saw the conference as a trap—a chance for the United States and the Arabs to gang up on Israel and force territorial concessions.

As for the Palestinians, most of those living in Israel who were not formal members of the PLO seemed to believe that carving a separate Palestinian state out of the territories occupied by Israel was beyond the realm of possibility. To them the pragmatic approach seemed to be to work for a degree of autonomy within the state of Israel.

The truth of the matter was that for the Palestinians—a people without a state—a seat at the table was itself a victory.

The Madrid conference opened with "salvos of intransigent oratory from both sides." The Arabs demanded that Israel immediately cease settling Soviet Jews in the occupied territories and agree to the return of those territories. Israel, in turn, demanded that the Arabs acknowledge Israel's right to exist. Each accused the other of deception, brutality, treachery, and aggression.

The one encouraging note was that even when the Palestinians identified themselves with the PLO, the Israeli delegation did not walk out.

The first of the follow-on, one-on-one meetings in Madrid was between the Israelis and the Palestinians. To the surprise of some observers, both sides agreed to discuss self-rule for the West Bank and the Gaza Strip. Everyone agreed that these talks between the Palestinians and the Israelis went well.

At first Syria took a very tough stand, balking at further talks. Then it relaxed its position and came to the table—although several hours late. However, the face-to-face talks between Syria and Israel got nowhere.

In spite of all the rhetoric on both sides, the overall judgment was that the Madrid talks did make progress. The Palestinians reversed their thirteen-year-old rejection of autonomy within the Jewish state, which had been called for years before in the Camp David accords, consenting to talks for at least an *interim* self-government.

Probably because of this, Arafat and the PLO lost ground to the "local" Palestinians—those living in Israel or Israeli-occupied territory. The local Palestinians, in fact, seemed to be becoming an alternative to the PLO. In an election in the Gaza Strip at about the same time, the local Palestinians gained significantly, which suggested that the Palestinian people had begun to swing away from hard-line Islamic fundamentalists toward more moderate groups.

However, the Madrid talks adjourned with uncertain prospects for the next phase.

The first question was where the next round of talks should be held. Syria and some of the other Arab states wanted the follow-on talks to be in Madrid, where the aura of great-power sponsorship would linger on. Israel, however, wanted the next round of talks in the Middle East, alternating between a site in Israel and a site in one of the Arab states. The idea was that this would show that Israel's existence had at least symbolically been recognized.

The Palestinians appeared to split with Syria over this question of where the next round of talks should take place. However, Syria permitted the PLO to reopen its office in Damascus, ending a ten-year rift between the two.

Also, immediately after the Madrid meetings, Israel opened a new settlement for Soviet Jews in the Golan Heights. Secretary of State Baker was obviously upset, and publicly chided Israel for actions that were not likely "to build the kind of climate that would serve the cause of peace."

However, the Israeli Labour party took a decidedly dovish stand. It abandoned its long-standing objection to direct negotiations with the PLO and called for compromise on territorial questions, such as the Golan Heights.

Then, in a surprise move that seemed to many to be a sort of ultimatum, the United States invited Israel and the Arab states to hold the next series of talks in Washington, to begin on Wednesday, December 4.

Shamir voiced Israel's strong irritation. What made Shamir particularly angry was that the United States issued the invitation for talks in Washington just before Shamir met with President Bush, and he made no secret of the fact that he regarded it as an insult. In addition, Shamir thought that this action by the United States suggested to the Arabs that at any time that the talks stalled, the United States would intervene, which encouraged the Arabs to be intransigent.

Israel was also annoyed that the United States' invitation included a series of specific suggestions on how some of the issues could be solved.

The Palestinians also saw a problem with the Washington site. For its part, Syria indicated that it would go along only if Israel agreed beforehand to surrender territory, which everyone understood to mean the Golan Heights.

After some internal agonizing, the Israeli government announced that it would go to Washington for the talks, but at its own pace and not necessarily when the United States leaders said so. The implication was that Israel regarded any future talks as being one-on-one, with only an occasional hand from the United States. Israel said that its delegation would arrive in Washington not on December 4, as the United States' invitation specified, but on December 9. It also insisted that these first talks would be preliminary, lasting for only a day or two. The talks should then be moved to a site or sites in the Middle East.

In response, Syria, Lebanon, Jordan, and the Palestinians all agreed to meet in Washington on the date specified by the United States. Syria, in particular, made a point of accusing Israel of seeking to sabotage the peace talks entirely.

The Syrian, Lebanese, Jordanian, and Palestinian negotiators arrived at the State Department in Washington at the appointed day and time, but the Israelis never showed up. The Israelis, to demonstrate their independence of the United States, said that they would be ready to meet on December 9. But the Palestinians and Jordanians said that

December 9 was not acceptable, since it was the fourth anniversary of the *Intifada,* the Palestinian uprising, and because they did not want to give in to Israeli dictates. The U.S. government in private expressed its disgust at the "petty, juvenile games" that both sides were playing.

The second round of talks began on December 10 with a rehash of previous arguments. The highest hopes were held for the talks between the Israeli team and the Jordanian-Palestinian team. The Palestinians insisted on negotiating with the Israelis separately from the Jordanians. But the Israeli delegation insisted that the talks be held with the Israelis on one side of the table and the Jordanians and Palestinians on the other. Both sides refused to enter the conference room until the seating question was settled. So the chief delegates for Israel, Jordan, and Palestine discussed the matter for three hours while seated on a couch in the hallway. The rest of the delegates from both sides milled around the hallway avoiding each other until the Israeli ambassador to the United States suggested to one of the Palestinian delegates that the one thing both sides could easily agree on was that the coffee supplied by the State Department was terrible. After that the delegates began to mix, although everyone remained in the hallway. The second day, the same thing happened: the chief negotiators sat on a couch discussing seating arrangements while the rest of the delegates milled around in the hall. In meetings with the press, the Israelis repeated their demand that the next meetings take place in the Middle East, where the press could be better controlled, rather than in Washington, and the Palestinians reported the latest Israeli moves against Palestinians on the West Bank.

In the meantime, talks between the Israelis and the Syrians and the Israelis and the Lebanese continued.

The Palestinians proposed two compromises on December 16, but the Israelis would have none of it. The Israelis concentrated on seeing that any subsequent meetings would be held in the Middle East and resisted engaging in any substantive talks until that meeting.

The talks broke up two days later with no real progress made on any of the other goals that the various parties sought. The goal of the Lebanese and Syrians had been to trade their lands now occupied by Israel—Syria's Golan Heights and Lebanon's territory that Israel occupied as a security zone—for peace. The Israelis wanted the Arabs to accept Israel's existence, to provide ironclad security guarantees, and to withdraw forty thousand Syrian troops from Lebanon. The Palestinians wanted self-government within Israel and an immediate freeze on Jewish settlements in the West Bank, the Gaza Strip, and East Jerusalem, which Israel categorically refused. Jordan apparently wanted peace and an end to the Palestinian problem, which it saw as a long-term threat to its own existence.

On December 22 Israel agreed that the next talks would be held in Washington, to begin on January 7.

Before the talks could begin, however, Israel announced it would expel from the occupied territories twelve Palestinians accused of inciting terrorism. The Arab countries responded by refusing to attend the talks until after the U.N. Security Council passed a resolution condemning the Israeli action. The Muslim sabbath and the Jewish day of rest postponed the meetings two more days, so the talks did not begin until January 13.

The seating dispute that had kept everyone in the hallway for six days at the last meeting was solved by having the Israeli, Palestinian, and Jordanian delegations meet together for about half an hour and then having the Israelis meet separately with the Palestinians, but with two Jordanians present.

The Israeli delegation had announced before this series of talks began that it would stay only until January 15. The reason was apparently that Israel anticipated trouble from the two right-wing parties whose five seats in parliament gave Shamir his two-seat majority. These two parties had threatened to resign if the Shamir government offered even to discuss Palestinian self-rule in the Gaza Strip and the occupied West Bank.

The talks between the Israelis and the Palestinians deadlocked immediately over the agenda. The same thing happened in the talks between the Israelis and the Syrians. The Israelis refused to discuss exchanging all or part of the Golan Heights for peace unless Syria recognized Israel; the Syrians refused to do anything unless Israel committed itself to withdrawing in advance. The talks with the Lebanese met the same obstacles. The only talks that were encouraging were those between Israel and Jordan, mainly because Jordan said that if the peace talks were successful, it was prepared to establish diplomatic relations with Israel.

By the end of this third round of talks, the disagreements between the Israelis, the Palestinians, and the Jordanians about the shape of the table had been resolved, but there was no agreement about a future agenda for talks. The most encouraging development was that the Palestinians submitted a plan for self-rule in the West Bank and the Gaza Strip and the Israelis agreed at least to discuss it. Since both sides had refused any consideration of such a plan in the past, both actions marked a significant step forward.

But no progress was made in either the Israeli-Syrian talks or the Israeli-Lebanese talks. What was worse was that in all the talks, the exchanges were increasingly bitter—as were each side's attacks on the other in their press briefings.

The talks resumed in Moscow on January 29, 1992, to discuss broad regional issues. No major decisions were made, nor was there a date and place specified for the next meeting.

What seemed most likely at the time of this writing was that no progress at all would be made until the political crisis in Israel caused by the resignation of the right-wing parties from the coalition was solved. Shamir's government no longer commanded a majority and is vulnerable to a no-confidence motion. Although the next election is not scheduled until November 1992, it could be moved up. But unless either the Labour party, headed by Shimon Peres, or Shamir's Likud party wins a substantial majority, progress toward an overall peace in the Middle East is likely to be very, very slow—if it can be achieved at all.

=CHAPTER 16=

The Political Consequences of the Gulf War

When Saddam Hussein invaded and conquered Kuwait, almost all the world—the Arab countries, Israel, the countries of the industrialized world, and the developing countries of the Third World—seemed to agree that such blatant aggression was unacceptable. There was no question as to whether or not something should be done about it, but *what* that something should be was another matter entirely.

The Goals Achieved by the Gulf War

As discussed earlier, President Bush had several alternatives—before and after sending American forces to the Gulf—to making the struggle an American war. Instead of taking any of these alternative roads, President Bush chose war, a war in which American forces played the major role. The results were mixed. Some of the goals stated by the United States and its allies were clearly achieved, some were just as clearly not achieved, and two remain uncertain.

The clear accomplishments were two: Iraq was forced to withdraw from Kuwait, and Iraq's facilities for making chemical and biological weapons were severely damaged, if not destroyed. The U.N. teams apparently accomplished what the bombs left unfinished.

Three goals were either *not* achieved or not *fully* achieved: Saddam Hussein not only remained the head of Iraq, but his position seemed to have been strengthened; the hard-core elite of Iraq's military—the Republican Guard and its armor—was damaged, but remained essentially intact; and Iraq retained a considerable proportion of its helicopter gunships.

Finally there were two goals whose status remained uncertain: The best of Iraq's jet warplanes were flown to Iran, and only time would tell if they would be returned to Iraq, and it remained uncertain whether or not Iraq's potential for making nuclear weapons at some time in the future had been eliminated. Iraq's single most vital asset for building nuclear weapons—the scientists and engineers who have the necessary knowledge—was unharmed. Israel destroyed Iraq's only nuclear reactor in a 1981 bombing raid, but Iraq developed an even more impressive capability in just ten years. In mid-January 1992, CIA director Robert M. Gates testified before Congress that Iraq could rebuild its nuclear, chemical, and biological weapons and ballistic missile installations within a relatively few years.

Only two developments could guarantee that Iraq could not do so. The first would be if the United States and its allies reopened the war, repeated their victory, and then subjected Iraq to a military occupation—all of which seemed to be highly unlikely. The second would be if the international community established some sort of worldwide international control of nuclear facilities.

Iraqi Casualties

The Bush administration approached the question of Iraqi casualties with official disinterest, according to the American press. United States intelligence agencies said that they had simply not addressed the issue. So just how many casualties Iraq suffered still remains a mystery.

On June 4, 1991, the Defense Department in a report to Congress estimated that 100,000 Iraqi soldiers were killed and 300,000 were wounded. However, the report was filled with qualifications. Complaining of a serious lack of information, the report said that the actual number could be 50 percent greater or 50 percent less.

General Schwarzkopf's headquarters arrived at a figure of 100,000 dead Iraqi soldiers, and Schwarzkopf used this figure when testifying to Congress. In answers to reporters, however, Schwarzkopf would say only that Iraq suffered a "very, very large number of dead."

Some intelligence people questioned both the Pentagon and Central Command estimates. They pointed out that if the dead numbered 100,000, the number of wounded should be several times that figure. Yet there is no evidence so far of such massive numbers of wounded. Unofficially, those same officers estimated that the number of dead Iraqi soldiers was between 25,000 and 50,000. The counterargument is that for armies in retreat, the ratio of dead to wounded is usually much higher than for armies that are attacking or defending. If so, the number of wounded to be expected from a death toll of 100,000 could be anywhere between 100,000 and 300,000.

Les Aspin, chairman of the House Armed Services Committee, estimated that 65,000 Iraqi soldiers were killed. Colonel Trevor Dupuy, a retired army officer who writes extensively on military affairs, estimated that Iraq suffered between 100,000 and 150,000 military casualties, of whom about one-third were killed.

Military sources in Saudi Arabia believe that Iraq suffered 85,000 to 100,000 military killed. Other Saudi sources think these figures are much too low.

Iraqi Civilian Casualties

There are simply no authoritative estimates on total Iraqi civilian casualties. The Iraqi government published casualty reports for specific incidents, such as the bombing of the Al-Amiriya air raid shelter in Baghdad that the Allied command claimed was being used as a military communications center. But it has not published any figures for the entire war. The environmental activist organization Greenpeace estimated that the civilians killed numbered between 5,000 and 15,000. Gary Sick, an authority on the Middle East who worked on the National Security Council staff during the Carter administration, "guessed" that no fewer than 1,500 civilians were killed.

Several observers also pointed out that the number of civilians killed and wounded by bombs and shells would probably be only the tip of the iceberg. The bombing destroyed the water purification plants, and U.N. public health authorities reported that cholera, typhoid, and gastroenteritis probably claimed tens of thousands more lives. The health authorities expected that the coming summer heat would multiply the 1991 figures horrendously. Greenpeace estimated the total number of Iraqi civilians dead from war-related diseases rather than from bombs and shells at between 70,000 and 85,000.

The very first wave of bombers on the night of January 17 used a new weapon against Iraq's electrical generating plants. It consisted of thousands of metallic filaments—very fine wire the size of a human hair—that were dropped on key points in Iraq's electrical network, causing short circuits throughout the plants and the electricity distribution system. This was followed by precision strikes on power plants. In April 1991, 80 percent of the power grid was still out. A Harvard University medical team that visited Baghdad immediately after the war said that the collapse of the electrical generating capacity had been a crucial factor in what had become a "public health catastrophe." The team predicted tens of thousands of war-related deaths by the end of the year—a prediction that the Bush administration did not dispute.

"Without electricity," the report said, "hospitals cannot function, perishable medicines spoil, water cannot be purified and raw sewage cannot be processed."

Because of the lack of generating capacity, daily blackouts lasting eight hours were required. This caused water to be recontaminated and hampered the ability of hospitals to operate, because of the loss of medicines through lack of refrigeration.

Inflation put the price of baby formula out of reach of the mass of the people. This, plus the closing of local clinics and the lack of transport to places where sick babies could be treated, led the U.N. team to expect a very high infant mortality rate for a long time to come.

Commenting on the death rate among Iraqi children, a Palestinian Arab repeated that no one had yet offered a satisfactory explanation of why it was necessary to bomb the electrical generating plants and water purification plants in Iraq. He argued that the bombing of facilities of that kind did not contribute to military victory but only to civilian deaths, mainly children. "You Americans court-martialed Lt. Calley for killing Vietnamese women and children at My Lai. But you let a president order the deaths of thousands of Iraqi women and children without a second thought. Just how do Americans define a war crime?"[1]

To all this must be added the casualties from illness and malnutrition among the refugees—Kurds, Shiites, and many thousands of other Iraqis who had either been bombed out of their homes or had fled to avoid the fighting. The total according to BBC estimates was about three million. A U.N. team reported that about 9,000 civilian homes were destroyed by Allied bombing, including 2,500 in Baghdad and 1,900 in Basra, and that as a result about 72,000 people were homeless.*

---

*A distinction is usually made between refugees and people *displaced* by a war. The *New York Times* (June 16, 1991: 3) estimated that a total of five million people had been displaced by the war, including people from Iran, Kuwait, Yemen, Sudan, Egypt, Jorday, Syria, Pakistan, India, Sri Lanka, Bangladesh, Vietnam, and the Philippines.

The total civilian dead, counting both those killed by bombs and shells and those killed by disease and malnutrition, seems likely to come very close to the total military dead—that is, about 100,000. Thus the total Iraqi dead, both military and civilian, was probably about 200,000 out of a population of 18 million. If the same percentage of Americans died as the result of a war, the total would be about 2.8 million.

Physical Damage

A survey conducted by the U.N. in late March 1991 called the war damage in Iraq "near-apocalyptic." In the words of the report, "Iraq has, for some time to come, been relegated to a pre-industrial age, but with all the disabilities of post-industrial dependency on an intensive use of energy and technology."

The authors of the book *Iraq Since 1958* estimated during a radio interview that the physical damage to Iraq was about $100 billion.[2] The news media reported that the CIA, on the other hand, estimated the repair bill at $30 billion, to which has to be added the $8 billion that Iraq owes each year on its external debt of $80 billion plus whatever it has to pay in war reparations to Kuwait. According to the same reports, other U.S. officials concluded that it would take Iraq years to rebuild. They said that still-classified studies had found lasting economic harm, with the total damage still unclear.

In April 1991 reporters visiting Iraq said that economic hardship was widespread. Among ordinary people, the tendency was to blame the United States more than Saddam Hussein for their troubles. The feeling was that Bush was punishing the people of Iraq for what Hussein had done. They were particularly upset that the United States had destroyed the country's electrical generating and telephone systems, some of which served only local needs. Their feeling was that most of the bombing had no military purpose but was designed to demoralize the Iraqi people.

In late June the Iraqi minister of industry said that as a result of the bombing, Iraq's electrical generating industry was in a state of crisis. He admitted that Iraq had been able to restore only a third of its prewar capacity. Equipment failures and blackouts were consuming the available supply of spare parts and, since they were running out of spare parts, the amount of electricity generated would decline to less than a third of prewar levels in the months ahead. Furthermore, all six of the plants that produced chlorine to purify water for drinking were put out of production by the bombing, and only one offered any hope of being repairable any time soon. As a result, Iraq was also down to about one month's supply of chlorine.

"War Is Politics" and "Too Important to Be Left to Generals"

In the Korean War, President Truman forbade any bombing of the Chinese supply lines north of the Yalu River, in spite of the Chinese intervention. In the Vietnam War, President Johnson went over the list of targets selected for bombing each day, approving some and scratching out others. Many in the military, especially in the air force, resented Truman's decision as forcing the military to fight with one hand tied behind its back and Johnson's as unwarranted nitpicking. Others, however, recalled Clausewitz's dictum that war is an extension of politics by other means and Georges Clemenceau's remark that war is too important to be left to generals. They thought that both Truman's and Johnson's interventions were proper exercises of political responsibility. George Bush, on the other hand, gave the military carte blanche.

Understandably, when there is any doubt about whether or not to bomb a particular target, the military usually opts to bomb. If there is any possibility at all that the target contributes to the enemy's war effort, military leaders feel an obligation to knock it out if possible—for the perfectly understandable reason that they are anxious to keep casualties among their own forces to an absolute minimum. The long-term political consequences of a decision to bomb particular targets are not the responsibility of military leaders, nor is the military equipped to make such judgments by either training or experience.

However, many in the American military question whether demolishing Iraq's electrical generating capacity, its water purification systems, and its sewage systems made any useful contribution to winning the war. On the other hand, the number of civilian deaths caused by bombing these particular installations was large—especially among children—and continued long after the war was over. Not just the Iraqi people but almost all Arabs and many among Third World peoples regard hitting these particular targets as just one more illustration of the West's wanton disregard for Arab and Third World life. In any case, there is little question that Bush's failure to provide the kind of supervision that Truman did in Korea and Johnson did in Vietnam brought political consequences that will haunt the United States for a long, long time.

The Question of Continuing Sanctions

The U.N. report mentioned above pointed out that Iraq normally imports about three-fourths of its food supply, especially wheat, and recommended that the ban on food and other supplies be lifted immediately to avoid "imminent catastrophe." In response, the U.N. lifted the ban on food and medicine, but the situation remained unchanged. The trouble was that Iraq had no way of paying for imports of any kind. The Western countries—including the United States, Britain, and Switzerland—where most of Iraq's assets remained frozen, refused to release the funds.

In mid-April 1991 Iraq asked the U.N. committee monitoring sanctions to permit it to sell $1 billion in oil to buy food and medicine, but the request was denied. Iraq later sought permission to sell $2.4 billion worth of oil so it could buy food. A White House official said that if the U.N. Security Council approved the request, the United States would do all it could to prevent Saddam Hussein from distributing the food in a way that would strengthen his political base.

The Remaining Sanctions

The U.N. specified that before the rest of the economic sanctions would be lifted, Iraq must satisfy two U.N. demands. First, it must dismantle its chemical and biological warfare facilities, its ballistic missile stockpile, and the facilities that gave it a potential for developing nuclear weapons. Second, it must agree to use 30 percent of its future oil revenues to pay reparations to Kuwait, an increase of 5 percent over the 25 percent payments previously called for by the U.N. Iraq claimed that it was complying with the military conditions, but it objected to the condition about committing such a high proportion of its future oil revenues to pay reparations.

On March 20, 1991, President Bush went further, stating that the United States would oppose lifting sanctions until Hussein no longer remained in power. Since the power to lift sanctions rested with the U.N. Security Council and since the United States had a veto power in the Council, sanctions would presumably remain until Saddam Hussein was no longer in power, President Bush changed his mind, or Bush was no longer president.

Clearly, continuing the sanctions would prevent Iraq from recovering from the war damage. Estimates were that $1.5 billion worth of equipment from abroad was needed to get the oil industry back in working order. Sanctions prevented Iraq from buying the necessary parts.

Iraq's telecommunications system would have to be completely rebuilt. Again, it could not be done without foreign equipment and experts, which continued sanctions prevented.

Both the highway and rail system were badly damaged. About forty major bridges across the Tigris and Euphrates rivers have to be replaced and another ten bridges that were seriously damaged repaired. All these repairs would require imports that sanctions prevented.

The *New York Times,* in a June 9, 1991, story entitled "Sanctions on Iraq Exact a High Price From Poor," said that sanctions had helped force Iraq to make a deal with the Kurds, to promise a kind of democracy for its people, and to show a readiness to comply with U.N. demands for the destruction of its chemical and biological warfare plants and its potential for making nuclear weapons. But sanctions, the *Times* argued, had had no effect on Hussein's power and position. The question, then, was whether continuing the sanctions would persuade the Iraqi elite to do something about Hussein, or whether continued sanctions would do only what they had done so far—bring yet more hardship to the poor while causing only modest inconvenience to the rich and powerful.

Iraq's ration system gave the poor a minimum amount of food and the other necessities of life. But the private market was supplied by trucks from Jordan and by smugglers operating from Turkey, Iran, and Syria, and the rich could get almost anything they wanted by paying the high prices demanded.

In the late spring of 1991 the CIA estimated that if sanctions were lifted Iraq could, by the end of the summer, export one million barrels of oil a day, about a third of the prewar level. If Iraq could find $1.5 billion to spend on repairs to its oil facilities, by the end of 1992 this figure could be raised to 2.7 million barrels a day.

Environmental Costs

No overall estimate has yet been made of the war's environmental costs. The environmental and ecological damage caused by Iraq's releasing millions of gallons of Kuwaiti crude oil into the Gulf was local. The remaining concern about the environment was what the damage would be from the 650 Kuwaiti oil wells that were burning when the war ended (an additional 99 wells had been damaged). By August 1991, only 200 of these wells had been successfully capped; the remaining fires were burning about six million barrels of oil a day. At the time, it was estimated that it might be two more years before the remaining fires could be brought under control. However, twenty-seven fire-fighting teams— a total of ten thousand workers from thirty-four countries with 125,000 tons of heavy equipment—made better progress than expected, and the last fire was put out on November 6, 1991.

Before the war Kuwait's OPEC quota was 1.5 million barrels a day, and it often pumped more. Before the last fire was put out, Kuwait was pumping 320,000 barrels a day and expected to be pumping 800,000 barrels a day by the middle of 1992 and 2,000,000 barrels a day by the end of 1993.

The Kuwaiti oil ministry estimated that the total loss of oil was $12 billion, equal to approximately six hundred million barrels or the equivalent of three months' worth of worldwide consumption. The total cost of the operation to put out the fires was between $1.5 billion and $2.2 billion. In the end the fires consumed about 3 percent of Kuwait's oil reserves.

The vast majority of the fires were set by retreating Iraqi troops in an attempt to hamper Allied military operations or simply as an act of cruelty against Kuwait. However, a report in the magazine *Scientific American* said that the Allied bombing of refineries and oil reserves in Iraq had started fires that created smoke clouds comparable to those in Kuwait, and any U.S. comment on the environmental effects of fires was "gagged" by order of the White House.[3]

New York Times columnist Tom Wicker believes that the United States shares another kind of blame for the fires, although an indirect one. Hussein set the fires, Wicker wrote, and he was responsible for this threat to the environment. "He had plainly warned that he would do it, however; so the U.S., by its decision to launch the war anyway rather than rely on non-combat pressures, bears some responsibility."[4]

Whatever the case, a number of scientific studies have concluded that the effects of the oil fires will largely be confined to the Gulf region.[5] The reason is apparently that the fires' strong, hot updraft formed large cumulus clouds, and these clouds "scavenged" the soot particles from the atmosphere, usually depositing them locally in the form of rain.

The Political Costs of the War

On the question of the longer-range accomplishments of the Gulf War, many observers were skeptical. An "Andy Warhol War" was how Professor John Shy of Michigan described it. "A quarter-hour of fame and maximum attention and, in retrospect, horrendous losses of life on the other side, but remarkably trivial in its consequences otherwise." Another professor, Alan Brinkley of Columbia University, said, "The threats we face now aren't primarily military threats, they're economic ones. In the long run, this wasn't the kind of thing that could transform America's political outlook. That's why it just seems to be vanishing into the mist."

Along the same lines, in both the United States and among its allies, a number of observers have wondered aloud how a military victory in the Middle East, achieved with American troops, could be turned into a political victory—a stable Middle East in which all can live in peace, including Israel. The answer would have to wait at least until the last of the many meetings of the peace conference that Secretary Baker labored so long and so hard to bring about. But among skeptics the suspicion was that the unbelievable destruction caused by the bombing, the extensive attacks on targets that were not directly related to the military situation, the use of American troops rather than having Arabs as the cutting edge of the attack, the apparent indifference in the West to the loss of Arab life—all would militate against efforts to bring lasting peace to the Middle East. The American intervention with its seemingly wanton killing, they speculated, was likely to bring even more hatred and violence for decades to come.

What was just as bothersome to many of the critics of the war in the Persian Gulf was that the United States was spending its time, attention, and treasure on petty little Middle East dictators, while the Soviet Union had 27,000 nuclear warheads and the missiles to deliver about 10,000 of them to the American homeland. The Soviet Union was in turmoil. Another Stalin—or even a madman—might seize power. Imagine a madman, these critics said, with control of 10,000 nuclear warheads and the missiles to deliver them!

Arab Reaction

It seems obvious from the reactions described earlier that Sunni Muslims in Iraq tend to blame the United States rather than Saddam Hussein for what happened to them. As described above, the Kurds and Shiites continued to fear and dislike Hussein. But because they felt that President Bush encouraged them to rebel and then failed to give them the support they expected, they were also bitter toward the United States.

As we have seen, the Jordanians and the Palestinians were on Iraq's side from the beginning and, if anything, were even more so after the war ended. The editor of Jordan's *Al Destour* newspaper, Mahmoud Sherif, summed up the situation: "The destruction of Iraq is going to be an ugly scar that will continue to bleed for some time and create a deep sense of guilt in the hearts of the Arabs."[6]

Yemen placed itself firmly on Iraq's side in spite of the United States cutting its aid 90 percent. In Algeria and Tunisia, pro-Iraqi sentiment forced the governments in effect to support Iraq's cause. King Hassan of Morocco was presented with popular petitions urging a cease-fire.

A distinction must be made between the rulers and the ordinary people in the rest of the Arab states. No public opinion polls are available that give the attitude of the masses, so the only gauge of this attitude is such events as street demonstrations, conversations with individuals, the opinion of Arab personalities who are in a position to assess opinion in various segments of the population, and the opinion of journalists and academics who specialize in Middle Eastern affairs. The government of Egypt was an ally in the war against Iraq, for example, but there were street demonstrations in support of Iraq, and the Egyptian government kept the universities closed out of fear of student riots.

From this sort of data it is clear that the Arab masses did not have high regard for Kuwait and its rulers. As mentioned earlier, many ordinary Arabs regard Kuwait as the spoiled rich kid of the Arab world—self-indulgent, investing its great wealth mainly in Europe and America, and indifferent to the troubles of the rest of the Arab world. Not surprisingly, some Arabs privately cheered when Iraq invaded Kuwait, and it was only after news of Iraqi atrocities began to circulate that some Arabs began to sympathize with the Kuwaitis.

After the Gulf War was over Kuwait again began to import foreign workers, especially women household workers to replace those who had fled. Reports of their exploitation again began to circulate in both Arab and Third World countries. In January 1992, Western newspapers reported that 130 Filipino women workers had taken refuge in the Philippine embassy in Kuwait and that the Sri Lankan, Indian, and Bangladeshi embassies said that 15 to 20 women a day were seeking refuge at each of those embassies.

Professor Peter Awn, a Columbia University Middle East specialist, wrote that the early responses among Arabs after the war ended were based more on ethnicity than religion. In some quarters of the Islamic world the United States and Allied opposition to Saddam Hussein was received sympathetically. But the extraordinary devastation inflicted on Iraq by the bombing, especially the bombing of Baghdad, which is one of the primary cities of Islam in terms of history, culture, and intellectual life, brought forth a negative reaction. "There is clearly the sense among the broad-based Islamic population," Awn wrote, "that there is something amiss when there is so little concern for the lives and property of Muslims."[7]

Christine Helms says that for Middle East specialists like herself, the first question is whether the United States went too far in devastating Iraq's armed forces and destroying its economy. The second question concerns the long-term consequences of the United States encouraging a premature uprising and then backing off from supporting it. President Bush said that he had nothing against the Iraqi people, Helms points out; yet even after a U.N. team reported that Allied bombers had reduced the country to a "preindustrial age," Bush was, because of his insistence on continuing the sanctions, in effect asking the Iraqi people—who had nothing to do with Hussein's rise to power—either to challenge Hussein's rule at great personal risk or to suffer the consequences of preindustrial deprivation indefinitely.[8] A year after the war, Bush again called for the people and army of Iraq to rise up and oust Hussein, and he repeated the call even more frequently as the 1992 election campaign heated up.

As widely reported in the press, on July 27, 1991, a senior Egyptian official in Washington said that public opinion in the Arab world had turned markedly sympathetic to the plight of the Iraqi people. A widely repeated joke was that the United States benefited from so few Arab states being democratic; otherwise all the United States' Arab allies would have been Iraq's allies.

In the words of a prominent Arab political scientist, Kamel Abu Jaber, spoken during the bombing, "If the United States continues with what it's doing . . . , there is no question that the region is in for a long period of terrorism, Islamic fundamentalism and terrific hatred."[9]

The same point was made by Mohammed Milhme, a PLO official in Amman, Jordan, who said, "You can flatten Iraq. But no American plane will be safe in the sky, and you will need five bodyguards for every American in the Mideast."[10]

Again, from an American who had been born in Lebanon: "If the United States succeeds in removing Saddam Hussein, as they did Noriega or by assassination, then all over the Middle East, fifteen Husseins will arise to take his place."[11]

Third World Reaction

The Third World reaction to the war in the Persian Gulf had a surprising twist. President Bush hailed the war as having put an end to the "Vietnam syndrome." Just exactly what he meant by this is not crystal clear, but to most of the developing world what he seemed to mean when speaking of the "Vietnam syndrome" was the feeling that great powers that intervene in Third World quarrels are likely to fail. Analysts of international affairs, pointing not only to the failed U.S. intervention in Vietnam but also to the failed Soviet intervention in Afghanistan, argue that the reason is the end of colonialism in the Third World and the rise of nationalism.[12] A superpower can *kill* all the inhabitants of a country such as North Vietnam or Afghanistan if it chooses to use nuclear weapons, and do it in a matter of minutes. But, as Gen. Matthew Ridgway once said regarding U.S. military intervention in Vietnam, military power is useless in trying to change a people's political attitudes.[13]

To the Third World, then, the end of the Vietnam syndrome seems to suggest the increased likelihood of American military intervention.

To many people in the Third World this is the most portentous and disastrous legacy of the Gulf War. The lesson of Vietnam was that other than the Soviet-American confrontation, communism was no threat. The cause of the upheavals in places such as Vietnam and Afghanistan was not really communism or anticommunism but Third World nationalism, and against Third World nationalism the awesome military might of the superpowers was meaningless.

The United States could have won in Vietnam, but it would have done nothing to lessen the threat posed by the Soviet Union. The United States would have had to occupy Vietnam with American troops for generations. No American walking the streets of a Vietnamese town or village at night would have been safe.

If the Gulf War indeed marks the end of the Vietnam syndrome, as Bush believes, and if the end of the Vietnam syndrome means what the Third World thinks it means, the United States will come to regret the Gulf War. This will be especially true if Bush and future presidents are encouraged to intervene in other Third World problems and against other Third World dictators.

Bush's talk of a "new world order" also bothered the Third World. As mentioned earlier, many Americans understood Bush's phrase to mean a new strategic balance of power in which the more powerful countries would join the United States in dealing with future threats by countries such as Iraq under Saddam Hussein. But to many people in the developing countries Bush's "new world order" suggests a "new American imperialism." It sounds especially ominous because of the turmoil inside the Russian commonwealth. When there were two superpowers, the developing world speculates, one restrained the other. When there is only one, what will happen?

Commenting on the staggering Iraqi casualties, Washington's apparent disregard for Arab life, and the fears that the United States under Bush's leadership sees itself as the policeman of the world, a Third World diplomat wryly commented: "President Bush has said that what awaited Hussein was a new set of Nuremburg trials, but if the Third World were in charge, there would be two war criminals in the block—Saddam Hussein and George Bush himself."[14]

=EPILOGUE I=

How Did It All Happen?

The history of the war in the Persian Gulf leaves the observer with three unanswered—and fundamentally important—questions:

The first is: Why did Saddam Hussein choose the course of action he did?

The second is: Why did George Bush turn his back on at least four alternatives to making the Gulf conflict an American war as described in an earlier chapter and decide instead on what a number of members of Congress and other observers have called a "headlong rush to war"?

The third is: Why did the war go so well for Bush, the United States, and its allies and so badly for Hussein and Iraq?

The Choices Facing Hussein

In fact, Hussein had three choices. First, he could have acceded to the U.S. and Allied demands and promptly withdrawn from Kuwait. If he had done so, Iraq would have been spared both the enormous, mind-boggling physical destruction of the weeks of constant bombing and the approximately three hundred thousand military and civilian casualties—killed, wounded, and dead from malnutrition and disease.

Second, Hussein could have fought. If so, the damage and casualties might have been even greater, but he probably would have exacted a high price. The Americans alone could easily have lost ten thousand killed and the Allies an equal number.

Instead, Hussein chose neither to accede to the Allied demands nor to fight, but to retreat without either surrendering or putting up any more than a token resistance to cover the withdrawal.

The Choices Facing Bush

As we have seen, one alternative for Bush was to midwife negotiations that would provide an Arab solution to Iraq's grievances and, hopefully, head off an Iraqi invasion of Kuwait. The argument for this alternative was that Iraq's grievances were serious and that, given Saddam Hussein's aspirations to be a leader of the Arab world, he would not be likely to resort to violence in the face of a settlement worked out by the Arabs themselves.

Once Iraq invaded and occupied Kuwait, the problem changed. Given the long history of Western countries oppressing Arabs, it was crucial to the future peace of the Middle East that if anyone had to kill Arabs it should not be Americans and Europeans but other Arabs.

Keeping this criterion central, the second alternative open to Bush was not to send American troops to protect Saudi Arabia from a possible Iraqi invasion, but to send an international force, mainly from Arab and Third World countries, backed up by American sea power and carrier-based air power. An economic boycott could also have been imposed, sponsored not by the United States but by the Arabs.

Again, the goal would not be war but a settlement negotiated by the Arabs, presumably satisfying Iraq's grievances at the price of Iraq withdrawing from Kuwait.

After the original U.S. and Allied force designed to defend Saudi Arabia had been deployed, the problem became more difficult. But a third alternative for Bush was at least theoretically possible: letting the U.N. take over the entire Middle East operation and replacing the American ground forces and land-based air forces with contingents from the Arab states and other Third World countries.

If the U.N. could not have been persuaded to accept the responsibility, a fourth alternative was available: for the Arab and Third World states to take over, as in the second alternative above. Again, the result would be, hopefully, not a war but a settlement negotiated by the Arabs.

If such a policy did not persuade Iraq to withdraw from Kuwait, the stalemate might have gone on for several years—with Iraq's conquest of Kuwait eventually being accepted by all the countries concerned. This would not have been a very satisfactory result, but it can be argued that the ordinary people of Kuwait are no better off under the feudal rule of the emir and his family than they would have been under Iraq.

A second possibility is that Iraq might have waited until the U.S.

forces had departed and then attacked both Saudi Arabia and the emirates. In such circumstances it seems likely that Egypt and the other Arab states would have come to the aid of Saudi Arabia and the emirates. If they failed to do so and Iraq had defeated and annexed both, the result would have been a tragedy.

But it would not have been a world-shaking tragedy. Iraq would have then been in control of 21.5 percent of the present global oil production and conceivably an even higher proportion of the known reserves. But the oil would have done Iraq and Hussein no good if they could not sell it. As discussed earlier, in the short run what determines the price of oil is the production costs of other producers, such as Canada, Venezuela, and Texas. In the long run what determines the price of oil is the "substitution price." It has been estimated that, with oil at twenty-five dollars a barrel, Venezuela, Canada, and Texas could supply all the oil that Kuwait, Saudi Arabia, and Iraq supplied before the war. If the price goes only a few dollars higher than twenty-five dollars a barrel, substitutes would begin to be competitive.

Furthermore, it is doubtful if Hussein would have been able to forge his conquests into a single homogeneous nation. Even if he had been able to do so, its population would have been less than 50 million and its industrial capacity limited. Egypt and the rest of the Arab states would have been thoroughly alarmed and hence much more likely to take the major responsibility for containing any further Iraqi expansion. The odds against Iraq would then have been 130 million Arabs against 50 million citizens of the new Iraq—citizens whose loyalty would be uncertain. The 55 million Iranians would certainly join in opposing Iraq; given the changed circumstances, even the 4.7 million Israelis might have found it possible to join an anti-Iraq coalition. The total would then be 239.7 million Arabs, Iranians, and Israelis against 50 million citizens of Iraq, many of whom would not have been ethnic Iraqis.

Why Did the War Go So Well?

At least some parts of the answer to this third question are fairly obvious.

One part of the answer is the stupefying odds against Iraq—in terms of the number of people on each side, in terms of industrial might, and in terms of both the number and sophistication of the weapons. No one had any doubt whatsoever about the ultimate outcome. Saddam

Hussein himself told a foreign visitor that he fully understood that Iraq could have no hope. A total of twenty-eight countries sent military forces of some kind to Saudi Arabia or naval forces to the Gulf as part of the coalition: the United States, Great Britain, Egypt, Saudi Arabia, France, Kuwait, Syria, Morocco, Pakistan, Bahrain, Oman, the United Arab Emirates, Qatar, Argentina, Bangladesh, Niger, Senegal, Sierra Leone, Australia, Belgium, Canada, Denmark, Greece, Italy, the Netherlands, Norway, Portugal, and Spain. A twenty-ninth country, Turkey, did not send forces to Saudi Arabia or the Gulf, but it joined the opposition to Iraq, provided bases for the U.S. Air Force, and, because Turkey borders on Iraq, Turkish troops tied down a substantial number of Iraqi troops.

Although the forces that many of the twenty-eight countries sent to the Gulf were essentially token, the population differences between the two sides must have had at least a psychological effect on Hussein and the Iraqi people. The total population of the states opposing Iraq came to 1.3 *billion,* whereas the population of Iraq was about 18 *million.*

Several other countries, including Germany and Japan, did not send military or naval forces to the Gulf but contributed money and arms. So the countries lined up against Iraq together controlled very close to 90 percent of the world's military industrial production. Iraq, on the other hand, was almost entirely dependent on buying its weapons from other countries—countries that had aligned against it or, in the case of the Soviet Union, were no longer supporting it. The only native Iraqi war industry consisted of a few factories manufacturing conventional small arms and artillery ammunition, some small capacity for manufacturing chemical and biological weapons, and a *potential* for manufacturing nuclear weapons at some time in the future.

Another reason the war went so well was the total absence of a great power with any interest whatsoever in coming to Iraq's aid, which made the odds against Iraq even more staggering.

During the Korean War, the United States drove back the North Korean troops who invaded South Korea and pushed right up to the Yalu River, North Korea's border with China. But the Chinese then intervened with massive armies, using "human-wave" attacks to hurl the American and South Korean troops back to the 38th Parallel, the original dividing line between North and South Korea. When the U.S. and South Korean forces finally stemmed the Chinese attack, the United States was deterred from invading the North again not only by war-weariness and the fear of still more casualties, but also by the possibility of Soviet intervention.

Again, during the Vietnam War the possibility that China might repeat its Korean intervention acted as a powerful deterrent to the United States, making it reluctant to either invade North Vietnam or even use its air power to its maximum potential.

In the Gulf War, on the other hand, the Soviet Union was in the midst of internal turmoil that made it not only impotent but anxious to do nothing that would jeopardize its good relations with the United States. China, for its part, remained aloof, with Deng Xiaoping, China's leader, sneering that the war in the Gulf was between a "big bully" on one side and a "little bully" on the other. What is more, China also made the political task of intervening with military force much easier for the United States and the coalition by abstaining when it could have vetoed the U.N. resolutions that formed the international legal basis for the U.S. and Allied intervention.

But even though the Gulf War was a war of almost the entire industrialized world against one tiny country, it still went much better than anyone expected.

Before-the-War Casualty Estimates

Before the United States and its allies launched their ground offensive, most military specialists—in and out of uniform—estimated that American and Allied casualties would be significant.

Two former chairmen of the Joint Chiefs of Staff, testifying before Congress during the air campaign, opposed a ground offensive because they were convinced that American casualties alone would be greater than any potential gain. Most people familiar with either modern war or the Middle East agreed with them. Vietnam was often cited as an example. If Vietnam proved anything, the argument went, it was that even determined peasants "clad in black pajamas" can inflict an enormous number of casualties.

A few generals and outside specialists were optimistic, thinking that the victory would be quick and overwhelming and that casualties would be no more than two or three thousand Americans killed, perhaps twice as many wounded, and somewhat smaller figures for the Allies, principally because they were providing fewer troops.

Another small number of generals and outside specialists were pessimistic. In private, some generals said that they thought that casualties would be about the same as in Vietnam, even though the fact that the United States was starting out with a large force rather than gradually escalating as in Vietnam probably meant that the war would not last so long. Some outside specialists also thought that casualties would be about the same as in Vietnam.

The majority of both the responsible military officers and outside experts settled on an estimate of about 10,000 Americans killed. This was the figure that U.S. commanders forecasted for the first twelve days of ground combat. General Schwarzkopf himself thought that the figure would be slightly lower—between 5,000 and 10,000 killed. Outside specialists came to similar conclusions. The Center for Strategic and International Studies, for example, calculated that if Iraq fought hard, 30,000 American soldiers would be killed or wounded, which presumably works out about the same—10,000 killed and about twice that many wounded.

Actually, not just in terms of casualties but in every other respect, the war went much, much better than anyone expected. In an awed tone, General Schwarzkopf himself said, "We certainly did not expect it to go this way." Generals Powell and Schwarzkopf both said that the Iraqi forces were much less formidable, and American casualties were substantially fewer than they had thought they would be.

Why were all of these expectations so wrong? The first reason usually cited was that the quality of the weapons on the Allied side was vastly superior—and that Allied soldiers were better trained in the use of their weapons.

Second, contrary to the belief of intelligence experts, who estimated that the Allies were outnumbered at the time they launched their invasion, the Allies may well have achieved the desired doctrinal 2:1 or 3:1 advantage General Schwarzkopf in his postwar briefing said had eluded them.

Evidence obtained by the Allies after the war indicates the Iraqi divisions were almost all below strength and that the total number of troops facing the 750,000 Allies may have been no more than 350,000—a far cry from the more than half a million troops estimated in the Kuwaiti theater of operations and 300,000 more along the Turkish border.

One authority on the Iraqi army, Ahmed Hashim, an American of Egyptian birth, maintains that documents captured during the war show that the Iraqis' leave policy was very generous and that many Iraqi soldiers simply stayed home. Hashim believes that, as a result, Iraqi frontline forces at the time of the Allied assault may have numbered as few as 200,000.[1]

Third, as already mentioned, all of the Iraqi forces except those in the Republican Guard were second- or third-rate reservists.

Finally, the laser bombs worked better than anyone had expected— but *not* as well as the administration's press managers had sought to make it appear. Apparently, only 15 percent of the laser bombs hit their targets. But these were point targets such as bridges and command and control centers rather than area targets such as industrial targets, and 15 percent is a huge increase in accuracy over the bombs of previous wars. The laser bombs and the conventional bombs combined were enough to destroy bridges, supply dumps, and much of Iraq's infrastructure.

But bombing, even laser bombing, is not all that effective against troops that are well dug in. Some other factor must also have been at work.

The evidence is overwhelming that this other factor was that Hussein decided not to fight. His decision was to withdraw with only token resistance rather than to either surrender or make a stand in prepared positions.

Historically, a retreat has always brought more casualties than any other kind of military operation. A retreating force almost always suffers more casualties than a defending force that either succeeds in holding its ground or pulls back step by step fighting as it goes. A force in full retreat has *always*—without exception—suffered many more casualties than its pursuer. And the losses are multiplied manyfold if the retreat becomes a rout. The Iraqi retreat did not become a rout, but no attempt was made to stand and fight or conduct a fighting retreat. Thus Hussein's decision to neither surrender nor stand and fight but to retreat without surrendering cost Iraq both the damage and casualties of resisting but left the Allies with only a handful of either dead or wounded.

George Bush vs. Saddam Hussein

The common element in all three of the unanswered questions is that the crucial decisions on each side were made by the opposing leaders acting pretty much on their own. Thus the missing answers lie in the personality and background of George Bush and Saddam Hussein.

More than any other war in modern history, the war in the Persian Gulf was a personal struggle between two men. The great Napoleonic wars were born of the rise of nationalism, which permitted the *levée en masse* and a "nation in arms" rather than the small professional armies fielded by rival monarchs. The Napoleonic wars lasted so long because the development of modern artillery and Napoleon's brilliant concept of the infantry-artillery team together offered France the tantalizing dream of an empire.

The American Civil War was a bloodbath over the two questions of slavery and whether the United States should remain one nation or become a confederation of essentially sovereign states.

World War I began as just another of the several wars rooted in the balance of power of Europe, with almost all of the players on both sides expecting it to last no more than a few weeks. It became one of history's most wrenching agonies largely by accident—because the machine gun and magazine-fed rifle had temporarily given the defense a decisive edge over the offense and because so much blood was spilled so quickly that both sides thought that a compromise, negotiated peace would be a betrayal of the dead.

World War II was in one sense and on one front a continuation of World War I, with Germany seeking to avenge its defeat and establish an empire in Central Europe that would include at least such parts of the Soviet Union as the former Baltic republics and the Ukraine. World War II was also a deadly and cataclysmic struggle between two rival ideas about how humankind should be governed: on the one side, by the Nazi concept of totalitarian dictatorship feeding on megalomaniac notions of racial and national superiority or, on the other side, by some form of democracy in which the mass of the people have a significant voice.

But the war in the Persian Gulf had no such momentous roots as these earlier conflicts.

Saddam Hussein really made two decisions in the Gulf crisis. The first was to invade and occupy Kuwait. Reprehensible though it may be to invade and occupy a weak neighbor, the decision did have a rational basis, given the facts of international politics in the Middle East. Furthermore, it was clearly supported by a significant number of the Iraqi people.

Iraq had always thought that Kuwait was rightfully a province of Iraq. It was previously noted that Britain drew the line between Iraq and Kuwait so as to deny Iraq an outlet to the sea. Kuwait had siphoned oil from Iraq's side of the Rumaila oil field. Iraq had accumulated a massive external debt that could be paid only by revenues from oil. Kuwait, however, had sold more than the share allotted to it by OPEC and at lower prices. What is more, it was continuing to do so, making it impossible for Iraq to sell enough oil to earn the foreign exchange it needed. Kuwait had refused Iraq's request for financial aid to reduce the burden that Iraq carried as a result of its war with Iran—a war that Iraq believed had been waged to protect all Arabs from the militant priests who ruled Iran. All of these factors helped turn Iraqi public sentiment against Kuwait. To further confuse the issue, as we have seen, Hussein had reason to believe that President Bush and the United States had given him a green light for his plans to invade Kuwait.

But Hussein's second decision—not to withdraw from Kuwait when confronted by the massive alliance assembled against Iraq—could certainly *not* be understood as a decision by the people of Iraq. Given the forces arrayed against it, Iraq could not possibly win. It was a foregone conclusion to everyone everywhere that Iraqi casualties would be enormous if Iraq did not immediately give in to the U.S. and Allied demands. But in the near-total dictatorship that is Iraq under Saddam Hussein, the decision was not the people's to make. It was made by Saddam Hussein, and it was obviously made for his own, very personal reasons and not for the good of the Iraqi people.

As for George Bush, he talked of not allowing aggression to stand, of nipping in the bud the rise of a new Hitler, of destroying Iraq's potential for building nuclear weapons, and of preventing a Middle Eastern dictator from controlling the oil on which the industrial world was so heavily dependent.

But these are obviously rationalizations—"good" reasons rather than "real" reasons.

On Bush's first point, not permitting aggression, the United States fought in Korea and Vietnam against what it considered at the time to be communist aggressions on the grounds that the ultimate enemies in both cases were the Soviet Union and world communism. Yet it did not fight when Soviet troops invaded Czechoslovakia, Hungary, or Afghanistan. When it comes to aggressions such as that of Iraq against Kuwait, the United States has tolerated dozens in recent history: the Indian takeover of Goa; the Vietnamese invasion of Cambodia; Israel's occupation of the Gaza Strip and the West Bank, its attack on Lebanon, and its occupation of the Golan Heights; the Indonesian attack on East Timor; and the Iraqi attack on Iran, to name but a few. The United States itself has invaded a few countries when it believed that its interests were threatened, the most recent being Cambodia, Grenada, and Panama.

Bush's second point, that Saddam Hussein was a new Hitler, was discussed in Chapter 4. Suffice it to say that although Hitler was a threat to the entire world, it is very doubtful whether Iraq—a country that is, after all, a comparative midget of a nation—could *ever* be a threat to anyone except its immediate neighbors.

The question of Iraq's potential for building nuclear weapons was discussed earlier, and the conclusions were twofold. The first was that although Iraq's nuclear program was much more extensive and further along than the United States and its allies realized, it was still limited. Iraq might well have been able to build a few nuclear bombs similar to the fourteen-kiloton bomb dropped on Hiroshima. But it would be quite some time before Iraq could develop the means to deliver those bombs anywhere except in its immediate neighborhood. The second conclusion was that several other countries pose a similar threat, and the only hope for a long-term solution to such threats is not unilateral military action by the United States but some sort of international control of nuclear energy, perhaps through the U.N.

Bush's point regarding the dependence of the United States and the developed world on Middle Eastern oil was also discussed in an earlier chapter. Here it need only be said that even if Saddam Hussein did come to control a large share of the oil produced in the Middle East, it would do him no good unless he could sell it. He would undoubtedly have raised the price, but if he raised it too high, the United States and the other industrialized nations would have turned to other sources of oil—such as Canada, Venezuela, Mexico, and Texas—and to other sources of energy, such as coal, solar power, and nuclear energy. In any case, as more than one observer has remarked, the people of France and the United Kingdom for many years have been paying three or four times what an American pays for a gallon of gasoline, and the difference hardly seems worth the risk of so many lives.

The point is simply that the reasons President Bush offered in his public statements for his swift and massive reaction to the Iraqi takeover of Kuwait are not really persuasive. There must have been deeper reasons.

It seems clear that this war—unlike most wars in recent times—can be understood only by looking at the deeper personal motivations of these two men, Saddam Hussein and George Bush.

════════EPILOGUE II════════

Saddam Hussein

Pursuing the notion that the missing elements in all three of the unanswered questions about the war in the Persian Gulf seem to lie in the personality and background of George Bush and Saddam Hussein, consider first Saddam Hussein.

Earlier chapters have told the story of Saddam Hussein's struggles to gain power and to retain it. What does this story tell us of the man himself that might help us understand why he pursued the course that he did in the Gulf War?[1]

First, the story tells us that Saddam Hussein is both able and extraordinarily ambitious. Clearly he set his sights very high from the beginning of his career. Given the nature of Iraqi politics—its intricate ins and outs, its Machiavellian maneuverings, and its bewildering gyrations—anyone who managed to reach the top in Iraq and to stay there as long as Saddam Hussein has stayed there must have exceptional native cunning and ability.

But Hussein's ambition is undoubtedly realistic. His flights of rhetoric have alarmed Westerners—threatening the Allies with the "mother of battles"; warning the Americans that they would "swim in their own blood"; threatening Israel that if it tried to do anything against Iraq, "By God, we will make the fire eat up half of Israel . . ."; and much more. But these phrases are in fact rather standard Arabic figures of speech, and should be recognized as boilerplate. Saddam Hussein's ambition is great, but it is realistic in the sense that his most grandiose dream has probably been to become the head of a unified Arab world, rather than the conqueror of an empire beyond that world.

A Hobbesian View of Life

Saddam Hussein also clearly has a Hobbesian view of life. The world is one of all against all. It is a violent and hostile world, one in which the will to self-preservation rules. Life is a ceaseless struggle to survive. Hussein clearly would heartily agree with Hobbes' description of life as "solitary, poor, nasty, brutish, and short."

Efraim Karsh and Inari Rautsi, in their biography of Saddam Hussein, point out that he is also suspicious to the point of paranoia. He is certain that no one can be completely trusted. Everyone is an actual or potential enemy. One must remain constantly on the alert. The only way to prevent people from attacking you is to dominate them and make them cower in fear. To avoid being killed you must be the first to kill.

Survival requires nothing short of absolute power for one's self and complete subservience from others. As Hussein himself said: "I know that there are scores of people plotting to kill me, and this is not difficult to understand. After all, did we not seize power by plotting against our predecessors? However, I am far cleverer than they are. I know they are conspiring to kill me long before they actually start planning to do it. This enables me to get them before they have the faintest chance of striking at me."[2]

Karsh and Rautsi, writing after the attack on Kuwait, argue that the attack had more to do with Hussein's perennial sense of insecurity than any premeditated grand design. In the case of both Iran and Kuwait, war was not Hussein's first choice, "but an act of last resort, taken only after trying other means for shoring up his position in the face of great adversity."[3]

In both cases, Hussein's choice of war was made at the last minute after a long period in which he felt increasingly threatened. In the case of Iran, Ayatollah Khomeini had waged a fanatical campaign calling for Hussein's overthrow. In the case of the attack on Kuwait—for which, as we saw, Hussein thought he had been given a green light—Hussein saw it as a rather inexpensive operation that would provide the means to reconstruct Iraq's economy, "on which Saddam Hussein's political survival hinged."

From Hussein's point of view, Iraq was in debt because it had defended the Arab world against Iranian fundamentalism, and the other Arab states could not expect "to take a 'free ride' on Iraq's heroic struggle." What was more, Hussein argued, the continued violation of the oil quotas really amounted to a declaration of war on Iraq. War, he said, is fought not only by soldiers but also by economic means. What was being done was "in fact a kind of war against Iraq."

At the same time, Karsh and Rautsi argue, Hussein was convinced that Israel would never allow an Arab state to draw even with it technologically. He believed that the massive movement of Soviet Jews to Israel would boost Israel's self-confidence and lure it into military adventures against the Arabs.

The "Butcher of Baghdad"

Saddam Hussein is called the "Butcher of Baghdad," a title that he well deserves. Part of Hussein's ruthless, kill-or-be-killed attitude undoubtedly stems from the troubled and insecure childhood already described. But part of it comes from the chaotic, violence-ridden social and political state of the Middle East. Hussein's behavior is typical of a very large percentage of the people involved in politics in most of the countries there. In Iraq, this tendency to violence is magnified because the Iraqi body politic is divided into three segments whose hostility and hatred for each other have roots that go back centuries: the Sunni Muslims, the Shiites, and the Kurds.

To repeat briefly the recent political history of Iraq, in Qassim's coup that overthrew the monarchy, everyone in the royal family, including the children, was butchered in the palace courtyard. Howling with delight, mobs dragged the regent's body through the streets. The body of the former prime minister was dug up from its grave and treated the same way.

When the army first attempted a coup against Qassim, he responded with a bloodbath that dwarfed all the previous purges in modern Iraqi history.

When Qassim was overthrown in yet another coup, his opponents took him to a TV studio, executed him, and lifted his limp head in front of the cameras and let it drop so everyone watching could see that he was truly dead.

Springing as Saddam Hussein does from such brutal and violent social and political roots, it is not surprising that he is equally brutal and violent. Indeed, it would be surprising if he were not. How could anyone who was not brutal and violent rise to power in such social and political circumstances?

If Saddam Hussein's brutality and violence stem from the social and cultural environment in which he lives as much as from the circumstances of his childhood, it would be a mistake to see him as a sadist in a psychological sense. According to an American diplomat who knew him well, Hussein was not in any way a maniac or out of his wits. "He's clearly a tough, extraordinarily determined man."

There are other scraps of information that suggest that beneath the brutality and violence runs at least a vein of humanity. One example is related by Karsh and Rautsi.[4]

In the early 1970s, a member of the Iraqi Jewish community, Na'im Tawina, now an Israeli citizen, was arrested as a "Zionist spy" and taken to the Baathist torture chambers. Just as he was about to be tortured, Saddam Hussein came into the room, glanced at Tawina, and said to the interrogator, "Do not touch this man. He is a good man. I know him. Let him go." Tawina was released and fled to Israel. But he had no memory of ever having met Saddam Hussein, and for years was unable to solve the puzzle of why Hussein had freed him. Then Tawina saw a picture of Saddam Hussein as a youth and remembered that he had frequently bought cigarettes from the young Saddam—and had often tipped him handsomely.

Saddam Hussein's Innate Caution

In addition to being brutal and violent, Saddam Hussein is also cautious. Part of his caution is related to his paranoiac view of the world. He is cautious in the sense that he trusts no one, not even his closest companions. When Hussein suspects that someone is becoming even a potential rival, he eliminates him at the first opportunity.

But Hussein is also cautious in the sense that he postpones action until either the time seems to be entirely right, or, even more often, when he comes to believe that he no longer has the choice of waiting—when he comes to believe that to wait is to lose.

An example is his delay in taking over the office of the presidency. Not only did he wait until he was absolutely sure that he had eliminated the opposition and enlisted all the support he possibly could, but he waited until circumstances—the threat of Iran under Ayatollah Khomeini—made further delay dangerous.

Another example is probably his invasion of Kuwait. Iraq's financial situation was desperate. From Hussein's point of view, he had tried everything from persuasion to bullying to get Kuwait to give him what he believed Iraq needed to survive. But the effort failed. Furthermore, Hussein thought that he had a green light from the United States.

Pragmatism

Along with brutality and caution, another of Saddam Hussein's characteristics is pragmatism. He shifts easily between the traditional pan-Arabism of the Baathists to putting the state of Iraq above all else.

In another example of pragmatism, when Hussein saw that Iraq could not win its war with Iran, he took the first opportunity—the Israeli occupation of the Golan Heights—to pull his troops out of Iran and propose to Khomeini that Iran and Iraq join forces in an attack on Israel. Khomeini refused, but the incident illustrates not only that Hussein is pragmatic but that he is devious as well.

Another example of Hussein's pragmatism is the way he flip-flopped on the Shatt-al-Arab issue. After years of contention Hussein signed a treaty with Iran, when it was still ruled by the shah, dividing the Shatt-al-Arab between Iraq and Iran. Then Hussein began the war with Iran by appearing on TV and tearing the treaty to shreds. Eight years of horribly bloody war ended in a stalemate. Later, when Iraq was faced with the Allied coalition, Hussein quickly reversed himself and acknowledged Iran's right to half the Shatt-al-Arab after all.

Operator, Not Thinker

Another characteristic of Saddam Hussein is that he is an operator rather than a thinker. He is introverted and constrained. Nasser had Hitler's gift as a rabble-rousing speaker, and Nasser would sometimes be carried away by his own rhetoric. Hussein has no talent as a public speaker. His delivery is wooden and uninspired. If a comparison with a modern dictator is necessary, Hussein should be compared to Stalin, whom he is said to have admired. Like Stalin, Hussein is a backroom manipulator rather than a rabble-rouser. Like Stalin, Hussein's major characteristic is ruthless pragmatism. Also like Stalin, Hussein collaborates with people he despises, is endlessly patient in waiting for the right moment, calculates intensely, and then strikes with utter ruthlessness.

Saddam Hussein's technique for domination is two-sided. First, he is completely without mercy in destroying enemies and potential enemies. Second, he makes sure to involve his associates in purges, so that if he is the victim of vengeance, they too will be. If Saddam Hussein dies, his associates will die with him.

For example, immediately after Hussein became president in July 1979, he began a purge of the Baathist party. He convened an extraordinary session of senior party members. It was then announced that a sinister plot had been uncovered, and that the principals of the plot were present in the room. Hussein then took the podium and read the names of 66 alleged plotters, all of whom were arrested on the spot.

Of the 66 arrested, 55 were found guilty. Of these, 22 were sentenced to death, and 33 were given long prison sentences. In an effort to make sure that the remaining party members would share in any retribution—and so refrain from joining any plot—Hussein decreed that the executions would be "democratic." What he meant was that the executions would be carried out by firing squads composed of members of the Baathist party—not just the senior members but delegates from party divisions and branches from all over the country.

A Politician Wooing the Masses

It is also clear that Saddam Hussein is a politician, in the sense that he cultivates not just particular groups that have power, such as the military, but that he also cultivates the masses. One example, already described, is that when Hussein decided the time had come for him to replace Bakr as president, he toured the country making speeches in cities, towns, and even villages as if he were an American presidential candidate on the campaign trail.

But Hussein's effort to cultivate the masses had more substance than just a campaign tour. Since the Baathists and Hussein came to power in Iraq, women have gained more rights and freedom than anywhere else in the Arab world. Twice as many women attended primary schools in Iraq before the Gulf War as in Kuwait—three times as many as in Saudi Arabia. Of the 250 members of the Iraqi parliament, 15 were women. Voting rights are universal at age eighteen, which is much more liberal than in most Arab states.

In Kuwait, for example, the vote is limited to males who lived in Kuwait before 1920 and their male descendants twenty-one years old or older. The result is that only one-tenth of the male population has the vote. In Saudi Arabia, to give another example, there is no vote at all.

People who actually know Saddam Hussein, according to *New York Times* reporter R. W. Apple, Jr., disagree with the pundits who picture him as erratic, eccentric, and mad. Those who know him think he is "cunning, ruthless, vain, bloodthirsty, but not demented in the slightest—a man whose motives and goals are quite comprehensible, even if the world considers his methods despicable."[5] Apple quotes Prof. Jerrold Polst of George Washington University, a psychiatrist who specializes in developing psychological profiles of political figures, as saying that Hussein "is no psychotic megalomaniac. He is a highly rational man—dangerous but well focused." Speaking after the invasion but before the attack to oust Iraq from Kuwait, Polst said that Saddam Hussein was a person who was willing to wait very patiently, to use time as a weapon. "If he sees a way out of this [the position Hussein found himself in after his invasion of Kuwait] with a fig leaf, he'll take it, and then two years from now, five years from now, his appetite for power will be undiminished and he'll strike again somewhere."

The point that Hussein is not neurotically compulsive but pragmatic and adaptable was also made by BBC correspondent John Simpson.[6] Stationed in Iraq before the war, Simpson returned to find that Saddam Hussein had changed from his old brutal methods to much more subtle ones. He had replaced his "rhetoric of aggression and power" with a "rhetoric of meekness." Explaining his new policy of liberty for the press, Hussein told a group of journalists that if they got their stories right, they would get the credit. "If you get things wrong," he went on to say, "I'll take the blame."

Simpson notes that both after and before the war, the central factor in Iraq had been Saddam Hussein's personality—his "demonic energy, his obsessive notions about the dignity and honor due Iraq, his lack of careful and balanced forethought, his willingness to sacrifice anyone and anything to protect his own position. . . ."

Another factor is Saddam Hussein's deep distrust and hatred of the Western countries that have dominated and humiliated Arabs for so long. To some extent, *all* Arabs share these feelings—the result of ruthless treatment dating back to the Crusades and intensified enormously by the aggressive imperialism of the nineteenth century and the subjugation of so many Arab countries through colonialism. Hussein was weaned on tales of the injustices inflicted on Arabs by the West. In the midst of the Gulf crisis, in a speech given on November 3, 1990, he reminded his listeners that it was the British who had drawn Iraq's border so as to deny it access to the sea. "Is it possible," he asked, "for a civilization which is 6,000 years old to have been isolated from the sea? A part of Iraq's land was cut off by English scissors."

For Saddam Hussein these feelings, which are shared by most Arabs, were inflamed and reinforced by his family's personal experience. As already recounted, in his childhood Saddam Hussein lived with his uncle, whom he regarded as a father. The uncle was one of the Iraqi army officers who rebelled against the British troops who occupied Iraq in World War II, and he was cashiered from the army and imprisoned for five years—all of which instilled in Saddam Hussein a life long hatred of the West.

Saddam Hussein's Reasoning and Strategy

What light can this description of Saddam Hussein's personality and background shed on the puzzle of why he chose neither to accede to the Allied demands nor to fight, but to withdraw without either fighting or surrendering—a course that would maximize Iraqi casualties and minimize those of the United States and its allies?

As described in the preceding chapter, when the United States intervened, Hussein seems to have reasoned that he had three alternatives. His first alternative was to agree to the Allied demands at the very outset. If he had chosen that option, Iraqi casualties would have been minimal. But the thought of Iraqi casualties had never bothered Hussein in the past. What must have seemed more important to him was that if he gave in at the outset, he himself would not be the hero to the Arab masses that he has since become. As it is, many Arabs see Saddam Hussein not only as one more victim of the brutality of the Western infidels, but also as a victim who at least tried to stand up and resist. In Jordan during one week in January 1991, for example, more than four hundred newborn males were given the name "Saddam."

Second, he could order his troops to resist. If he had done so, according to several American generals and outside military experts, as many as several thousand Americans would probably have been killed and two to three times that many wounded. But even so, Hussein seems to have understood that if Iraq did fight, it would only be a matter of time—a rather short time—before Hussein's troops would have been defeated.

What Hussein also seems to have realized was that the Americans and their allies would then have had both the excuse and the incentive to drive on to Baghdad and occupy the whole of Iraq. If so, Hussein must have concluded, the result may well have been the breakup of Iraq as a state and almost certainly his own demise.

Elaine Sciolino reports in her biography of Saddam Hussein that a few days before the invasion Hussein told some Palestinians that he was in a "lose-lose" position.[7] If he fought the United States and its allies, he would surely lose militarily. On the other hand, if he capitulated and withdrew from Kuwait without fighting, he would lose politically. "Shall I lose militarily or politically?" he asked rhetorically. "I shall lose militarily."

Saddam Hussein's third alternative was to refuse to surrender but at the same time order his troops to withdraw while putting up only token resistance.

To some extent this decision stemmed from an almost mystical— and very Arabic—pride and sense of self. Sciolino says that Hussein knew that defeat was inevitable but that he also believed that "Iraq's unique place in world history had grown, not diminished." Over and over in interviews with foreign reporters, he expressed the "importance of dignity—*haidba* in Arabic—for himself and the Iraqi people." The imposition of sanctions and the public condemnation and threat of war by the United States, Britain, France, and fellow Arabs had been deeply humiliating. Hussein said that dignity was more important than peace. "'We gave rivers of blood in a war that lasted eight years [the Iran-Iraq war], yet we did not relinquish our humanity, . . .'" By this, Sciolino explains, Hussein meant Iraq's right to live with dignity. As he said to one reporter on January 3, 1991, "I know I am going to lose. At least I will have the death of a hero."

His decision not to surrender but at the same time to withdraw without fighting also offered a chance not only to avoid his own death but to gain a victory of sorts.

His reasoning seems to have been along the following lines. Although their motives were different, neither America's Arab nor European allies relished the idea of the Americans occupying Iraq. Hussein could be fairly confident that they would probably succeed in persuading the United States to stop short of driving on to Baghdad. Withdrawal with only minimal resistance would mean high Iraqi casualties, but, again, Hussein did not seem to care.

This third alternative of refusing to surrender but withdrawing with only token resistance would give Iraq a very good chance of surviving as a state. Bush publicly encouraged both the Shiites and the Kurds to rebel, but none of America's allies and friends in the Middle East— whether Arab, British, French, or Israeli—wanted to see Iraq balkanized into separate Kurdish, Sunni, and Shiite states. They much preferred a united Iraq to stand between them and the fifty-five million Iranians led by religious zealots, even if the cost was that Iraq's leader continued to be Saddam Hussein!

As it turned out, both the Arab and European allies opposed continuing the offensive to Baghdad and insisted that Bush halt well short of it. The Turks went even further, warning that they themselves would invade Iraq to prevent the formation of an independent Kurdish state.

Hussein also seems to have reasoned that this third alternative offered the possibility not only of letting him evade a hangman's noose or a firing squad, but of giving him a fairly good chance of surviving as Iraq's ruler.

So far, it looks as if Hussein's judgment was sound, at least from his own, personal point of view. The troops manning the front lines were Hussein's "throwaway divisions," 70 percent of whom were Shiite and 30 percent Kurds. The best trained and equipped divisions, such as the Republican Guard and armored divisions, were composed of the more loyal Sunni Muslims, who were held in reserve. The fact that Hussein was able to put down both the Shiite and the Kurdish rebellions indicates that most of the military casualties were suffered by the "throwaway divisions."

In any case, a substantial portion of the tanks, helicopter gunships, and other military equipment needed to put down the rebellion survived. The Republican Guard, Hussein's elite force, was certainly damaged, but not enough to prevent it from dealing with the rebellion. Some of Hussein's air force was destroyed, and he sent some aircraft, which have yet to be returned, to Iran. But a substantial number seem to have survived in bunkers, especially the helicopter gunships that were so vital in putting down the rebellion.

Iraq suffered terribly, both in terms of physical damage and casualties. It will not be a threat to Kuwait, Saudi Arabia, or any of its other neighbors for some time to come. But it avoided being dismembered and continues to survive as a state—a state that still has a significant military capacity.

As for Saddam Hussein himself, he not only remains the dictator of Iraq at the time this is written, but he seems to be more strongly in power than he was before. What is more, to many among the Arab masses throughout the Middle East, Saddam Hussein is a hero—an Arab leader who defied the United States and the entire industrialized world and survived.

═══════EPILOGUE III═══════

George Bush

The question now is, what was it in George Bush's background and personality that led him to turn his back on at least four alternatives to making the Gulf conflict an American war and instead to pursue what many people called a "headlong rush to war"?

George Herbert Walker Bush was born into an old, wealthy, Republican family from Connecticut that had been listed in the social register for generations. His father, Prescott Bush, served as the U.S. senator from Connecticut from 1952 to 1963. Educated at one of the most prestigious private schools for boys, Phillips Academy Andover, and at Yale University, Bush, not surprisingly, "looks every bit the pinstriped Ivy Leaguer."[1]

World War II was in full swing when Bush graduated from Andover. He put off college and became a U.S. Navy aviator. At age eighteen he became the navy's youngest pilot, and he was later shot down in the Pacific and rescued by an American submarine.

Bush went to Yale when the war ended—as members of the Bush family had done for generations—worked hard, got good grades, made Phi Beta Kappa, excelled at sports, and graduated in 1948.

After graduation Bush moved to Houston, Texas, to get into the oil business. His first job was sweeping out a warehouse. In spite of this humble start, Bush was no Horatio Alger. A friend of his father's gave Bush his first real job as a salesman with Odessa's Dresser Industries, an oil supply firm (Bush's father was also a director of the company). Shortly afterward, in 1951, Bush helped start the Bush-Overby Development Company—backed by Bush family money. Two years later he co-founded the Zapata Petroleum Corporation, and became president of the Zapata Off-Shore Company in 1954.

Bush's real ambition, however, was to follow in his father's footsteps to high political office. In Houston, he immediately joined the Republican party and was very active in its affairs, becoming chairman of the Harris County Republican party organization.

In 1964, Bush sought the Republican nomination for the U.S. Senate so that he could compete for the seat then held by liberal Democrat Ralph Yarborough. In spite of being almost unknown to the general public in Texas and carrying the stigma of being a "carpetbagger" from the East, Bush won the Republican primary.

The general election was a different matter. Defeating an incumbent is always difficult, but Bush faced two additional obstacles. The first was that it was a presidential year and the incumbent president was a Democrat, Lyndon B. Johnson. The second handicap was that the Republican presidential nominee was Sen. Barry Goldwater. A general in the air force reserve, Goldwater was perceived as something of a warmonger and was accused of wanting to settle the Vietnam problem with bombs. Johnson won by a landslide, which provided coattails for even unknown Democrats running for lesser office, and Bush lost by 330,000 votes.

In 1966, redistricting created a new congressional district in the Houston suburbs where Bush lived. Not only was there no incumbent, but the district, the 7th, remains today the most heavily Republican district in all of Texas. Bush won the seat easily.

Bush gave up his House seat in 1970 to try once more for the Senate.

During his four years in the House, Bush generally scored high in the ratings of the conservative *Americans for Constitutional Action* and low in those of the liberal *Americans for Democratic Action.* His voting record on fiscal matters was conservative, yet he also supported liberal causes such as the Civil Rights Act of 1968 and the Open Housing Act. In 1970, however, Bush took the position that no more civil rights legislation was needed.

Although Bush hoped his opponent would again be the liberal Yarborough, the more conservative Lloyd Bentsen defeated Yarborough in the primary. Bush lost the general election to Bentsen by nearly 160,000 votes, receiving 46 percent of the vote to Bentsen's 54 percent.

If defeated candidates and the incumbent president are members of the same party, it is customary for the president to appoint them to some federal office, most often ambassadorships. Accordingly, in December

1970, President Nixon appointed Bush to be ambassador to the United Nations. Bush had argued in his 1964 campaign that if mainland China were admitted to the U.N., the United States should quit the organization. As ambassador, however, Bush loyally tried to carry out Nixon's so-called two-China policy—giving communist, mainland China a seat in the U.N. but retaining one for the nationalist government on Taiwan. In the end, the effort failed; mainland China was seated and Taiwan was expelled.

Bush remained at the U.N. for only two years. In 1972 Nixon named him national chairman of the Republican party, a post Bush held during Nixon's Watergate troubles. Bush remained loyal to the end, when Nixon resigned in order to avoid being impeached. Later, in 1980, Bush claimed that he had privately urged Nixon to resign—a statement that was greeted with considerable skepticism from both the general public and members of the Republican party.

When Gerald Ford succeeded Nixon as president in 1974, Bush lobbied hard to be appointed vice president, but Ford preferred Nelson Rockefeller. He offered Bush the post of ambassador to mainland China, and Bush accepted. He was ambassador for slightly more than a year—until President Ford fired CIA director William E. Colby, with whom he was at odds. Ford then offered the job to Bush, and he again accepted.

Bush, however, encountered trouble during his Senate confirmation hearing. Frank Church, chairman of the Senate Intelligence Committee, opposed Bush's confirmation for two reasons. The first was because of Bush's past political jobs, especially his tenure as chairman of the Republican National Committee. The second was because Bush was being mentioned as Ford's running mate for the 1976 presidential campaign, which Church thought would be inappropriate for the person who was head of intelligence. Ford promised that he would not select Bush as his running mate, and the Senate voted to confirm Bush in January 1976. Bush served as head of the CIA for about a year.

As the *Congressional Quarterly* remarked in a review of Bush's career, Bush often touted his government background when campaigning, but "he actually spent very little time in any of the jobs he held."

Out of a job following Jimmy Carter's election to the presidency in 1976, Bush concentrated on winning the Republican presidential nomination. He campaigned hard in Iowa, while Republican front-runner Ronald Reagan campaigned hardly at all. Bush won in the caucases and Reagan, realizing the threat, began to campaign in earnest.

The next big contest was in New Hampshire. Bush performed badly in the debate at Nashua, and he spent the weekend before the primary resting. Reagan, however, kept on campaigning and won by a two-to-one margin.

Bush's campaign had few boosts in the weeks that followed. Then, on May 20, Bush won the Michigan primary. But news media tallies reported that Reagan already had enough delegates to win the nomination on the first ballot, despite his loss in Michigan. Bush, bowing to the inevitable, withdrew from the race.

During the campaign Bush said he had always tried to avoid being labeled as either a conservative or a liberal. Where Bush's Republican orthodoxy was most apparent was on the role of the federal government and fiscal policy. For example, Bush backed such proposals as the Human Investment Act, which was designed to combat poverty through incentives rather than government grants. Bush said that as a member of Congress—and in every job he had held since—he refused to take extreme positions and shunned rhetorical hyperbole. However, to the delight of the press, he spurned his own advice, calling Reagan's supply-side economic policies "voodoo economics."

The 1988 Presidential Campaign

Both the Republican and Democratic candidates for president are nominated by conventions whose delegates are mainly state and local politicians. Governors, elected state government officials, mayors, and nongovernmental party officials from cities and towns are the usual delegates. A Republican senator or member of the House will usually be a delegate to the Republican convention and a Democratic senator or member of the House to the Democratic convention. Nominees, as a result, are chosen mainly by local politicians.

When Lyndon Johnson was the Senate majority leader during the Eisenhower administration, he did legislative favors that earned him the gratitude of the major industries, the labor unions, the farm organizations, women's organizations, the National Association for the Advancement of Colored People (NAACP), and a long list of other organizations of almost every kind. Senator John F. Kennedy, on the other hand, spent every moment he could during those years giving speeches at state and local fund-raisers for the Democratic party all over the country, meeting the local party faithful, finding out their concerns, and doing everything he could to convince them that he was the man who would satisfy those concerns if he was in the White House.

When the convention met, Johnson had a substantial bloc of votes, but Kennedy got the nomination on the first ballot.

During the eight years of the Eisenhower administration, Vice President Nixon followed the same strategy, spending every moment he could with state and local party officials. He, too, got the nomination on the first ballot.

As vice president, George Bush followed the Kennedy and Nixon formula, traveling all over the country to speak at local Republican fund-raisers and other events. As a result, by the time of the 1988 Republican convention, he had the nomination sewed up.

Cultivating the party faithful at the local level affects the candidate's behavior as much as it does the potential delegates to the upcoming convention. The candidates learn what the party faithful want and then alter their views—whether cynically and deliberately or because they have been persuaded that the party faithful are actually right. When Kennedy was beating the backwoods bushes, Martin Luther King was battling for civil rights, and Kennedy moved from being a lukewarm supporter of civil rights to being a staunch advocate. Nixon, responding to the fears of local Republicans, made the cold war with the Soviet Union his central theme.

For George Bush, getting the nomination posed a somewhat different problem. The center of gravity of the Republican party at the local level is where Richard Nixon had stood. Nelson Rockefeller and George Bush were both perceived as being to the left of that position. Rockefeller never succeeded in allaying the fear that he was too "liberal" to be a good Republican, but Bush did. On abortion, for example, at one time, Bush was "pro-choice"; then he became adamantly "pro-life."

The 1988 campaign was replete with examples of Bush's efforts to appeal to the right wing of the Republican party: the flag burning brouhaha, his opposition to gun control measures, his description of Democratic presidential candidate Michael Dukakis as a "card-carrying member of the American Civil Liberties Union," and his selection of Indiana senator J. Danforth Quayle, a Republican with impeccable conservative credentials, as his running mate.

In any event, George Bush overcame his liberal image and won the support of both the conservative and liberal wings of the Republican party, although Quayle's selection caused some uneasiness in the party's moderate and liberal wings. The subsequent media frenzy surrounding the Quayle selection led many to question Bush's rationale for choosing his running mate.

Why *did* Bush pick Dan Quayle? A few male chauvinists jokingly suggested that Quayle's youthful good looks might attract some of the women's vote, but no one—Republican or Democrat, conservative or liberal—seriously argued that Quayle was anything other than a political lightweight who would bring no additional votes to the Republican ticket. The general conclusion was that Bush did not want a vice president who might in any way become a rival or even share the spotlight.

As it happened, however, the choice of Quayle turned out to be a big plus during the election. Dukakis was a virtual unknown outside of New England and he desperately needed the attention he would get from the press following the Democratic convention. Unfortunately for him, reporters were too busy investigating Quayle's background during the two or three weeks after the convention to give Dukakis the coverage normally devoted to the presidential candidate earning his party's nomination.

The Quayle selection is not momentous in itself, but it may shed some light on an important aspect of Bush's personality. Peggy Noonan, in her autobiographical account of her years as President Reagan's speechwriter, says that when she began writing speeches for Bush, she learned he hated to say "I."[2] The staff speculated that his reluctance came from his youth, when his New England mother would rap his knuckles whenever he bragged—used the first person singular as the subject of a sentence. The trouble was that, in going over a draft speech, Bush would cut entire sentences rather than reword them to eliminate the "I." So, rather than write, "I moved to Texas and joined the Republican party," in a Bush speech, Noonan would simply write, "Moved to Texas. Joined the Republican party." At some point during the campaign, she recalled, Bush changed his style and no longer cut sentences including the first person singular.

Listening to Bush since he became president suggests a profound change, indeed. Most presidents are very sensitive to the possibility of being charged with having an imperial attitude or of being egocentric. They avoid saying "I decided" this or that and instead say, "the administration decided," "the government" has done this, "the executive branch" has done that. But listen to the tenor of George Bush's remarks during the Persian Gulf crisis:

On August 5, three days after Iraq invaded Kuwait, as Bush stepped off a helicopter, reporters asked if the United States was going to move militarily. Bush replied, "I will not discuss with you what my options are or might be, but they're wide open, I can assure you of that." Pressed by reporters, Bush snapped, "Just wait. Watch and learn."

Waving his finger at reporters and obviously angry, he said, "I view this very seriously, our determination to reverse out this aggression. . . . This will not stand. This will not stand, this aggression against Kuwait."

Referring to his campaign line, "Read my lips—no new taxes," Bush responded to a reporter's question while he was out jogging with, "Read my *hips*." Asked about the possibility of permitting Saddam Hussein the option of peacefully pulling out of Kuwait, Bush said, "There can be no face-saving. I'm not in a negotiating mood." On yet another occasion, speaking of the fact that Hussein was still in power, Bush said, "There will be no normal relations with this man as long as I'm President of the United States."

Most presidents since the days of Franklin D. Roosevelt have worried about media overexposure, especially on radio and TV. The belief is that too many appearances would lessen their impact on important issues. Instead, they have tended to husband their appearances to maximize that impact. Not so President Bush. His almost constant image on the TV screen was perhaps understandable during the Gulf War, when it was the United States that was the principal actor in events. But throughout the crisis in the Soviet Union in the summer of 1991 Bush's image appeared on TV almost as often as did those of Mikhail Gorbachev and Boris Yeltsin. As newspaper columnist David S. Broder pointed out, Bush held more press conferences, delivered more public speeches, and appeared on TV more often during his first two years in office than Reagan did in eight.[3]

The Foreign Policy President

In January 1991 *Time* magazine named President Bush its "man of the year" but the magazine's editors gave Bush two faces on its cover. One depicted his foreign policy profile: a picture of resoluteness, mastery, and determination; the other was Bush's domestic policy profile: a portrait of confusion, indecision, and waffling. Bush was understandably furious, but *Time* had a point.

On the domestic side, the Bush record has given many pause for concern. Time and again he has taken stands on issues only to change his position when he encounters a negative public response, taken only tentative steps toward solving problems, or seemingly ignored domestic issues in favor of dealing with problems in the foreign policy realm.

President Bush clearly thinks that his major expertise is in foreign affairs, in spite of the fact that his experience consisted of two years as ambassador to the U.N., slightly more than a year as ambassador to China, and a year as director of the CIA. But even though the time he actually spent directly dealing with foreign affairs was short, his four years in Congress, the years of his appointive positions, and his two years as president gave Bush the opportunity to meet and talk with most of the world's leaders. One result is that he developed a personal style for dealing with foreign affairs that is totally different from any previous president in history. The Bush style is based on personal contact— on making "friends" with the leaders of other countries. In his first three years in office, Bush made more foreign trips than any other president in history.

Because Bush came to know so many of the world's leaders and because he placed such great value on person-to-person or, more accurately, leader-to-leader contact, Bush used the long-distance telephone in a way that was unique. It is said, for example, that during the Gulf War he made more than thirty telephone calls to the president of Turkey alone and many, many more to some of the other coalition leaders.

There are obvious advantages if a president knows other leaders and makes personal contact with them during crises. In the course of human relationships people build up considerable expertise in judging others, their motives, and their sincerity. It is because of this that every newly elected president since World War II, at least, has put high on his agenda a personal meeting with the leaders of the Soviet Union and other major powers.

But there are also disadvantages to the person-to-person approach. One is that it leads to giving more weight to leader-to-leader relationships than state-to-state relationships. In other words, countries whose leaders President Bush regards as personal friends tend to be treated well even if the states behave in ways contrary to American interests. For example, during his year as ambassador to China, Bush got to know and become "friends" with the country's top leaders. Later these same leaders ordered the massacre of Chinese students protesting in Tiananmen Square. The world was outraged, and most democratic countries took concrete measures to give meaning to their feelings. But the Bush administration confined itself to a rather mild expression of disapproval. A number of congressional leaders, for example, wanted at least to withdraw China's "most-favored-nation" trade status, but Bush would have none of it. Many members of Congress regard the president's failure to take such action as rewarding tyrannical and brutal behavior and fear that this is exactly the way that the Chinese interpret it.

Giving leader-to-leader relationships more weight than state-to-state relationships works the other way as well. No one except President Bush's psychiatrist can know for sure, but the evidence suggests that this emphasis on personal relationships played an important role in Bush's decision to send troops to the Gulf and to use military force to drive Iraq out of Kuwait. The evidence suggests that Bush thought he had made at least some progress in making a "friend" of Saddam Hussein. He also seems to have concluded that Saddam Hussein had given some sort of assurance that if he used force to deal with his problems with Kuwait, it would be limited to taking the two uninhabited islands blocking Iraq's access to the sea and the tip of the Rumaila oil field that Kuwait had used to siphon off oil on the Iraqi side of the border. When Hussein took all of Kuwait, Bush seems to have felt that Hussein had lied to him and betrayed their budding friendship.

In other words, if you look at the relationships between states as if they are relationships between individual leaders, not only does personal friendship play a big role in determining policy, so does going back on a "promise" made by one leader to another. This personal, emotional reaction seems to have been an important factor in President Bush's decision to turn his back on the alternatives and to make the Gulf conflict an American war.

Another disadvantage of giving leader-to-leader relationships more weight than state-to-state relationships is that it leads President Bush to try to be his own expert. No one can be equally expert on all of the more than 130 countries of the world, and it is dangerous to ignore the real experts: people who spend their entire lives studying a particular country. One example, already cited, was when Bush called upon the Iraqi people and the military to overthrow Saddam Hussein after watching Baghdad crowds on TV celebrating what they thought was a peaceful solution to the crisis. Bush did not consult U.S. intelligence agencies or anyone else. In fact, U.S. intelligence, Allied intelligence, and Israeli intelligence all thought that his interpretation was wrong, that the Sunni Muslims were very loyal to Hussein, that the Shiite Muslims preferred Hussein to domination by the Shiite priests ruling Iran, and that only the Kurds were actively hostile to Hussein. The intelligence agencies also thought that if Saddam Hussein was overthrown, his successor might be worse. Israeli intelligence, in particular, held this view.

Bush's emotional reaction to Saddam Hussein is, in a sense, the mirror image of emphasizing leader-to-leader rather than state-to-state relationships. A state "behaves" out of considerations of national interest, and states sometimes find it in their national interest to conceal their future plans. But a "friend" who misleads a friend has betrayed that friend and should be treated with contempt and, if possible, punished. Bush apparently thought he was on his way to making a friend of Saddam Hussein. But Hussein, in Bush's view, misled or even betrayed him, thus justifying Bush's turning his back on negotiated solutions and launching a war.

When pressure from the Allies ruled out making the occupation of Baghdad and the removal of Hussein as head of government one of the goals of the Gulf War, Bush's frustration was obviously almost unbearable. As the 1992 election campaign got going, Bush again began to call upon the Iraqi army and people to oust Hussein, making it a minor campaign theme. He made a pledge to the Iraqi people that the United States stood ready to work with a new regime. At the same time, Saudi Arabia also pressed Bush to organize a large covert action campaign aimed at dividing the Iraqi army, and Bush, in a letter to King Fahd, reaffirmed his determination to see Hussein overthrown.[4]

In early February 1992, CIA director Robert M. Gates traveled to the Middle East. The media reported that President Bush had ordered him to meet with Arab allies to discuss plans for fomenting a coup to remove Saddam Hussein. The White House acknowledged that in November 1991 Bush had notified the appropriate congressional committees that he was directing the CIA and the Pentagon to help plot a coup against the Iraqi leader, supported if necessary by U.S. bombing raids, and that he had signed a "finding" to that effect. "Findings" are formal statements that national security justifies covert action and are required by law before the CIA can use restricted funds for that purpose.

Middle East specialists criticized the decision as demonstrating too much concern about the effect stopping the war with Hussein still in power would have on the upcoming election and too little understanding of the Middle East. In the first place, these critics argued, when and if Hussein is overthrown, he will—inevitably—be killed. Few Westerners or Arab leaders would shed many tears over this, in spite of the congressional prohibition against assassinating foreign leaders. But Hussein's death as a result of a CIA plot would undoubtedly be regarded by ordinary Arabs as still another example of the low value the West places on Arab lives, a point already driven home by the Iraqi death toll attributed to the Gulf War. As if confirming the point, Egypt flatly refused to have anything to do with the plot.

Finally, they argued, if George Bush better understood the politics and passions of the Middle East, he would realize that if Hussein were killed in a plot supported by the U.S. government, Bush himself would then become the target of Middle Eastern fanatics. Bush's actions, far from promoting peace and stability, these critics contend, are helping push the world toward violence and savagery.

Inside Information

According to Maureen Dowd of the *New York Times,* even though Bush seemed "baffled by the inscrutable and seemingly suicidal behavior of Saddam Hussein," he did not have a Middle East expert to whom he could turn for advice.[5] Instead, he preferred to talk to the handful of people in his inner circle—Scowcroft, Baker, Cheney, and Sununu—or directly to Arab leaders such as the king of Saudi Arabia. In the period before he decided to attack Iraq, there was only one occasion on which Bush invited outside Middle East specialists to the White House, but afterward a number of them said that he did not seem to be paying attention.

As reporter Andrew Rosenthal wrote, personal diplomacy has its perils. Bush's knowledge of the Middle East came from his long association with its oil-rich, conservative royal families and this left him with "a blind spot in assessing the currents of the Arab street and the intentions of President Saddam Hussein of Iraq."[6]

On the point of Bush's failure to consult experts, the most serious of all concerns top military officers. When Bob Woodward published his book, *The Commanders,* about the way that decisions were made during the Gulf War, what disturbed some reviewers even more than Bush's failure to consult Middle East experts was the degree to which he failed to seek military advice from his senior military advisers. Clay Blair, for example, reviewing the book for the *Washington Post,* noted that Woodward described Bush and Scowcroft as hammering out military policy in the Oval Office. "Cheney and Powell," Blair wrote, "appear to be glorified messenger boys who must keep tuned to CNN to find out what decisions are evolving at the White House."[7]

Another aspect of Bush's failure to consult the experts was his tendency to act impulsively during the crisis. Bush's call for Hussein's overthrow after he watched Baghdad crowds celebrate the false peace, his decision to assume an offensive posture without first consulting the military, and his spur-of-the-moment decision to invite the Iraqi foreign minister to Washington and to send Secretary Baker to Baghdad—a move some experts contend Hussein interpreted as a sign Bush would back down—are all good examples. Still another example was the president's sudden decision on August 12, 1991, to order the navy to interdict Iraqi shipping—an order that took several days of frantic diplomatic maneuvering to straighten out.

Bush Limited His Own Options

Fouad Ajami, a Middle East expert at the Johns Hopkins University School of Advanced International Studies, pointed out that Bush had limited his own options by the stark choices he presented to Hussein. When Bush declared that "This [aggression] will not stand," he made war virtually inevitable. Bush's continued personal attacks on Hussein made it even more inevitable. As Ajami said, "once you describe Saddam as Hitler, not merely the thief of Baghdad," you further close the door. If Saddam Hussein is another Hitler, then you can't make deals without being charged with a sellout such as the Munich agreement.[8]

Edward N. Luttwak, who holds the Arleigh E. Burke chair in strategy at Georgetown University's Center for Strategic and International Studies, argued along the same lines. "Happily leaving behind all serious concern for the economy," Luttwak wrote, "and even more happily content to see photographs of Saddam Hussein replacing those of Neil Bush on the front pages, George Bush threw himself into crisis management on a full-time basis with boyish enthusiasm, barely turning aside to explain, most unconvincingly, the reason for it all."[9]

The "Kick-Him-in-the-Ass" Approach

During the 1984 presidential campaign that pitted Ronald Reagan and George Bush against Walter Mondale and Geraldine Ferraro, the two vice presidential candidates had a debate. Talking about the debate afterward to a group composed entirely of men, Bush said that he had "kicked a little ass." At the time, news commentators described it as the case of a blue-blooded Yankee aristocrat in a rather crass and bumbling attempt to be "one of the boys." But it is now clear that such talk is part of the Bush style.

Everyone—even the president of the United States—is entitled to a few minor vulgarities, but when this is combined with a tendency to rely on an inner circle of advisers and telephone calls to world leaders without consulting the experts in a field, the results can be unfortunate. This seems to have been what happened in Bush's dealings with Saddam Hussein.

Ruth Sinai of the Associated Press interviewed a number of people who specialize in Middle Eastern affairs, as well as prominent Arabs with international experience, to see if Bush's spicy language was a negative factor.[10] One of the people Sinai interviewed was Marshall Wiley, a former U.S. envoy to Baghdad and one of the few Americans who has met Hussein. The "kick-him-in-the-ass approach," Wiley said, is "counterproductive." By personalizing the dispute, making it not a quarrel between two countries but one with Hussein himself, by comparing Hussein to Hitler, by threatening Hussein with a war crimes trial, and by calling him a liar, Wiley said, Bush hardened Hussein's resolve to remain in Kuwait and to refuse to accede to Allied demands.

The Arab League ambassador to Washington, Covis Maksoud, told Sinai that Saddam Hussein "seeks respect and recognition more than approval or acceptance. . . . It's ingrained in the Arab psyche." Using language that humiliates Hussein, Maksoud said, is a "prescription for intransigence."

An Iraqi-born American businessman explained that the Arab language is flowery and full of hyperbole, such as the "mother of battles." Using the first name of the leader of another country is viewed as an insult, yet Bush often spoke of Saddam Hussein as simply "Saddam" (Bush also usually mispronounced the name, which only added to the insult). "For Bush to put down an Arab leader in front of his people is a cardinal sin," he said. "It stabs our national ego."

As described earlier, during the last-minute efforts for peace, Secretary of State Baker met with Iraqi Foreign Minister Tariq Aziz. Baker delivered a letter from Bush to Hussein; Aziz read it over and returned

it to Baker, refusing to deliver it to Hussein himself. Aziz later explained why he refused to accept the letter: "The language of that letter
was contrary to the traditions of correspondence between heads of state,"
Aziz said. "If he really intends to make peace . . . he should use po-
lite language."

Elizabeth Drew, Washington correspondent for *The New Yorker*
magazine, also addressed the question of whether Bush's spicy language had a negative effect on the Gulf situation.[11] One of the people
she interviewed was a Pentagon Middle East specialist who put the
point even more strongly: "You don't talk to Arabs like they're dogs
in the street; you don't say you're going to kick their ass." Even if
Bush had consulted experts and been more sophisticated about Middle
Eastern mores, Saddam Hussein might have continued to be intransigent, the official added, but even so, "that level of discourse isn't conducive
to a diplomatic solution."

Bush's "Tendency to Self-Victimization"

In *The Commanders,* Defense Secretary Cheney is quoted as telling Admiral Crowe that Bush had a long history of "vindictive political actions." If you cross Bush, Cheney allegedly said, "you pay." Then
he supplied the names of some victims. "Bush remembers," he added,
"and you have to be careful."[12]

Part of Bush's vindictiveness is apparently related to his tendency
to rationalize and justify his own actions. They are out to get me, seems
to be what Bush is saying to himself, so anything I do to retaliate is
okay.

Bush's vindictiveness and tendency to rationalize seem to be related
to what columnist David S. Broder calls the "art of self-victimization"—
an art, Broder says, that Bush has mastered.[13] Bush carries in his own
head what he thinks of as "a gentleman's rule of the political game."
But he finds "frequent and convenient reasons" to believe that others
have violated the rule, and he feels justified in adopting "all-out scorched
earth tactics" against them. When Bush sees himself as a victim of
foul play, according to Broder, he feels he has a right to lash out.

Broder cites as an example the time when House Majority Leader
Richard A. Gephardt said, "The Bush foreign policy . . . [is] adrift, without
vision, without imagination, without a guiding light save precious
public opinion polls." Bush, Broder says, was already angered by

Gephardt's statement that Bush's stand on the capital gains tax was a reward for his rich supporters. So Bush decided to squash Gephardt. He asked his old friend Senate Minority Whip Alan Simpson to deliver a floor speech written in the White House attacking Gephardt as a "frustrated font of trivia" and a man driven by an "obsessive and overweening" presidential ambition. The vehemence of the attack and the White House eagerness to take credit for it "raised eyebrows" in Washington. As Broder says, Bush's talent for self-victimization lets him launch "retaliatory" strikes that scar not just his opponents but the country as well.

Confronted with criticisms such as Gephardt's, Bush responds that he is uncomfortable with what he calls "the vision thing." Presumably it was because it seemed visionary that Bush brushed aside the proposal that the problem that Saddam Hussein presented should be solved by the U.N. But to many observers, whether it is the U.N. or some other international mechanism, there are too many Saddam Husseins in the world for the United States to handle alone. It seems obvious to these observers that humankind must find some sort of political mechanism that will perform the social and political functions that war has performed in the past. The observers' argument is that if humankind is to survive in a world of sovereign states armed with the diabolical military weapons it has invented, "the vision thing" is our only hope.

The "Wimp" Label

In about the middle of his tenure as vice president, Bush acquired the reputation of being a "wimp," which is defined as "An introverted, boring, overly solicitous person; a meek, passive person; one who is out of touch with current ideas, trends, fads, etc. . . ."[14]

The way the press applied the word to Bush, however, did not imply an introverted, boring, or even an overly solicitous person. Neither did the press' use of the word imply being out of touch with current ideas and trends. Meek and passive comes somewhat closer but not exactly. The context in which the press used the word seemed to suggest a somewhat different definition: A person who tries to ingratiate himself or herself with the powerful and is subservient to those of higher rank (for example, President Reagan); who switches positions on issues (such as abortion); who waffles on just where he or she stands on an issue; who tries to be all things to all people and attempts to please everyone, rather than taking a stand on principle (for example, letting the public opinion polls determine one's policy position).

Understandably, President Bush reacted strongly to the charge of being a wimp. In June 1991 he angrily told reporters in response to a question, "You're talking to the wimp. You're talking to the guy that had a cover of a national magazine [*Time*], that I'll never forgive, put that label on me."

Apparently what people who call Bush a wimp mean is something more akin to the press' seeming definition cited above. But if this is what people mean when they call Bush a wimp, there is a reverse to such personality traits. In just over two years as president, Bush led the United States into an invasion of Panama and an invasion of Iraq.

Why would a wimp lead the United States into two military invasions in just over two years? One answer might be that if someone is taunted enough about being a wimp, eventually he is likely to lose patience and try to prove the charge untrue with an act of violence.

On the other hand, in both instances it was a case of the world's strongest military power attacking a very small country. Iraq had a lot of weapons, to repeat an earlier point, but it lacked the necessary spare parts to fight for more than a few days. When faced down, a bully often turns into a coward. Similarly, it may be that, given a weak opponent, a wimp may become a bully.

According to Elizabeth Drew, a number of senators in both parties believe that Bush was trying to prove to himself and to the world that he was a tough guy. "When he personalized the issue as one between him and Saddam Hussein," Drew wrote, "when he swaggered and did his Clint Eastwood routine, when he said that Hussein is 'going to get his ass kicked,' he gave credence to the idea that he was proving something."[15] Drew says that a senator "reluctantly" told her that "we all know instinctively that this is not a strong man. It's greatly disturbing. I try not to think about it. I don't know anyone who's honest with himself who doesn't think this." Another member of Congress told her that a good many people in Congress were disturbed about Bush's "obsession" with Iraq, his "fixation" on it.

Conclusion

The purpose of this examination of George Bush's background, career, and personality is to try to find an answer to the question asked in Epilogue I: Why did George Bush turn his back on at least two alternatives to a negotiated settlement of the Persian Gulf crisis and two alternatives to making the Gulf conflict an American war—and instead, in the view of many people, "rush to war"?

The evidence suggests, first, that Bush seems to be firm in his commitment to only a handful of principles. It is not so much that he is unprincipled as that he switches positions easily and without any apparent psychic cost. To many observers the explanation seems to be opportunism.

It is, of course, pure speculation to relate Bush's personality traits to his decision to turn his back on the opportunities for negotiation and to "rush to war." But it remains true that the war in the Persian Gulf, more than any other war in modern times, was a personal clash between two men. It may be that the situation came to war because of only one personality trait that is common to both Hussein and Bush: a simplistic, black-and-white view of international affairs that leads them to see it as a personal struggle between rival leaders and that leads them to choose force because it seems to offer a clear-cut solution rather than the muddied, convoluted compromises offered by negotiation.

This is a disturbing thought, implying as it does that such leaders may too quickly turn their backs on negotiations in future crises and jump to the use of force as they have done in past crises. But the evidence also suggests that, in the case of President Bush at least, something more may be at work.

Mark Shields, on the CBS program "Face the Nation" on June 16, 1991, may have put his finger on the crucial point during a discussion of President Bush's continuing failure to come up with a domestic program that is more than pro forma. Shields remarked: "A boy wants to *be* something. A man wants to *do* something." His record during the Persian Gulf crisis suggests that George Bush does not have an agenda of things he wants to *do,* only that he very much wants to *be* president.

Notes

Introduction

1. The following account draws on Judith Miller and Laurie Mylroie, *Saddam Hussein and the Crisis in the Gulf* (New York: Times Books, a division of Random House, 1990); Efraim Karsh and Inari Rautsi, *Saddam Hussein: A Political Biography* (New York: The Free Press, 1991); *The Middle East,* 5th ed. (Washington, D.C.: The Congressional Quarterly, 1981); Elaine Sciolino, *The Outlaw State: Saddam Hussein's Quest for Power and the Gulf Crisis* (New York: John Wiley & Sons, 1991); Simon Henderson, *Instant Empire: Saddam Hussein's Ambition for Iraq* (New York: Mercury House, 1991); Micah L. Sifry and Christopher Serf, *The Gulf War Reader: History, Documents, Opinion* (New York: Times Books, a division of Random House, 1991); David Fromkin, *A Peace to End All Peace: Creating the Modern Middle East, 1914–1922* (New York: H. Holt, 1989); Albert Hourani, *A History of the Arab People* (Cambridge: Belknap-Harvard University Press, 1991); Samir Al-Khalil, *Republic of Fear: The Politics of Modern Iraq* (Berkeley: University of California Press, 1989, 1990); Jean P. Sasson, *The Rape of Kuwait: The True Story of Iraqi Atrocities Against a Civilian Population* (New York: Knightsbridge, 1991); Thomas L. Friedman, *From Beirut to Jerusalem* (New York: Farrar, Strauss, Giroux, 1989); and Daniel Yergin, *The Prize: The Epic Quest for Oil, Money, and Power* (New York: Simon and Schuster, 1991).

Chapter 1

1. Karsh and Rautsi, *Saddam Hussein,* 85. This account of how Saddam Hussein replaced Bakr is drawn from their work.

Chapter 2

1. The following account of events in Iran is drawn from my *The Politics of Policy Making in Defense and Foreign Affairs, Conceptual Models and Bureaucratic Politics,* 2d ed. (Englewood Cliffs, N.J.: Prentice-Hall, 1990).

2. On the hostage crisis, see Pierre Salinger, *America Held Hostage: The Secret Negotiations* (Garden City, N.Y.: Doubleday, 1981); Paul B. Ryan, *The Iranian Rescue Mission: Why It Failed* (Annapolis, MD:

Naval Institute Press, 1985); Hamilton Jordan, *Crisis: The Last Year of the Carter Presidency* (New York: Putnam's Sons, 1982); and Amir Taheri, *Nest of Spies: America's Journey to Disaster in Iran* (London: Hutchinson, 1988).

3. See my *The Politics of Policy Making*, 28–29.

4. For a rundown on the struggle inside Iran, see Robert D. McFadden, *No Hiding Place: The New York Times Inside Report on the Hostage Crisis* (New York: Times Books, a division of Random House, 1981). For a very full account of what went on inside the policy councils in Washington, see Warren Cristopher, et al., under the editorial guidance of Paul Kreisberg, Director of Studies, Council on Foreign Relations, *American Hostages in Iran: The Conduct of a Crisis* (New Haven: Yale University Press for the Council on Foreign Relations, 1985). This book is a prime historical record of the crisis. Seven of its nine authors were direct participants in the resolution of the crisis as policy makers and negotiators. See also Gary Sick, *All Fall Down: America's Tragic Encounter With Iran* (New York: Random House, 1985), and Robert Parry and Peter Kornbluh, "Iran-Contra's Untold Story," *Foreign Policy* (Fall 1988).

5. James Reston, the *New York Times* (April 27, 1980).

6. Digby Whitman, "52, Yes, But How About the 52,000?" the *New York Times* (February 8, 1981), Op-Ed.

Chapter 3

1. This account draws on Dilip Hiro, *The Longest War, The Iran-Iraq Military Conflict* (New York: Routledge, 1991); Miller and Mylroie, *Saddam Hussein;* and Roy Mottahedeh, *The Mantle of the Prophet: Religion and Politics in Iran* (New York: Pantheon, 1986).

2. The following account is drawn from my *The Politics of Policy Making*.

3. Seymour H. Hersh, "U.S. Secretly Gave Aid to Iraq Early in Its War Against Iran," the *New York Times* (January 26, 1992): 1, 12.

4. For further information on the Iran-Contra affair, see Jonathan Marshall, *The Iran-Contra Connection: Secret Teams and Covert Operations in the Reagan Era* (Boston: South End Press, 1987); William S. Cohen and George J. Mitchell, *Men of Zeal* (New York: Viking, 1988); Donald T. Regan, *For the Record: From Wall Street to Washington* (San Diego: Harcourt Brace Jovanovich, 1988); Noam Chomsky, *The Culture of Terrorism* (Boston: South End Press,

1988); and Philip Henderson, *Managing the Presidency* (Boulder, CO: Westview Press, 1988). For an account of Lieutenant Colonel North's testimony at the congressional hearings on the Iran-Contra affair, see Daniel Schorr, *Taking the Stand* (New York: Simon and Schuster, 1987). The Tower Commission report on the Iran-Contra affair is available from Bantam Books, 1987, and from Times Books, 1987. In addition, twenty-seven volumes of source documents were published by the U.S. House of Representatives Select Committee to Investigate Covert Arms Transactions with Iran and the U.S. Senate Select Committee on Secret Military Assistance to Iran and the Nicaraguan Opposition.

Chapter 4

1. Leslie Gelb, the *New York Times* (July 17, 1991): A21.

2. In addition to newspaper accounts, see Gary Sick, "The Iraqi Invasion of Kuwait" (New York: Research Institute on International Change, Columbia University, September 18, 1990).

3. Jean Edward Smith, *George Bush's War* (New York: Henry Holt, 1992), 63.

4. Bob Woodward, *The Commanders* (New York: Simon & Schuster, 1991). This account of the meeting is drawn from Woodward's book.

5. *Ibid.* 261.

6. Both quotes are taken from "Hussein's Belligerence Touches Arabs' Pride and Old Wounds," the *New York Times* (August 17, 1990): 11.

7. Edward Said, Op-ed, the *New York Times* (August 13, 1990).

8. Harrison J. Goldin, general partner of Goldin Associates, which advises corporations on restructuring, "Hussein's Support: Deeper Than We Think?" the *New York Times* (August 28, 1990): 21.

Chapter 7

1. Todd Robberson, "The Sanctions Noose is Too Loose to Pinch," *Washington Post National Weekly Edition* (January 7–13, 1991):16.

2. This account is drawn from Woodward, *The Commanders*.

3. Anthony Lewis, "On His Word Alone," the *New York Times* (January 12, 1992): 19.

4. "Special Report: Hollow Victory," *U.S. News and World Report* (January 20, 1992): 42.

Chapter 8

1. The *New York Times* (January 28, 1991): 11.

2. The *New York Times,* (February 2, 1991): 23.

3. The *New York Times,* "The Week in Review" (January 27, 1991): 2.

4. "Let's Think This Over Before It's Too Late," *Washington Post National Weekly Edition* (January 14–20, 1991): 23.

5. Thomas L. Friedman, "What the United States Has Taken On in the Gulf, Besides a War," the *New York Times,* "The Week in Review" (January 20, 1991): 1, 3.

6. The *New York Times* (February 3, 1991): A15.

Chapter 9

1. The *New York Times* (February 26, 1991): 12.

2. This and what follows are from Steve Call and William Branigan, "Spin Control on the 'Highway of Death,' " *Washington Post National Weekly Edition* (March 18–24, 1991): 12ff.

Chapter 10

1. The *New York Times* (April 16, 1991): 9.

2. The *New York Times* (April 4, 1991): 1, 10. See also April 6, 1991, pp. 1 and 5, for an account of both these views and those described below.

3. Jonathan C. Randal, "A Painful Case of Deja Vu," *Washington Post National Weekly Edition* (April 8–14, 1991): 19, 20.

4. John Simpson (a BBC correspondent in Iraq), "Saddam's Plan 'B', " *World Monitor* (August 1991): 20ff.

5. Bill Snead, "Children Are Dying in the Mountains," *Washington Post National Weekly Edition* (May 13–19, 1991): 9.

6. Jonathan C. Randal, "Limbo on the Long Road," *Washington Post National Weekly Edition* (May 13–19, 1991): 11.

7. The *New York Times* (May 7, 1991): 1, 17.

Chapter 11

1. The accounts of the views of Colonel Henderson and those of Judith Coburn given below are drawn from Tom Wicker's column, " 'Marketing' the War," the *New York Times* (May 8, 1991): A23.

2. David E. Rosenbaum, "Press and U.S. Officials at Odds on News Curbs," the *New York Times* (January 20, 1991): I16.

3. Patrick J. Sloyan, "The War the Administration Isn't Going to Let You See, Why coverage of combat in the gulf will be restricted," *Washington Post National Weekly Edition* (January 21–27, 1991): 23.

4. Jason DeParle, "Keeping the News in Step: Are the Pentagon's

Gulf War Rules Here to Stay?" the *New York Times* (May 6, 1991): A9.

5. James LeMoyne, "Pentagon's Strategy for the Press: Good News or No News," the *New York Times* (February 17, 1991): E3.

6. Jason DeParle, "Long Series of Military Decisions Led to Gulf War News Censorship," the *New York Times* (May 5, 1991): 1, 20.

7. DeParle, "Keeping the News in Step."

8. *Ibid.* DeParle's article is also the source for the following paragraph.

9. Rosenbaum, "Press and U.S. Officials at Odds."

10. DeParle, "Keeping the News in Step."

11. *The Day* (July 6, 1991): A6.

12. "The Military Vs. The Press," the *New York Times Magazine* (March 3, 1991): 27ff.

13. R. Michael Schiffer and Michael F. Rinzler, "No News Is No News," the *New York Times* (January 23, 1991): A19.

14. DeParle, "Keeping the News in Step."

15. Sloyan, "The War the Administration Isn't Going to Let You See."

16. John Leo, "Lessons from a sanitized war," *U.S. News & World Report* (March 18, 1991): 26. Also the quote that follows.

17. The *New York Times* (January 21, 1991): A18.

18. Rosenbaum, "Press and U.S. Officials at Odds."

19. Robin Toner, "The Senator, The Press and Crossed Swords," the *New York Times* (February 12, 1991): A14.

20. Lewis H. Lapham, *Harper's* (May 1991): 10ff.

Chapter 12

1. "The Day We Stopped the War," *Newsweek* (January 20, 1992): 19.

2. Barton Gellman, "Gulf War's Friendly Fire Tally Triples," *Washington Post* (August 14, 1991): 1, 26.

Chapter 13

1. "The Week in Review," the *New York Times* (May 12, 1991): 2.

2. Patrick E. Tyler, "Health Study Says Child Mortality Rate in Iraq Has Tripled," the *New York Times* (October 22, 1991): A6.

3. Walter Goodman, the *New York Times* (November 5, 1991): 18.

Chapter 14

1. Transcript of the MacNeil/Lehrer Newshour, September 23, 1991, WNET, New York, Show No. 4166, 5.

2. Seymour Hersh, *The Samson Option: Israel's Nuclear Arsenal and American Foreign Policy* (New York: Random House, 1991).

3. William A. Broad, "In Russia, Secret Labs Struggle to Survive," the *New York Times* (January 14, 1992): 1, 9.

Chapter 15
1. The *New York Times* (September 25, 1991): A1, A15.

Chapter 16
1. Personal communication.

2. Marion Farouik-Sluglett and Peter Sluglett, *Iraq Since 1958: From Revolution to Dictatorship* (New York: St. Martin's Press, 1987).

3. "Up in Flames," *Scientific American* (May 1991): 17–24; "US Gags Discussion of War's Environmental Effects," *Scientific American* (May 1991): 24 (box).

4. "Smoke Over Kuwait," the *New York Times* (April 3, 1991): A21.

5. *Science News,* Vol. 140 (July 13, 1991): 24–26.

6. *Washington Post National Weekly Edition* (March 18–24, 1991): 27.

7. *Columbia, The Magazine of Columbia University* (Spring 1991): 14.

8. Personal communication.

9. Alan Cowell, "Understanding Hussein: An Orphan Who Fights to Be Remembered," the *New York Times,* International Section (February 3, 1991): 17.

10. The *New York Times* (December 6, 1990): A11.

11. Personal communication.

12. See, for example, the chapters on Vietnam in my *To Move a Nation: The Politics of Foreign Policy in the Administration of John F. Kennedy* (Garden City, N.Y.: Doubleday, 1967); the chapters on the rise and consequences of nationalism in my *The Crouching Future: International Politics and U.S. Foreign Policy, a Forecast* (Garden City, N.Y.: Doubleday, 1975); the relevant case studies in my *The Politics of Policy Making in Defense and Foreign Affairs: Conceptual Models and Bureaucratic Politics,* 2d ed. (Englewood Cliffs, N.J.: Prentice-Hall, 1990); and the appendices on Vietnam and on guerrilla warfare in my *American Guerrilla: My War Behind Japanese Lines* (Washington, D.C.: Brassey's, 1990). See also my chapter "Two American Counterstrategies to Guerrilla Warfare: The Case of Vietnam," in Tang Tsou, ed., *China in Crisis, Vol. 2: China's Policies in Asia and America's*

Alternatives (Chicago: University of Chicago Press, 1968); and my chapter, "Vietnam: The Decisions to Intervene," in J. R. Adelman, ed., *The Superpowers and Revolution* (New York: Praeger, 1986).

13. In a conference on Vietnam sponsored by the Carnegie Endowment for International Peace held in Bermuda early in 1968.

14. Personal communication.

Epilogue I

1. *U.S. News & World Report, Triumph Without Victory: the Unreported History of the Persian Gulf War* (New York: Times Books, a division of Random House, 1992), 404–405.

Epliogue II

1. In the following analysis of Saddam Hussein's character I have drawn on Karsh and Rautsi, *Saddam Hussein: A Political Biography;* Miller and Mylroie, *Saddam Hussein and the Crisis in the Gulf;* Elaine Sciolino, *The Outlaw State, Saddam Hussein's Quest for Power and the Gulf Crisis* (New York: John Wiley & Sons, 1991); and Samir al-Khalil, *Republic of Fear: The Politics of Modern Iraq* (Berkeley: University of California Press, 1989, 1990).

2. As quoted in Karsh and Rautsi, *Saddam Hussein: A Political Biography,* from a personal interview by the authors.

3. Efraim Karsh and Inari Rautsi, "Why Saddam Hussein Invaded Kuwait," *Survival* (January/February, 1991). The quotes that follow are also from this article.

4. Karsh and Rautsi, *Saddam Hussein: A Political Biography,* 40.

5. R. W. Apple, Jr., "Gauging Next Move by Hussein: Search for a Face-Saving Route," the *New York Times,* International Section (September 2, 1990): 1, 20. The following quote is from the same article.

6. John Simpson, "Saddam's Plan 'B'," *World Monitor* (August 1991): 20ff.

7. Sciolino, *The Outlaw State,* 31.

Epilogue III

1. "Handyman of American Politics," a section on George Bush in a special 1981 publication entitled *President Reagan* by the *Congressional Quarterly,* as a guide to the new Reagan administration, from which much of what follows on Bush's background has been drawn.

2. Peggy Noonan, *What I Saw at the Revolution: A Political Life in the Reagan Era* (New York: Random House, 1990), 301–302.

3. *Washington Post National Weekly Edition* (June 17–23, 1991).

4. Patrick E. Tyler, "Saudis Press U.S. for Help in Ouster of Iraq's Leader," the *New York Times* (January 19, 1992): 1, 10.

5. "Bush at War," the *New York Times* (January 23, 1991): A8.

6. "The Golf Cart Crisis," the *New York Times,* International Section (August 26, 1990): 16.

7. Clay Blair, *Washington Post National Weekly Edition* (May 13–19, 1991): 35.

8. David Hoffman, "Two Stiff Necks That Would Not Bend: Misjudgments pushed Bush and Hussein into a corner," *The Washington Post National Weekly Edition* (January 21–27, 1991): 19.

9. "Saddam and the Agencies of Disorder," *Times Literary Supplement* (London) as reprinted in Micah L. Sifry and Christopher Cerf, *The Gulf War Reader: History, Documents, Opinion* (New York: Times Books, a division of Random House, 1991), 290ff.

10. AP dispatch dated January 11, 1991.

11. Elizabeth Drew "Washington Prepares for War, Letter from Washington," *The New Yorker* (February 4, 1991).

12. Woodward, *The Commanders,* 89.

13. *Washington Post National Weekly Edition* (June 17–23, 1991).

14. *Dictionary of American Slang,* compiled by Harold Wentworth and Stuart Berg Flexner (New York: Thomas Y. Crowell, 1967).

15. Drew, "Washington Prepares for War."

Index